Internet Commerce

Andrew Dahl

Leslie Lesnick

New Riders Publishing, Indianapolis, Indiana

Internet Commerce

658·84

By Andrew Dahl and Leslie Lesnick

Published by:
New Riders Publishing
201 W. 103rd Street
Indianapolis, IN 46290 USA

Copyright © 1996 by New Riders Publishing

Printed in the United States of America 1 2 3 4 5 6 7 8 9 0

Library of Congress Cataloging-in-Publication Data

```
Lesnick, Leslie, 1963-
   Internet Commerce / Leslie Lesnick.
      p.   cm.
   ISBN 1-56205-496-1
   1. Internet marketing.  2. World Wide Web
(Information retrieval system)  3. Electronic
funds transfers—Security measures.
   I. Title.
   HF5415.1265.L47  1995
   658.8'4--dc20
95-44994
CIP
```

Publisher	Don Fowley
Publishing Manager	Jim LeValley
Marketing Manager	Ray Robinson
Managing Editor	Tad Ringo

Product Development Specialist
Julie Fairweather

Acquisitions Editor
Alan Harris

Development Editor
Suzanne Snyder

Production Editor
Sarah Kearns

Copy Editor
Lillian Yates

Technical Editor
Pat Farrell

Associate Marketing Manager
Tamara Apple

Acquisitions Coordinator
Tracy Turgeson

Publisher's Assistant
Karen Opal

Cover Designer
Karen Ruggles

Book Designer
Sandra Schroeder

Manufacturing Coordinator
Paul Gilchrist

Production Manager
Kelly Dobbs

Production Team Supervisor
Laurie Casey

Graphic Image Specialists
Clint Lahnen, Laura Robbins
Craig Small, Todd Wente
Jeff Yesh

Production Analyst
Bobbi Satterfield

Production Team
Kim Cofer, Jennifer Eberhardt
Tricia Flodder, Aleata Howard
Tim Taylor, Christine Tyner
Karen Walsh, Robert Wolf

Indexer
Jennifer Eberhardt

About the Authors

Andrew Dahl and Leslie Lesnick are co-founders of L**3comm**, a content and applications development company specializing in the Web. L**3comm** helps companies develop a Web business strategy for their digital storefront and provides the content and applications necessary to make it successful.

Andrew Dahl is a graduate of MIT and has over 10 years of software development experience with companies like IBM and CompuServe. As an IBM consultant, Andrew specialized in designing client/server systems. While at CompuServe, Andrew helped develop tools that make a business on the Internet possible, from the GUI interface to billing and security systems. Andrew's author contributions include *Inside OS/2 Warp* and *Connecting NetWare to the Internet*. He is currently working on an administrator's guide for Lotus Notes. Andrew lives and works in Columbus, Ohio (102174,2004@compuserve.com).

Leslie Lesnick has contributed to numerous business and technology publications, including New Riders' *Inside OS/2 Warp* and *Connecting NetWare to the Internet*. She recently completed two manuals for EasyLink 3.0 for AT&T. She has also written proposals, reports, and technical manuals for technology and manufacturing companies like Owens-Corning. As a partner in L**3comm**, Leslie helps businesses develop their communication packages and Web content. Leslie continues to contribute to trade and educational publications, as well as magazines. Leslie lives and works in Columbus, Ohio (LLesnick@aol.com).

Trademark Acknowledgments

All terms mentioned in this book that are known to be trademarks or service marks have been appropriately capitalized. New Riders Publishing cannot attest to the accuracy of this information. Use of a term in this book should not be regarded as affecting the validity of any trademark or service mark.

Acknowledgments

A special thanks to Jim and Wendy Peters, Mike Burns, Edward and Mary Lesnick, Linda Davison, Kathleen and Victor Dahl, and Michael T. McKibben, all of whose inspiration, dedication, and entrepreneurial spirit made this book possible...

....and a very special thanks to Jim LeValley.

Contents at a Glance

Table of Contents

8 Alternate Technologies for Electronic Commerce   209

9 Planning Your Digital Storefront   233

10 Winning with Your Digital Storefront 247

11 Digital Storefronts 273

12 Agents in Commerce 295

13 Electronic Banking 309

14 The Future of Internet Commerce 325

Introduction

The World Wide Web's popularity continues to explode. Both the number of surfers and the number of servers continue to increase at a remarkable rate. The Web is quickly swallowing the other portions of the Internet and becoming the de facto standard for access.

As the only portion of the Internet where commercial messages are accepted (and even encouraged), the Web is a natural for digital storefronts. Until recently, digital storefronts were hindered by the inability to get paid directly over the Internet; however, the latest releases of Web browsers and Web surfers contain the technology needed to support secure payments over the Internet, and businesses are beginning to take advantage of the technology.

This book is based on the notion that clever graphics alone will not determine the winners and losers in cyberspace. Strategy, products, service, and price are the cornerstones of a successful digital storefront. It's one thing to publish company and product information on the Web, but quite another to set up and run a digital storefront. All of your "lessons learned" from setting up a Web site (if you have one) will apply to creating a digital storefront, but digital storefronts involve many additional issues. Digital storefronts are more than online catalogs with order buttons—they require their own business strategy, products, and support processes, all of which must reflect and be consistent with the rest of your business.

Accepting payments online requires the utmost attention to security, so whoever develops your digital storefront must understand how to make a site easy and fun, while simultaneously providing security for both the business and consumer. Also, order processing systems must be integrated into your traditional accounting and billing systems.

Of particular importance is the form of payment that you decide to accept online. Traditional credit card payments have several drawbacks that make them unsuitable for many digital storefronts, and many new online ventures will have trouble getting authorization to accept credit card payments. Other organizations will be hindered by the overhead charged by credit card companies. Some consumers are concerned with potential security and privacy problems inherent in credit card transactions. New forms of cash and electronic payment systems are thus being developed in response to these concerns. If you are interested in setting up shop on the Web, you must understand the risks and rewards of each payment scheme. Each payment system is unique, and you need to be able to make an informed decision about the payment system or systems you integrate into your storefront, while minimizing liability and risk.

Why Read This Book?

Internet Commerce was written to help ordinary people wade through the ever-increasing number of payment systems, Internet service providers, and Web server programs, so that you can put together a package that makes sense for your business.

If you're wondering...

➤ How do I set up a digital storefront?

➤ How do I evaluate different payment systems?

➤ What business strategies work on the Web?

➤ How will electronic commerce affect my company?

> ➤ What's different about a digital storefront from a traditional business?

> ➤ What's the difference between a digital storefront and a Web site?

> ➤ How do secure payments work?

> ➤ How can I evaluate different Internet service providers?

...then this book is for you.

Who Should Read This Book?

This book is for everyone interested in understanding the practical side of setting up a digital storefront. Setting up a digital storefront is a multidisciplinary project. Marketers, advertisers, public relations staff, product developers, software developers, and network administrators are all involved (or should be) in setting up a digital storefront. This book provides a common language that can be used by all of these disciplines. We have put special emphasis on the technical details that any project manager or administrator needs to actually set up a storefront.

How Much Should You Know About the Web?

Most people reading this book will have some experience with the Internet and the World Wide Web, so we skip some basic steps like finding a Web browser. Having some experience with the Internet and the Web is helpful, but not necessary, when reading this book. The book goes beyond simple explanations of netiquette (accepted manners on the Internet) or suggestions like putting your company name on all e-mail. This book introduces real business strategies that you can use to separate yourself from the pack.

Some sections of this book are very technical (Chapter 5, "Cryptography Basics," Chapter 7, "Secure Web Servers," and especially Chapter 6, "Web Server Capabilities"). If you are not an administrator, you can safely skip these sections.

Why is This Book Important?

It is increasingly important that managers of any business be technologically savvy. This is doubly important for any company venturing into online business. Business managers cannot surrender control of a digital storefront to the IS (information services) department. Online expertise can only be gained by "doing." This book will shorten your learning curve by explaining the issues that must be addressed, the strategies that you should consider, and the questions you must ask.

A digital storefront is no place for mistakes. Security loopholes can cost thousands or millions of dollars. We have included a detailed guide outlining the steps an administrator needs to follow when setting up a secure Web site. Word spreads fast on the Internet. One advantage of running a Web storefront is that you can fix problems quickly. One disadvantage is that you must fix problems quickly, often within a day. This book can help you avoid mistakes.

New Riders Publishing

The staff of New Riders Publishing is committed to bringing you the very best in computer reference material. Each New Riders book is the result of months of work by authors and staff who research and refine the information contained within its covers.

As part of this commitment to you, the NRP reader, New Riders invites your input. Please let us know if you enjoy this book, if you have trouble with the information and examples presented, or if you have a suggestion for the next edition.

If you have a question or comment about any New Riders book, there are several ways to contact New Riders Publishing. We will respond to as many readers as we can. Your name, address, or phone number will never become part of a mailing list or be used for any purpose other than to help us continue to bring you the best books possible. You can write us at the following address:

New Riders Publishing
Attn: Publisher
201 W. 103rd Street
Indianapolis, IN 46290

If you prefer, you can fax New Riders Publishing at (317) 581-4670.

You can also send electronic mail to New Riders at the following Internet address:

```
jfairweather@newriders.mcp.com
```

NRP is an imprint of Macmillan Computer Publishing. To obtain a catalog or information, or to purchase any Macmillan Computer Publishing book, call (800) 428-5331.

Thank you for selecting *Internet Commerce*!

Part I

Conducting Internet Commerce

Chapter 1

Doing Business on the Web

The Internet can no longer be ignored as a serious business tool, and the World Wide Web (WWW) is the vehicle that has brought the potential of the Internet to the masses. With its interactive, sexy look and business-friendly environment, it now accounts for about half the traffic on the Internet. People can wheel and deal on the WWW without impunity—something that is not tolerated on the Internet. New, emerging electronic payment systems (EPSs) available on the WWW are leading the way for an even more sophisticated business environment—a place for serious Internet commerce.

The WWW has captured the imaginations of business professionals. They now have another entertaining medium in which to showcase their store and products using text, a colorful company logo, video, music, and sophisticated graphics online, and better yet, they can GET PAID instantaneously with EPSs for their goods and services. The Internet is no longer just a vehicle for communication—it is a place of business.

Until now, conducting businesses (advertising, marketing, and selling) electronically was a "it will happen some day" proposition. The commercial network for businesses has arrived with easy-to-use interfaces and secure transaction capabilities. Instead of having to creatively hunt and search the Internet for desirable sites, the Web is making it easier and easier to get where you want to go.

Eventually, the Web will become part of a business's standard communications package, along with advertising, a Yellow Pages listing, telephones, voice mail, e-mail, and courier services. Will the WWW be the next "must have" for successful businesses? Will having a company's WWW page become a standard part of company letterheads and business cards? Probably.

The Current Status of Business on the Web

The WWW is a wide-open marketplace offering a hospitable and compelling environment for novices. Technically, it is raw, dynamic, and exciting. Companies have had tremendous success on the Web and yes, there have been failures. You are not guaranteed a profit, but—as far as anyone can tell—the potential for profit is unlimited. In many ways, doing business on the Web involves the same kinds of risks any business venture could face. Although no one has exact figures—only best guesses and estimations—it is known that unprecedented numbers of people are entering the WWW world.

The bottom line is that the audience is a huge and highly desirable one for businesses—well-educated, high wage earners with plenty of money to spend. Also, in today's world, information is a valuable commodity, and if used effectively, can be the key to faster, smarter, and more efficient business practices.

Essentially, the WWW is reshaping how the business world thinks about marketing, advertising, trading information, business partnering, and buying and selling. Many business owners are deciding right now whether to rush to market with a Web site, or wait for others to make all the mistakes, then put up a Web site. Many of the "big boys" are already there. Eight out of the top ten Fortune 500 companies have a Web site up and running. For smaller vendors, the WWW is still new enough that they can compete with the larger companies with some success. As the number of WWW sites increases, getting noticed requires over-increasing levels of investment. Small companies without an offline image to leverage may be priced out of the WWW if they wait.

The number of business professionals setting up shop and frequenting the Internet has increased dramatically over the last year. New WWW browsers are easy to use—they are graphical, conduct searches, and can seamlessly handle gopher, FTP, Veronica, and WAIS. New technologies, such as Java from Sun Microsystems, are adding even more excitement to the WWW.

Some business owners are overwhelmed by the unstructured, uncensored nature of the Internet. How could something so untamed and directionless be relevant to their business? The Web is simply another tool to use to reach your customer base. The Web accelerates the exchange of information between businesses and their customers—the customers feel well-served and the company gets quicker feedback about its products; it is yet another value-added service businesses can provide their customers. This kind of dynamic environment can foster a sense of community between businesses and their customers.

It's virtually a level playing field out there. Large companies are not dominating the Web environment like they do in the traditional marketplace with their name recognition. Some of the most widely recognized sellers of consumer products in traditional markets have uninspiring, static sites. Many small start-up companies have generated the most press in newspapers and magazines for having the most interactive, well-organized Web sites. Small companies that can adapt quickly and make the necessary changes to succeed in this new environment have the upper hand with the slower moving corporations. As the marketplace continues to grow, the current situation is unlikely to last— advantages abound for the quick movers on the Web. Sales for companies on the WWW are projected to reach 120 million by 1997.

Digital Storefronts

Digital storefronts are WWW sites that actually sell their wares online. The WWW is the place to be these days with your digital storefront, because people are window shopping in record numbers—the current guess, as reported by *The Wall Street Journal*, is somewhere around 24 million, but no one is entirely certain. If your storefront display is intriguing, customers will come in and look around. They want to see if your information and merchandise live up to your storefront image. If they like what they see, they may make a purchase or return later. Also, customers are not limited geographically, seasonally, or by time or place—the store is always open.

Currently, most businesses on the Web are there to offer better customer service, provide extensive product information, and be seen as an active participant on the Internet. For many businesses, setting up a Web page is a "me too" exercise—companies see their competitors set up a site and quickly put together one of their own. With the advent of EPSs, however, the Web is likely to become a serious profit turner for thoughtfully positioned digital storefronts. Software developers are in a mad dash to come up with the best software for cash transactions on the Internet. Banks are aggressively positioning themselves for what they see as an inevitable shift in how consumers buy goods and services. Anything can be sold on the Web: computers, travel financial information, paper publications, music, apparel, and so forth.

Businesses are using their Web pages to represent themselves, to market their products, and to sell their products, for the following reasons:

➤ Web pages can be far more entertaining and much more attractive than the text-based portions of the Internet.

➤ Information from widely disparate sources are becoming more interconnected every day. Searches are becoming easier.

➤ The Web is a low-cost way to distribute up-to-date information on a company and its products.

➤ Product demos can be distributed online.

➤ Businesses can improve customer service using the Web.

➤ Businesses can gather information about their customers through online surveys.

➤ Product distribution costs can be cut by using the Web in conjunction with seamless technology. This enables orders placed on the Web for hard goods to travel directly to the warehouse for filling and shipping, completely bypassing any intermediary processing. Information sales can be sent electronically.

➤ Marketing and selling is accepted practice on the Web.

➤ A global audience can be reached at little cost.

➤ Staying competitive is important, and statistics show that corporations are jumping on the Web bandwagon in droves. If you aren't already there, your competition probably is.

➤ Tracking their competition is easy. Just visit your competition's Web sites to keep up with their latest offerings.

➤ Market research is accessible, and new research can be easily conducted and performed.

➤ Businesses can try out new advertising campaigns without the cost of traditional media.

➤ Businesses can capture retail sales without the cost of opening a real storefront.

➤ The Web enables businesses to build closer associations and partnerships because of the ease of linking sites together in the Web environment.

➤ Businesses can improve their internal operations by making information quickly and easily available on a Web server for employees ONLY by locking out the general public to certain areas on the server, and employees can keep up by readily referring to the latest information being presented to the public by the business.

➤ A Web presence can be established for a reasonable investment.

A WWW digital storefront, when coupled with your other Web marketing strategies, could translate into significant revenue increases for your business. Let's examine each of the preceding bulleted items and explore in a little more detail the reasons businesses are jumping on the Web.

Web Pages are Attractive

WWW pages are inviting, because both the language and graphics are familiar. Many home pages have the look and feel of a slick magazine cover. Graphically interesting, dynamic pages are popping up daily. The design potential is limited only by your imagination. With full multimedia capability, audio, video, text, and graphics, the possibilities are endless.

An effective home page projects a professional, positive image of a business, uses sound and graphics to entice shoppers, and encourages customer interaction and questions about its services and products. Hewlett-Packard, for example, has an interesting and comprehensive home page. Every Monday a new comic strip appears on the home page as a little added bonus for checking in with them at least once a week.

Customers can do more than just look, however. The WWW is by its very nature a dynamic environment, which welcomes access and encourages exploration. You can explore a Web site in a variety of ways, making good use of the hypertext links throughout the site.

HyperText Markup Language (HTML) and HyperText Transfer Protocol (HTTP), the technologies that make jumping from spot to spot on the Web possible, are already old news. Although this exciting architecture has catapulted the Web's popularity, it is likely to be replaced by the Worldwide Transaction Web (WTW) in the near future. WTW will add even more technical sophistication to home pages by making military-level security, animation, interactive graphics, and sound a more integral part of the Web-site experience, making the Web experience even more secure, interactive, and entertaining.

Information is Easy to Find

Gone are the days of truly difficult Web navigation. Searches are becoming easier, so that potential customers will be able to find you, and you can easily keep an eye on your competition. As the amount of information on the WWW explodes, automated searches become more difficult. The amount of redundant or irrelevant information returned by a search grows as the amount of information searched grows. What is really needed is a pre-filtering process to screen out useless or irrelevant information. Hand-crafted hot lists are now popping up, which satisfy this demand. Getting your company listed on popular lists will enable customers to quickly find your Web site.

Conducting research and getting information online is easier with Web browsers, such as Mosaic, Netcruiser, and Netscape, than it ever was before. Even more advanced browsers are currently under development, but having statistically valid data on which to base research is still very difficult.

Latest Breaking News About Your Business

How many times have you wished that you could have squeezed one more bit of information into your current marketing materials before the brochures, ads, and press releases went out, or worse yet, wished that you had caught a printing mistake that marred your expensively packaged marketing campaign? Unlike print, if a mistake is discovered on the Web server, you can immediately correct the error. You don't need to make the correction and launch another expensive and unbudgeted print run.

You can set up a Web server that keeps everyone updated about your product information on a daily or even hourly basis. Get creative with daily, weekly, and monthly promotions. Your home page can be accessed by customers and your sales force in the field who need to stay on top of current product information.

Maintaining the information on your Web server does not have to be a difficult process. Think of it as a giant dynamic catalog of information. Make changes to your home page at will—update prices, add or remove products, and make special offers. New home pages, updates, and changes are mostly written with standard word processing packages, and automatically converted to the special format required by the WWW. The format required by the Web is accessible to any of the major computer platforms.

Most companies provide the following information on their Web servers: a company profile, press releases, extensive product information, promotions, special discounts, sales information, order forms, and support and technical databases (especially technology companies). Larger companies will often make their annual report available, along with information on special ventures with business partners.

Demo Your Products and Services

A great way of giving your customers a chance to see and try out your products and services on the Web is to set up demos of your products. This is a particularly effective sales technique for software vendors—you can save time and money by avoiding developing, printing, packaging, and mailing demos of your latest products; instead, make them available on your home page. Take advantage of recent advances in compression technology to show video clips of your products and services. Use audio for atmosphere and special messages. If you have a publishing or information service, provide samples of your databases for customers to explore. Customers are happy, because they can try out a product before purchasing it. Take advantage of all the vehicles and outlets available on the Web to get your business message across.

Improve Customer Service

Web access can actually increase communication between you and your customers, while simultaneously decreasing the number of direct calls you receive and process. How can this be? Customers can send e-mail directly to the sales reps, rather than playing phone tag or, worse yet, spending time on hold. Information on your products and services is easily accessible from your home page, as well as order forms. Your customers, for example, can order, pay for, and receive a product from your business without ever having to have a conversation with an actual person. Their orders are sent to the warehouse, where the product is immediately shipped. You have saved time and money, and your customers are happy.

You can construct databases of information that customers can search to find solutions to their problems. A common practice on Web pages is to provide a *frequently asked questions* (FAQ) document that customers can quickly review.

Gauge Customer Satisfaction

Encourage customer feedback on your Web sites by providing forms and e-mail, so they can quickly and easily offer comments and suggestions. Offer special discounts to motivate customers to complete surveys to add to your cadre of market research.

Cut Distribution Costs

Conducting business on the WWW makes it possible to cut out the middle man.

The dynamic environment of the Web lets other businesses enter the information market and compete with the big three online service providers. People who previously ruled out starting a publishing business because of the extensive overhead involved now have a new opportunity to jump on the Web with their offerings.

Other kinds of product-driven businesses can cut down their processing time by having catalog orders received and paid for on the Web and routed directly to their warehouses. The Web thus offers stress-free ordering for the consumer and low-cost processing for the vendor.

Market and Sell

By launching your Web site, loaded with information about your products and services, you have already expanded your market awareness potential by employing another medium to help get out your message. You can increase your odds of a successful Web launch by announcing your Web site arrival through the traditional media. Also, visit newsgroups that are likely to attract people who would have an interest in your products and services. Be careful, however—you cannot overtly advertise on the non-Web portion of the Internet, but it is perfectly acceptable to participate in newsgroup discussions and then mention your Web site. Most people include a signature file at the end of their messages: name, company, phone number, address, and WWW address.

Many companies encourage customers to visit their home page in their more traditional media campaigns by including their WWW address and a snapshot of their home page. Because Web pages are quite colorful and attractive, they are a nice asset to magazine ads and company brochures.

Currently, many businesses on the Web are accepting customer orders and credit card numbers. Customers are wary of sending out their credit card numbers over the Internet, however, so companies have developed more elaborate security systems and EPSs designed to make financial transactions more secure.

Secure HTTP (SHTTP) from Enterprise Integration Technologies and Netscape's *Secure Sockets Layer* (SSL) are new technologies that make it possible for customers to charge purchases online without worrying that their credit cards are going to get swiped in cyberspace. These technologies aim to do far more than enable encrypted credit card transactions. The eventual goal for these new encryption technologies is to replace checks, purchase orders, and most of the other existing business exchanges over the Web.

Companies have invested considerable time and money creating electronic payment systems in anticipation of the huge market that awaits them. Now that EPSs are a reality, they have the potential to make shopping on the WWW hassle-free for consumers as they conduct normal business transactions. Customers can shop the Web by visiting different storefronts and reviewing their options before making a purchase. In today's busy world, not many people have the time or the energy to drive around town and comparison shop. The Web will give consumers the luxury of comparison shopping from their homes.

Establish a Global Presence

The WWW is an international marketplace. Small companies can now have a global presence through their WWW home page—WWW makes distance irrelevant. For many companies, tapping into the international market before the advent of the Internet was impossible. Many business owners view the Web as a relatively low-risk way to tap a potentially vast national market that otherwise would be out of the question.

Stay Competitive

The world is changing. Telecommunication advances are changing the way we do business. Everything is faster. Time-based competition is a key feature of the modern business environment. People are conducting business over the Internet who have never met each other, because of convenience and increased speed. The commercial participation in the WWW is increasing sharply. With serious software investment and advances in Internet, the reality of conducting commercial transactions online is here. Can you afford to ignore the increased speed between businesses and their customers, and businesses and their partners, that the WWW offers?

Keep an Eye on Your Competition

Because of the volume of information available on the Net, you can monitor your competition closely. The Web is becoming the primary interface to the entire Internet, so you can do most of the searching from the Web.

The tremendous growth in the commercial sites appearing on the Web makes it easier to keep up with what your competition is offering. Building a comprehensive profile of a company's financial position and activities using Web browsers is not difficult. You can get press releases, marketing information, patent applications, news articles, digests, product details, and contact names and addresses.

Conduct Market Research

Businesses can build a list of prospects based on their Web page traffic. New tools are becoming available to better track Web server activity. For companies that normally do business anonymously, building a customer mailing list can be difficult. A Web site can be set up to collect this information easily. Of course, as is so often the case in life, the easy and cheap information comes with several caveats. There are two problems with relying on actual traffic at your Web site—Web site caching will cause you to underestimate the true number of customers, and new developments are making it difficult to correctly identify individuals.

Web site caching is the process of temporarily storing Web pages. All of the large Internet service providers (ISPs), such as CompuServe and America Online, use Web site caching to reduce the load on their networks. By storing Web pages on their own servers, when a second customer asks for a Web page from your server, the ISP uses the copy in their Web cache rather than going back to your server to get the page a second time. Thus, your server only sees one hit, even though two customers have accessed information from your site.

Anonymous proxies for Web browsers enable people to surf the Net without revealing their individual identity. A proxy takes requests from individuals, gathers the correct information, and returns it to the individual. Anonymous proxies do this without revealing the identity of any user and are used by businesses to help protect their internal networks. Most people still access the Internet from work or school, so anonymous proxies could turn out to be a major problem for merchants hoping to track individual access.

Experiment

The very nature of Web technology provides you with an opportunity to try out new ideas without racking up huge expenses. Just keep two basic rules in mind:

➤ Always keep your storefront professional

➤ Never promise more than you can deliver

Even if an idea turns out to be a dismal failure, you can make the necessary adjustments to your Web site immediately.

Try out advertising and marketing strategies on the Web site before launching a nationwide media campaign—offer innovative services, for example. Remember, though, that nothing is certain—something that works on the Web may still fall flat when taken to the masses; however, you do have an opportunity to get reactions from real consumers at a comparably small investment of resources.

Use the medium to test new products and services. Customers provide feedback and you can get a good feel for overall sales potential at a minimal expense.

Secure Desirable Retail Space without the Overhead

Essentially, you can just go to market. You don't have the same capital expenditures of building a storefront and all the headaches that go with it like codes, regulations, and building inspectors, but you do have to be concerned with security. Simply create your home page, make certain that your domain name is cleared, and start selling. If you don't want the hassle of setting up shop, there are plenty of Web service providers who would be glad to have your business. They will manage the process for you.

InterNIC registers and issues domain names on a first-come, first-serve basis. Set this up as soon as possible, because duplications are not allowed on the Net. You are not guaranteed a name that matches up well with your regular business name, which is obviously desirable so that customers can easily find you. Apply for your domain name at hostmaster@internic.com.

Another option is to join an online mall, which is a collection of online digital storefronts grouped together much like the traditional retail malls, and functioning similarly. The online mall houses the shops in one easy-to-reach location and provides entertainment, information, and interesting activities designed to draw a crowd. The advantage of joining an online mall is that you can benefit from the additional traffic generated by the other businesses.

If you find a mall on the Web that you like and you think it will be a good place for your business, inquire at the mall storefront about how to join. Most malls have a general information page on how to join, or you can send an e-mail request for more information.

Build Successful Business Relationships

Because the WWW structure encourages jumping about from one place to another, business are maximizing their Web exposure by creating links to each other's business sites. If you are a music vendor, you may want to partner with a book dealer and provide links to each other's sites from your home pages. A customer can then leap back and forth between your two sites in seconds. The more sites at which your business is listed, the more likely you are to receive additional traffic.

Improve Your Internal Business Operations

You can update your company information on the Web server daily, so that your remote employees have a cost effective way of

accessing the latest company information. Set up special databases with expert knowledge for sales and marketing personnel
on the road that isn't accessible by the general public.

Use the Web to conduct research that will help you to quickly put
together complex documents and reports—access libraries of
research information readily available from the academic community, search online bookstores, utilize corporate product
information databases, and explore other non-commercial sites
for business ideas.

Reasonable Investment

Not all Web pages are created equal—the more you spend, the
more bells and whistles you get. Remember, you don't have to
start out with the Cadillac version of a WWW site. Just establishing a presence on the WWW may be all you need initially as you
determine how doing business on the Web fits in with your
overall business plan. You can set up your own server and create
your own Web pages, or you can lease space and have someone
else develop and house your Web site for anywhere from $500 per
year for a single Web page to $25,000 for an elaborate hyperlinked
site. If you outsource all of your Web development, expect to pay
extra for online ordering capabilities, graphic design, programming, and sound. Having said that, it should be pointed out that
there are creative ways to spend less money. For example, you
can pay a graphic artist or programmer a percentage of your sales
generated from your Web site instead of a flat fee up-front. A
royalty arrangement guarantees that you and your consultant
have the same goals.

If you create an interesting and entertaining site, you will generate traffic. Word gets around, electronically speaking. When you
compare the cost of setting up a Web site to radio, television,
print ads, brochures, and so forth, a Web site expense pales in
comparison, but there are no guarantees that you will be successful. Don't develop a digital storefront if it is simply an after-
thought—you will be wasting valuable time and money. It takes
patience and nurturing to grow a Web site effectively.

The Web Clientele

Everyone is taking their best guess at the make-up and buying habits of the Web clientele. No one knows how many people are on the Internet—you will read or hear figures, such as 20 million or 30 million (*The Wall Street Journal* printed 24 million), but it really is just a best guess. The very nature of the Internet makes it very difficult to capture any definitive data about WWW users.

The reality is that demographics is a very big issue for media buyers. They are accustomed to knowing quite a bit about their target market, and are unlikely to invest in something for long that fails to pay for itself.

Nielson Media Research and Arbitron have both recently introduced a service that measures WWW usage. In addition, expensive software packages are coming on the market designed to measure server activity. As you wait for these services to develop and effective measurement tools and software to become less expensive, however, where can you turn for information?

One of the most widely quoted surveys available for free on the WWW is from the Graphics, Visualization, and Usability Center from the Georgia Institute of Technology. Their survey is the oldest and largest online survey to date in terms of the number of questions and the number of responses. They published their first survey in January of 1994, and have published a report every six months since that time. The intent of the survey is not to count the activity on Web servers, but rather to survey actual users of the WWW. The findings have been widely written about and reported, and a few of the points are included in the following:

➤ One of the exciting findings from their most recent survey is a substantial increase in the number of people seeking out Internet access providers, rather than just accessing the Internet through work or school.

➤ The average age is 35 for both men and women, and the estimated average income is $69,000.

➤ Overall, 50.3 percent of the users are married, with 40.0 percent being single. The users who reported being divorced was 5.7 percent.

➤ 82.3 percent of the respondents are white, with none of the other groups reporting over 5 percent of the responses. (This was not a multilingual study.)

➤ 15.5 percent of the respondents were women in this study, but other reports indicate that 34 percent of the users on the Net are now women.

Overall people spend a considerable amount of time on the Web, as follows:

➤ 41 percent use their browsers 6–10 hours per week.

➤ 21 percent use their browsers 11–20 hours per week.

➤ 72 percent use their Web browser at least once a day.

The respondents are actively using their browsers, and are drawn particularly to entertaining sites, as displayed in the following list—good information for someone just setting up a digital storefront.

➤ 82.6 percent of the respondents spend their time browsing the Web.

➤ 56.6 percent of the respondents use the Web for entertainment purposes.

➤ 50.9 percent of the respondents use the Web for work-related tasks.

➤ 10.5 percent of the respondents shop on the Web.

While the U.S. users are more likely to have a college degree (36.0% vs. 25.4%), European users are more likely to have Master's degrees (27.7% vs. 18%) and Doctoral degrees (13.7% vs. $4.06%). Although the percentages may differ, there are no significant differences between European and U.S. response profiles.

For marketing purposes, it's important to know that 50% of the users found out about this survey from other WWW pages, with 20.3% finding out via "other" sources, and 17.9% finding out via Usenet newsgroup announcements. WWW-based listserver/mailing lists (e.g. www-announce) accounted for nearly 6% of all respondents finding out about the survey. Additionally, most users find out about WWW pages from friends and other pages (95.71%). Other popular sources are magazines (64.3%) and Usenet (58.79%).

The Future of Internet Commerce

The WWW is still evolving. When you begin setting up your own digital storefront, patience is paramount. Although non-sophisticated users can easily access and navigate the Web, basic computer literacy does help. You need to remember that computers are still very new for a significant portion of the general public (two doctors living across the street from the author's house didn't know the difference between hardware and software until our picnic just after the launch of Windows 95). An extended adjustment period is to be expected.

The Internet still suffers from a lack of bandwidth and speed. Most Internet users are surfing at modem speeds of 14.4 Kbps or even 9600 Kbps. Graphic-intensive Internet sites will try the patience of these users as they wait for the wonderful graphics you created to display on their computers.

The media has put fear in the hearts of consumers concerning Internet commerce. People are reluctant to send their credit card or bank account information over a network that they really do not understand. The general buying public has no clue about electronic payment systems, and they will have a difficult time believing that they are secure. Whether the payment structure involves online credit, debit, or an option to use either, to most it feels like dropping your money and identity into a giant black digital hole.

Your internal staff will need training to understand the technology and to master the skills needed to get the most out of your Internet connection. In addition, once they become proficient at Web browsing, they may be tempted to use company equipment and time for their own personal gain and entertainment.

You are not guaranteed a return on your investment in establishing a digital storefront. The challenge is to turn Web surfers into your customers. Employing a multitude of strategies to advertise your storefront on the WWW is critical to success. You can't simply set up a digital storefront and sit back and watch the business roll in. People need a reason to visit your Web site—give them as many as possible. Savvy business owners are in fact aggressively learning how to best exploit the Web, believing that by being present on the Web as the market heats up, they have everything to gain and very little to lose.

The future for online business is very bright indeed. Everyone is preparing. Retailers and banks across the country are rushing to establish systems that will secure consumer trust. The government is trying to come up with standards for EPSs, and is monitoring commercial traffic over the Internet. The current commercial online services continue to expand their shopping areas. Thousands of copies of World Wide Web browsers are downloaded daily. City-by-city telephone lines are being upgraded to handle some of the increased bandwidth necessary to handle the sophisticated video, graphics, text, and sound commonly found on today's Web pages., but as is usually the case, the technology is ahead of the infrastructure.

In the next chapter, "Commerce on the Web," you will learn about some of the businesses on the Web and the strategies they employ to draw customers. Some of the online businesses are Web sites in transition to becoming digital storefronts, while others are already up and running and doing business online. The chapter will give you plenty of ideas for your own digital storefront.

Chapter 2

Commerce on the Web

Every kind of business you can imagine has entered the online world: wineries, bridal salons, toy companies, photography studios, software companies, publishers, music vendors, and so forth. And the truth is that most of them had no idea what they were getting into when they started; however, many companies do have a successful Web presence. Customers can sign up for automatic product updates, get customer support online, view demos of products and services, download free software, and tap into additional resources. Businesses are being very creative and using a variety of strategies to get noticed on the Web. These strategies are discussed later in the chapter, and include the following:

➤ Just the goods

➤ Leveraged information

➤ Unique services

➤ Coupons

➤ E-mail

➤ Subscriptions

➤ Contests

➤ Specials

➤ Free searches

➤ Free merchandise

➤ Compilation of strategies

➤ Malls

High-profile information sites are generating plenty of ink in the press and getting thousands of visitors every day. Remember, bragging rights go to the server with the most hits.

"Hits" is a commonly used term that is a bit misleading. The term "hits" refers to the number of files accessed at a Web site. Because each graphic is a separate file, each user will account for several hits with each page he visits. The ratio of hits to actual visitors is estimated to be 10-to-1 for most sites—ten hits per actual visitor. For example, if your Web site received 100,000 hits in a week, 10,000 different individuals visited your storefront.

Site caching, the process of temporarily storing recently accessed Web pages, can also make it difficult to track actual traffic on a Web server. Customers of CompuServe and AOL—two firms that cache their customer's actions—who access your Web server may be actually be hitting the site cache instead of your server. This will reduce the number of hits recorded at your server.

With the Web's flashy graphics, marketing and advertising are a natural fit. Companies with hot Web sites are capturing the business world's imagination. Every day, creative new marketing strategies are showing up, which in the long haul will translate into $$$ for these pioneers. Most companies are advertising, but not selling, on the Web—their emphasis is on telling, not selling. As the elements of electronic commerce are folded into these marketing and advertising sites, selling will take precedence over telling. Inevitably, companies will want to see a return on their Web investment. Electronic commerce, therefore, will be the next big push.

Both large and small companies are treating their Web sites as a market test. They are putting their lines in the water to see if the fish are biting. And like the inveterate fisherman, if they see someone getting an inordinate amount of bites, they will immediately move their poles to where the fish are and worry about tangled lines later.

Companies successfully selling on the Web today are marketing known commodities with consistent quality, such as CDs, magazines, and brand-name computer equipment. Clothing is more difficult, unless you are an established brand-name store or catalog company. Will it fit? What will it look like? Is the color on the screen the real color? But given the tremendous success of apparel catalog sales in recent years, one can only surmise that some of that business will move to the Web.

Risk Takers

Companies are betting that Web profits will eventually follow their Web presence. Web advocates believe that online commerce is the next natural progression.

John Werner, owner of Stauf's Coffee Roasters in Columbus, Ohio, recently launched his digital storefront as an extension of his hugely successful coffeehouse/retail store with the belief that if he first establishes a Web presence and invests some time and money in his digital storefront over the long-term Web, profits will follow.

John started his business in 1984 with just enough space for four tables. Now his store spans a quarter of a block and boasts a steady stream of regular customers. Rather than print up direct mail catalogs (selling coffee, coffee accessories, and miscellaneous items) like he did last year, John decided to invest his time and money in the World Wide Web (see fig. 2.1). He connected up with Tim Geraghty from SmartPages Direct (http://www.smartpages.com), a Web server service who helped him take his storefront to the online market. Stauf's has not done a brisk business; however, John didn't expect it to. He went to market with the knowledge that over 200 coffee shops have Web sites. His goal is to continue to improve and differentiate his site, spend time in Usenet groups, and take the risk that his relatively early presence on the Web will pay off down the road.

Figure 2.1

The Stauf's Coffee Roasters home page.

Will Internet commerce evolve as the television industry did? Some think so. The parallels are certainly there. Television makes its money through advertising. The Web is a marketing channel. Just as television shows quickly grew in sophistication as technology matured, so has the Web. As the number of television channels exploded, share of mind—getting consumers to immediately recognize and think about a product—among the viewing audience translated into marketing muscle. The early risk takers in television established a presence and still rule the industry decades later. In addition, television now has the Home Shopping Network. Can the Web be far behind? When Internet commerce standards emerge as they did for the credit industry with Visa, MasterCard, and American Express, presence will translate into cash.

Fear of the Competition and of What's to Come

Competition is a powerful motivator. While looking over their shoulders, businesses are rushing to the Web as they see their competition put up a site. Because the Web is a new medium, creativity abounds, and as new technologies continue to emerge, Web pages will continue to evolve. Creative sites are drawing attention. Already, a common strategy to encourage traffic on a site is to provide links to other interesting or "cool" pages. While surfing the Web, you will regularly stumble across links to a "cool" site of the day, week, month, or year decided on by one or two people, a committee, or a contest held by the company. Lists regularly appear in computer magazines, such as *Wired*, *Byte*, *Interactive Age*, and so on, detailing the hottest Web sites.

Small Businesses

You don't have to be rich and powerful to launch a business on the WWW. Like settlers in the Wild West, Web pioneers found that market share was free. Small companies could affordably stake out huge territories. As more people move in, the battle is changing. The fight is already on to defend territory. Will size matter more than speed? Probably not. Small companies can and are masquerading as big companies—the Web enables a small company to project a professional, interesting, wide-reaching global image. The battle will go to those with the best overall strategy, not the biggest budgets. Check out Chapter 9, "Planning Your Digital Storefront," and Chapter 10, "Winning with Your Digital Storefront," for a more in-depth discussion of storefront strategies.

Small companies thinking about a Web site should move quickly. The bottom line for small companies is that the longer they wait, the more expensive things become. Market share won't be free for much longer. As the Web continues to grow and get more crowded, distinguishing yourself from everyone else will become increasingly difficult. The Web hotlists in magazines will eventually lose their cachet, and sites won't automatically get thousands of hits because of an appearance on a Web hotlist, like they do today.

CDNOW (http://www.cdnow.com) was a small start-up company, but they are now one of the top nine music companies selling on the Web (see fig. 2.2). The Philadelphia-based retailer is accessible through the Web's Downtown Anywhere mall. If CDNOW had waited even one year before launching their business, they would have found themselves competing with the likes of SONY. But by developing an early presence, CDNOW was able to get a loyal following, developing their Web site into a fun place to shop.

Figure 2.2
CDNOW is an example of a small company success story on the Web.

 The CDNOW site is also featured in *World Wide Web Top 1000*, by R.F. Holznagel and Point Communications (New Riders, 1995).

Retail giant Home Shopping Network recently bought the Internet Shopping Network (http://www4.internet.net), the most prominent direct-marketing company on the Internet. At the time, Internet Shopping Network had just eight employees and one network server. Now the Internet Shopping Network is one of the largest retailing and mall operations on the Net, offering online shoppers access to a broad range of products, including over 25,000 computer products from more than 600 major companies like Lotus, Symantec, and Microsoft.

CDNOW, a purely Web-based business that receives over 5,821,0000 hits per month, was started in 1994 by 24-year-old twins, Jason and Matt Olin, in the basement of their parents' house. The idea grew from Jason's frustration at the lack of information about the music he was buying—thus the creation of CDNOW, where comprehensive music information and entertainment are unified to provide the largest inventory of readily available entertainment products. CDNOW sells CDs, magazines, T-shirts, and (soon) movies and videos.

The business that was started with seed money from their parents has grown to a multimillion dollar company with 11 employees at the main office and a few additional employees in Chicago and LA. CDNOW has successfully shipped items from an inventory of more than 150,00 products to customers in over 60 countries. The majority of their customer base is male, listening to Rock, Alternative, Urban, and Rap, and between the ages of 18–24; however, their female customer base is steadily increasing, as well as their customers in the 25–34 age group.

CDNOW success is attributed to several factors, as follows:

➤ Good information and a quality product.

➤ Small flexible company that can "turn-on-a-dime" to respond to customer interest and needs.

➤ Frequently changing site that keeps customers interested and coming back.

➤ Seamless technology that makes fast, efficient shipping possible.

➤ Responsive customer service that typically turns around all e-mail within 12 hours.

➤ Customer suggestions are taken very seriously and often implemented.

➤ Paying close attention to the competition, especially as the Web market continues to grow.

Large Businesses

The big boys from all industries are arriving in droves: Ford, Merrill Lynch, J.P. Morgan, Pizza Hut, General Electric, Sun Microsystems, Nordstrom, Xerox, Hyatt, Roswell Books, and more.

In the discount store world, Target and Wal-Mart are present and accounted for on the WWW; so is JCPenney (http://www.jcpenney.com), as shown in figure 2.3. It remains to be seen if K-Mart will join up.

Figure 2.3
JCPenney is among the top retail stores finding a home on the Web.

Big companies are not willing to let their competition get ahead for fear that the Web will take off, leaving them in the dust. One of the way Internet service providers know that they can hook new clients is to show them the competition's Web site.

Large companies have an advantage over smaller companies because they can more easily generate publicity for their sites through traditional media, such as by including their World Wide Web addresses in radio and television spots, sending out press releases, and adding an image of their Web pages to printed ads and brochures. Large companies also have a disadvantage— expectations for them are high, especially if their traditional advertising has created a strong company image. Large companies need to invest substantially more money in setting up a highly sophisticated site to satisfy people's expectations. For example, the movie industry has begun to create Web sites for some of its feature films, and includes the Web addresses in the print ads that appear in newspapers and magazines. They also are including them in the trailers for TV. *Get Shorty* is a critically acclaimed film from MGM with its own Web site. You can read about the actors, get a look behind the scenes, and visit other interesting pages for the diehard movie fan.

Figure 2.4

Check your local newspaper for Web addresses to your favorite recently released films.

Internet Service Providers

The Web has brought back the old business of *timesharing*—renting space on someone else's computer. About 55 percent of the Fortune 1000 companies are building their Web sites internally, while the other 35 percent are turning to Internet service providers. This percentage is likely to increase because the technology involved in building a Web site is complex and changing furiously. Businesses are turning to Internet service providers for the following reasons:

➤ To become a hot site, you must take advantage of the latest technology, which is time-consuming given the constant stream of updates that must be tested and installed.

➤ A full-time staff is often needed just to keep a site running. Because Web technology is often used solely for external customers, the employee time investment in this specialized technology cannot be justified. Playing with Web technology is a distraction for most businesses, especially if it is not one of their core competencies.

➤ Security is compelling concern for businesses. Specialists are required to truly isolate internal computers from the Internet. Most companies simply do not want to take the risk that a hacker will penetrate their internal systems.

➤ Real access security that ISPs can offer provides multistaged access control, monitoring of personnel with access to equipment, and 24-hour per day guards.

➤ Real physical security is taken care of by ISPs—floor rooms, power supplies, air conditioning, physical locations, and network links.

➤ Cost is a motivating force. Many Internet service providers can provide a Web site complete with graphics for less than the cost of the hardware and communications required to run your own site.

➤ Many companies start with slow lines, such as 14.4 or 56 KB lines. ISPs often have high-speed connectivity, multiple T1, and even T3 connectivity to main Internet hubs.

➤ ISPs offer headache-free management control with their pre-existing, proven policies for operations and security.

➤ ISPs can provide automated backup and off-site storage.

➤ System administrators (if applicable) do not need to learn obscure Unix commands and TCP/IP setup parameters.

➤ ISPs offer one-stop shopping—no need to talk to Internic for a domain registration, Telco for lines, router vendor for firewalls, and so on. The ISP does it all—you simply write the check.

Because everyone is rushing to the Web, most providers have more business than they can handle. Many new providers are arriving on the scene at a remarkable rate. Be selective. Make certain that the ISP you select can meet your individual business needs. Use the preceding list and Chapter 9, "Planning Your Digital Storefront," as your guide.

Many companies run their own Web sites because their sites have been developed by their IS departments, and IS departments are typically uncomfortable giving up control—timesharing is new for many of today's IS staff. In all likelihood, timesharing Web sites will become as common as having an advertising agency handle your companies marketing. New companies specializing in electronic commerce, in addition to advertising, will be important players.

Over 2,000 Internet service providers are currently doing business, and more will probably be available by the time this book goes to press. Besides the obvious "big boys" (Netcom, CompuServe, PSI, Prodigy, and AOL), many local providers are offering their services at very competitive prices. Mecklermedia's iWORLD offers "The List" at their WWW site (http://www.thelist.com). The long list of Internet service providers are searchable by state, area code, country, and country code.

Agents

More and more sites are now being established on the Web, covering nearly every conceivable topic. Manually searching through the maze is becoming a time-consuming and expensive proposition. Agents are being developed to help speed these searches. Agent-based search tools will enable customers to search for the most competitive price or find general points of interest on the Internet.

A *software agent* is a computer program that is a mobile autonomous entity traveling around cyberspace on your behalf. An intelligent agent can go off and do useful things for you as your representative in the marketplace, such as buying and selling goods and services. Individuals, groups, and institutions can own software agents and instruct them to access certain kinds of information and exchange information with other people and agents in cyberspace.

Agents take what customers want and automatically search the Internet for matches. As a customer, you fill out a 50–200-question survey about yourself and your buying habits. The results of the search will generate a home page on your browser. The agent searches continually, even while you sleep. The agent doesn't run on your workstation, but rather on an agent provider's machine. When you log on in the morning, the agent may have posted 30 items retrieved from all over the Web. You can quickly look at the results and determine which pertain to your life. The agent also learns from your online behavior—the agent becomes a highly personalized tool for you. Agent providers benefit also, because they now know things about you that they can sell to advertisers (see Chapter 12 "Agents in Commerce," for more information).

Web Site Business Strategies

Shopping on the Web is still new. A customer's natural tendency is to resist anything new, especially when money is involved—it took more than a decade, for example, before people were comfortable with ATM machines. People will need to see an advantage when doing business with a company on the Web. Successful merchants understand this and offer discounts. Once a presence has been established, prices slowly rise. Even when offering discounts, many companies come out ahead. By cutting out the cost of distributing goods to retail malls, a factor that can account for 70 percent of the final cost of many goods, firms can offer lower prices while maintaining higher margins.

When you ask the buying public to change its habits, there better be a payoff. Products must be cheaper than comparable goods sold at retail or through a catalog. Down the road, once the buying public gets comfortable, convenience may be enough to draw customers to the Web.

The progression for most Web sites is to first "tell, not sell." Next, they sell a small sample of products to test market interest. If successful, they launch a full-scale "tell and sell" site, and they may even establish a mall.

Just the Goods

Zaro's Bread Basket (http://www.nybagels.com/zaro/) is a very popular bakery chain in the New York City area, with 12 retail outlets (see fig. 2.5). According to *Inc.* magazine, Zaro's owner, Joseph Zaro, is keeping his total initial investment in his Web site to a modest $15,000. After six months, Joseph will compare his revenues to the cost of the Web site and decide whether he needs to invest more money.

Figure 2.5

The Zaro's Bread Basket home page.

No marketing gimmicks here. The home page for Zaro's Bread Basket is attractive, but not flashy. The home page welcomes you to Zaro's Bread Basket, where you have two choices: you can either review the menu, or send an order through e-mail. Prices are based on next-day shipping rates.

This simple and straightforward approach may be all that is needed to attract former New York residents reminiscent and anxious for some of Zaro's popular products. Zaro's Bread Basket is also reaching new clientele from around the world.

Leveraged Information

Clos LaChance Wines (http://www.commerce.com/clos/clos-top.html) offers a marketing newsletter on its Web site as a way to keep customers coming back, as well as get new ones. The site, also profiled by *Inc.* magazine, is a step above Zaro's in sophistication.

Upon entering the site, a brief company overview is provided, as well as a list of available wines, an order form (see fig. 2.6), and a list of restaurants where the wines are currently being served. Clos LaChance currently accepts three methods of payment: check, credit card number (currently offline only), and a customer charge account.

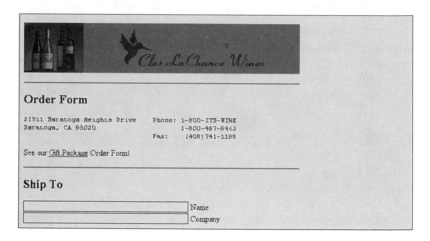

Figure 2.6

The Clos LaChance Wines Web site offers lots of information about its products and services.

The newsletter, published three times a year, describes gift packages, announces new products, and mentions the *Inc.* magazine article in which the business was briefly profiled. Copies are provided to interested customers; in the issue reviewed by the author, there was a lobster bisque recipe, as well as other bits of information.

The intent of the newsletter is to keep customers coming back to find out about new products and services—a visit to the site in exchange for information. Clos LaChance does not have e-mail built into its site, but posts its AOL address for customers to use.

Providing useful information of interest to your targeted customer group is a proven method of winning market share and establishing a Web presence. This is one variation on the strategy of offering something for free. Managing a successful Web site using this strategy is more like managing a small magazine than creating a successful advertising campaign. Little wonder that many of the popular Web sites are started by magazines or people with a publishing background.

Unique Services

Need help shopping? Nine Lives Quality Consignment Clothing (http://www.los-gatos.ca.us/nine.html) provides shopping assistants for free. You can fill out a profile of sizes and articles of clothing you are interested in locating. Your Nine Lives assistant will shop the entire inventory using your current profile and let you know what is available. In addition, you can browse the most popular items in the brand-name store inventory from the electronic storefront. The site also offers a free coupon good for 10 percent off purchases over $50 (see fig. 2.7).

Offering personalized service is another way to differentiate yourself on the Web. It's one thing to list products for sale, but it's quite another to help customers locate the perfect item. Nine Lives Consignment Clothing successfully combines personalized service with low prices to sell a product that may not otherwise appeal to the typical Web surfer.

Coupons

Online shoppers demand discounts when buying hard merchandise. One way that merchants can offset this cost is with online coupons. Online coupons, like their paper cousins, are a way of temporarily lowering prices to increase store traffic and encouraging purchases.

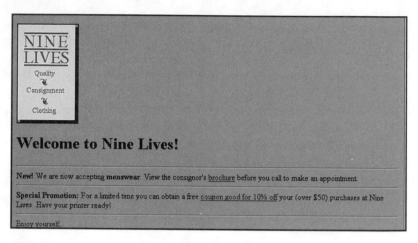

Figure 2.7

A personal shopping assistant can be a big draw if people see your service as an added benefit.

Online coupons are especially effective because they can be used to gather information about your customers—for example, you can have users of your electronic coupons fill out a survey about themselves, their buying habits, and their Internet connections in order to get the coupon. Given the lack of data about Internet shopping, this data is especially valuable and important to your business. It enables you to build a database for your own demographics study.

Customers love a good deal. They are likely to return to your site as long as you keep those coupons updated. When you later scale back the use of coupons, you avoid the shock of a price increase.

E-Mail

All digital storefront pages worth visiting offer a way of contacting a real-live human. Because digital storefront customers are already logged on, e-mail is a natural way of communicating with these customers. Using e-mail to open a channel for a two-way dialog shows you care about the customer, which is good for business. Many online businesses also use e-mail to handle administrative and billing questions, as well as for technical support. A company's response to its e-mail is critical. Most businesses attempt to respond within a business day to any messages they receive from a customer. Even if their only response is "I don't have an answer yet" or a simple "thanks for the input," they at least are providing some kind of response. When responding to e-mail promptly, the business sends a clear message that the customer is a priority and is being taken seriously. Customers can tell if you are sliding on responding to e-mail, and they can get just as impatient as the customer at the end of a long check-out line.

E-mail is a good example of the kind of planning required when setting up a Web site. You should try to respond to your e-mail within a single business day. Meeting this one-day turnaround may require special staffing arrangements. If multiple people are involved in answering online questions, make sure that the one-day rule isn't broken as a query is passed from person to person. This is especially important during vacation seasons. You should plan a way to measure your response times to e-mail inquiries.

You can't assume that all e-mail received will be properly addressed. Each person handling e-mail should know who to forward a message to. You should also expect general comments about your Web page. Take these to heart, as the people making comments are the ones who were attracted to your site and represent potential customers.

E-mail is a great way to communicate with your customers and show that you care. Just make sure you really do care, and take the appropriate steps ahead of time.

Subscriptions

There is an axiom in business that it costs at least five times as much to get a new customer as to retain an old one (due to the cost of advertising, negotiations, first-time order processing, and so on). Regular customers know who you are and what you are about, and for obvious reasons, more marketing and advertising dollars need to be spent to draw in new customers. Repeat customers are especially important for information companies, because the cost of finding a customer can outweigh the profit from a single sale. They need to build credibility and a following before any real return on investment can be realized.

Subscriptions are the way most information companies get repeat business. Electronic payment systems supporting automatic renewals that require little or no customer intervention are needed to support electronic publishing.

Quote.Com (http://www.quote.com) is a financial information service providing quotes on stocks, commodity futures, mutual funds, and bonds (see fig. 2.8). Also, Quote.Com adds value to their existing service by bundling other relevant business information with its financials. By providing limited access to its services, Quote.Com entices customers to subscribe to the service. Because every business has different needs in terms of accurate financial information, Quote.Com wisely offers a variety of subscription options to fit specific customer needs. You can pay directly online with your credit card, or request an invoice through e-mail. As electronic payment systems catch on, look for more payment options as well.

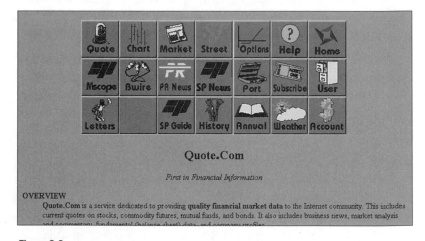

Figure 2.8
The Quote.Com home page.

Software companies have also been hugely successful, giving away promotional versions of their software. On the Web, software companies often distribute scaled back or "lite" versions of their product for free. Customers use a lite version of the product, want more, and purchase the full product. Purchasing software is more like purchasing a subscription than buying a tangible item such as a toaster. Like a quarterly magazine, new revisions are announced every few months, requiring a continuous investment to stay current.

Contests

An electronic storefront can market your retail stores, and you can use your retail store to spread the word about your Web site. JCPenney uses sweepstakes in their "What's New" section to encourage customers to visit their retail stores. For example, JCPenney at the writing of this book was encouraging people to come in and find out how to win a Jeep Wrangler Sahara, as shown in figure 2.9. "What's New" sections on Web sites are excellent places for contest announcements because this section, found on most Web home pages, updates customers on the latest company offerings and information about the new value-added features to its Web site; consequently, the contest draws the customer to the place on your site with the most current information.

Figure 2.9
A JCPenney sweepstakes offer.

Any digital storefront must be integrated with your company's entire business strategy. Digital storefronts must project the same personality as the offline part of your company. One common concern is that sales through a digital storefront will come at the expense of the same companies' traditional retail outlets—companies want to grow the business, not just shift customers around. Digital storefronts don't have to be competitors to your normal distribution channels. Contests are just one strategy for integrating your digital and retail storefronts.

Specials

Sale racks are on the Internet. When you select women's clothing on the JCPenney Web page, a list of selections appear with specially marked sale items (see fig. 2.10). Traditional marketing approaches can translate to the Internet—people are likely to click on the sale items first, and then compare their prices with those items not on sale.

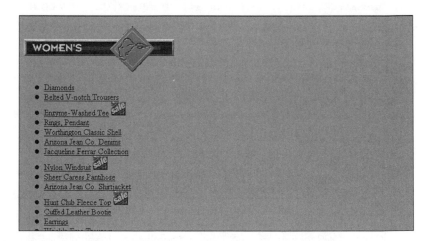

Figure 2.10

JCPenney's specially marked sale items.

Price competition is going to be fierce on the Internet. Comparison shopping is considerably easier online than it is even in a large mall. A customer can compare prices from a dozen stores in less than one hour online. Automated search agents will eventually reduce the cost of comparison shopping even more. Offering price breaks online will be a critical strategy for drawing customers to your site; however, consider integrating as many offerings as possible into your Web site that make the most sense for your business in order to keep your customers coming back to your digital storefront. If you have great prices and good quality, word travels fast.

Free Searches

San Jose Mercury Center is a daily Pulitzer prize-winning newspaper from San Jose, California. The Mercury Center offers standard newspaper copy and special expertise in business and computing through the Web. This site has a strong reputation for having a solid Web site with relevant articles about the computing industry, as shown in figure 2.11.

Figure 2.11
Check out *San Jose Mercury Center's* home page for articles of interest.

Searching the Mercury Center's current issue and its nearly one million archived articles is free. Charges apply only for downloaded articles. Discount rates apply for download request during off-business hours.

Free Merchandise

"Free" is a powerful and productive word in the advertising world. The word "free" can launch a customer stampede. The Free Offer Forum, a unique Web site from Venture Communications (http://www.shopping2000.com), offers free goods and services by category: apparel/gift, business, computer, sports, and so forth (see fig. 2.12). Some of the free offers in the computer category include demos, free downloads of software, and free issues of magazines. Businesses post free offers, samples, and services, and surfers are drawn to the site to check out all the free stuff—businesses want to be there to capitalize on the traffic.

Figure 2.12

Visit the Free Offer Forum for special offers from a variety of businesses.

Although the Free Offer Forum is a general-purpose site that capitalizes on people's natural appetite for free stuff, you can put the word "free" to work on your own Web page. Offering free samples is one way to avoid aggressive price cutting of regular merchandise. Draw people in with the word "free," and then advertise your other products heavily. Some price cuts on your other merchandise is also recommended. The regular merchandise is what will generate repeat business (and pay for all those freebies you just gave away).

You should consider forcing customers through several pages of your Web site, without frustrating them, before they get their freebies. Doing so enables you to advertise a few more goods than you can on one page. You should also consider asking customers to fill out some demographic information before getting their freebies. Avoid making it a requirement though—some customers are very sensitive to this kind of demand.

Compilation of Strategies

Some companies are investing heavily in their Web sites in order to create highly entertaining sites that will attract you and keep you there. Time Warner's Pathfinder (http://www.pathfinder.com) is just that kind of Web site, as shown in figure 2.13. Over 40 people were involved in the creation and development of Pathfinder.

Figure 2.13
The Pathfinder home page offers an array of entertaining options.

This site is a compilation of all the strategies described in this chapter, and then some. Pathfinder leverages information to get you to visit their site frequently by offering daily updates of the latest sport's scores and the latest headlines. You can chat on the billboards or take the unique Pathfinder tour, which automatically show you a succession of Pathfinder home pages. Subscribe to *COMPASS*, a free newsletter with the latest Pathfinder news sent to you weekly via e-mail. Enter contests and win prizes like a new HP printer. Visit the dream shops—a mall-like area that offers many fine name-brand stores: Eddie Bauer, Bombay Co., The Sharper Image, Spiegal, and so on. While you are visiting the dream shops, check out the special sales, or use the personal shopper search to find particular products. If you have an idea on how to improve the site, send your feedback to Pathfinder via e-mail.

Malls

Malls are popping up everywhere on the Internet, and some are attracting big name retailers. For the most part, they are simply an electronic model of the real thing. Being part of a hot mall is likely to generate additional traffic for your site. You can increase the odds that a mall browser will enter your storefront out of curiosity and maybe become a frequent shopper.

One of the "hot" malls on the Web is InternetMCI (http://www.internetmci.com), shown in figure 2.14. The mall houses a wide range of products and services: Aetna, Covey Leadership Center, Inc., Danmark, Dun & Bradstreet Information Services, Hammacher Schlemmer & Co., L'eggs, and Reiter's Scientific & Professional Books. The mall also provides a sneak preview of stores that will be arriving soon: FTD, The Timberland Company, and Lillian Vernon are just a few examples.

The mall itself leverages information and advertises sales to encourage people to come back. InternetMCI's Back to School home page promoted thematic freebies, such as an online dictionary, thesaurus, and encyclopedia. Reference tools and books were also available according to grade level.

InternetMCI offers CyberWarehouse—an online discount electronics superstore specializing in computer and consumer electronic products for the home and office. Orders are processed in 24 hours, and products are shipped within five business days.

Figure 2.14

InternetMCI houses popular retailers and services.

CyberWarehouse provides an electronic shopping basket to pick up a few things. The shopping basket holds all your purchases until you are ready to pay—you don't need to go through the payment cycle for each product. The shopping cart analogy will be an important part of retail online. Several software houses, such as Stydec (http://www.globalone.net/lionsden/stydec/) and Skeleton Development Corporation (http://www.upscale.com/skeleton.html), are offering products that will help companies build electronic shopping carts. The shopping cart symbol and process is proving to be an important part of a digital storefront (see fig. 2.15). Any general merchandise shopping site without a shopping cart will be projecting a cheap image.

CyberWarehouse offers technical assistance through e-mail for problems that cannot be resolved by the manufacturer's technical support department. This is one strategy that resellers can use to differentiate themselves from the competition. Service centers are a common strategy for electronics and appliance stores today. This same strategy also works online. Don't be fooled, however, into thinking that support online is the same as running a service center at a mall. Online support has several additional difficulties. Online support technicians, for example, will have more difficulty getting accurate information on the problem. In addition, customers may not understand enough about the product to accurately describe their problems. Your technicians will need some training in the use of e-mail, especially in how to avoid sounding rude, which is easy to do with e-mail.

Figure 2.15
Stydec can help you integrate the shopping cart model with your existing Web site.

You can securely shop the MCI Marketplace. All you need is a Netscape-compatible browser. Netscape Web browsers incorporate an encryption technology called *secure socket layer* (SSL), which is based on technology licensed from RSA Data Security. Credit card transactions are protected using public-key cryptography. If an MCI customer wants to make a purchase, but does not have a Netscape-compatible browser, MCI enables them to download one for free at their Web site. Visa, MasterCard, Optima, and American Express are all accepted.

Making Money

Setting up a Web site is not a guaranteed revenue generator by any stretch of the imagination. The Web in many respects is still in its infancy; however, secure electronic payment systems are believed to be the definitive ticket to unleashing the business potential of this medium.

For most businesses, the WWW is still a side show to their main business as they determine if long-term opportunity really exists on the Internet. So, you may ask, if the dollars aren't rolling in, where's all the hype coming from? Somebody must be cashing in or there wouldn't be so much commotion.

Some companies are making substantial profits from this new technology, and those companies are the usual suspects: software and hardware companies, computer publishers, Internet service providers, and consultants. The people making the money today are the people with the expertise or equipment to establish a business on the Web.

Netscape is a perfect example (http//www.netscape.com). In only two years, Netscape has established itself as the Web browser of choice. The company's profits have catapulted. Netscape is also profiting hugely from selling temporary advertising space on its browser. Companies are paying thousands of dollars for a banner about their company that pops up—for example, every time you do a search (see fig. 2.16).

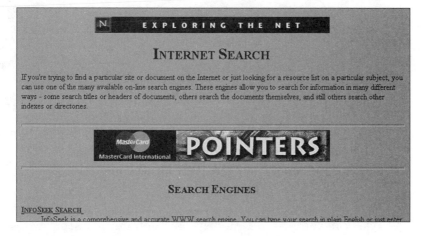

Figure 2.16

Netscape can charge a competitive rate for its advertising space.

Bookstores are crammed with books and magazines about the Internet and World Wide Web, and people are gobbling them up in record numbers. Because the Internet is so large and untamed, people take comfort from a book—a medium they understand—that will help them navigate through all the confusion.

Visit the widely written about Macmillan site (http://www.mcp.com) for a look an interesting marriage of the online world and the traditional book world that writes about the online world. Visit the Macmillan Information Super Library for a complete online catalog of computer resources. Read sample chapters and view tables of contents that give you an in-depth look at all the computer books from the various Macmillan computer imprints: New Riders, Que, Que Education and Training, Sams, Sams.net, Hayden, Adobe Press, and BradyGAMES (see fig. 2.17).

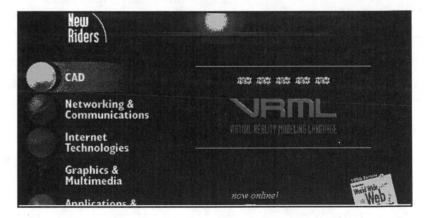

Figure 2.17
Check out New Rider's site for the latest in computer reference material.

With the new medium comes an array of hardware and software needs, including faster modems, better monitors, security system hardware and software, and programs that will add even more glitz to the WWW. These products are hot, and the craze is not showing any signs of slowing down any time soon. Sun Microsystems, for example, is a company that is truly capitalizing on the Web craze with its array of products, which extend from its server technology to its new product, Hot Java—not to mention their hugely successful Web site that boasts over 100,000 hits a day.

In addition to the hardware, software, and ISP frenzy, there are the consultants, who always benefit when people have no clue what they are doing. People are willing to pay great sums for the security and comfort of getting guidance from someone "in the know" who has a solid list of references.

With a few exceptions, the people responsible for getting the Web to its current state are the ones that have made money so far, with the exception of a few extremely successful sites like CDNOW.

Summary

The Web is now ready for the next generation of companies. Secure electronic payment systems are the defining factors that will enable companies, large and small, to profit by selling online.

Soon, it will no longer be about who is doing business on the Web, because nearly everyone will have a presence, but rather who is doing it well. Who are the true visionaries? What do customers really want? Will the large companies gobble up the small ones? Predictions abound, but the story is still unfolding. Smart businesspeople are keeping a close eye on their competition as they continue to refresh and re-energize their own digital storefronts.

Chapter 3

The Electronic Commerce Revolution

"In God we trust, all others pay cash." Have you seen this statement on the WWW? If the new breed of payment systems is successful, you just might. Electronic payment systems are being touted as the technology that will transform the Web from an advertiser's dream into a viable commercial arena.

The whole world of electronic commerce is overwhelming, even for regular Web surfers. Electronic commerce has suffered from several daunting obstacles: the challenge of forming contracts, the inability to sell to unknown parties, and, most of all, the difficulty of getting paid. Some companies have been accepting credit cards over the Internet, but customer resistance to this is high because of the possibility of having credit card numbers stolen. Businesses have been using electronic payment systems for some time, but these are cumbersome and involve long and difficult contract negotiations.

In this chapter, you are introduced to the new technologies obliterating the obstacles of doing business on the Web and enabling a new form of electronic commerce—a particular emphasis is placed on electronic payment systems. Different payment systems currently available are discussed and a method of evaluating those competing systems is presented. The chapter ends with a discussion of issues facing companies that want to accept electronic payment systems. Chapter 5, "Cryptography Basics," takes a closer look at the technology that makes these systems possible.

Public Key Cryptography

The big breakthrough that made advances in electronic commerce possible happened in the late seventies, when a group of researchers developed what is now known as public key cryptography. *Cryptography* is the science of scrambling messages so that they cannot be read. Ordinary cryptography schemes rely on a high-tech "secret-decoder ring," which, just like the matching secret-decoder rings buried in cereal boxes, is needed by both the sender and the reader in order to read messages.

Public key cryptography splits the decoder ring into two parts (called *keys*)—one key is made public (the *public key*) and the other is carefully guarded (the *private key*). The two keys always come in pairs. If the private key is ever compromised, the whole system breaks down.

All of the technologies discussed in this chapter rely in some way on public key cryptography. For more in-depth detail on public key cryptography, see Chapter 5.

Electronic Data Interchange

Electronic cash is just one application of advanced cryptography revolutionizing the field of Electronic Data Interchange (EDI). EDI specifies the format for a set of standard messages. Businesses exchange EDI messages with other businesses to order and pay for goods, check on parts availability, ship supplies, and more. EDI is essentially an electronic document—there are EDI purchase orders, EDI quotes, EDI authorizations, EDI verification of delivery, and so on. A clearinghouse collects various EDI payment authorizations from customers and settles accounts once a day. Until recently, EDI messages exchanged between businesses were sent over leased lines, not the Internet. The following is a description of a probable EDI scenario:

1. A buyer prepares an authenticated message, authorizing the transfer of funds to a merchant.

2. The message is sent to the merchant, who forwards it to the bank.

3. The merchant's bank checks the validity of the message and credits the merchant's account.

4. The merchant's bank sends a message to an electronic clearinghouse, indicating a payment is due from the buyer's bank.

5. Overnight, the clearinghouse settles accounts among participating banks.

6. The buyer bank debits the buyer's account.

EDI offers several advantages to businesses. Big businesses have been participating in these clearinghouse payment schemes for a number of years. For example, a typical paper order may involve a purchase order, a confirmation, a shipping bill, and an invoice. Multiple signatures are often necessary for each piece of paper involved in the process; therefore, a single order can easily cost several hundred dollars to track using a paper system. While EDI does eliminate unnecessary paperwork for businesses, the real advantage of EDI is that it gives a business increased capability to track orders and inventories electronically. This helps companies to improve their management, and in some cases save millions of dollars. Another huge benefit of EDI is that companies control their money at all times, preventing banks from collecting interest on customers' money as it "floats" in between accounts. When huge sums are involved, the interest is nontrivial.

You may be wondering, "If EDI is so great, why isn't it more widely used?". There are two barriers preventing EDI from being more widely used, as follows:

➤ Before businesses participate in EDI, they negotiate very detailed contracts. Involved negotiations are only practical when large sums of money are involved with a long-term partner. The cost of setting up EDI outweighs any benefit for small transactions.

➤ Because all EDI arrangements to date have relied on pre-negotiated contracts, established rules for electronic commerce do not exist. Only pre-existing contracts have been enforced by the courts.

The new technologies (electronic payment systems, digital signatures, and digital notarizations) will eliminate these barriers, enabling transactions between parties that may never meet, and making EDI possible for small money exchanges and consumers. These technologies represent a new way of doing business, one that the courts have not previously dealt with. The "big defining liability case" for EDI has not yet occurred. In the author's opinion, the benefits of participating in the new world of electronic commerce—speed, efficiency, and cost savings—greatly exceed the potential risks. If you happen to work for a large or successful company, you should analyze carefully the kind of risk your company is taking on before plunging ahead with an electronic payment system. These advances in EDI will help small companies compete with larger firms. As EDI is extended to the Internet and enhanced with new capabilities, small firms will be able to take advantage of automated systems that were previously cost-prohibitive. Soon, small and large companies alike will be able to electronically track orders and payments, enter into contracts, and get paid over the Internet.

A six-month pilot project to test the practical and security aspects of making payments via the Internet is currently underway by BankAmerica Corp. and Lawrence Livermore Laboratory, using EDI. BankAmerica is using the trial to test out the new technology, while Livermore's motivation is to cut down on direct costs involved in paying vendors.

In addition to electronic cash, two other advances in EDI will play a key role in electronic commerce: digital signatures and digital notarization. These advances enable companies to enter into binding contracts over the Internet. These contracts have several efficiency, security, and validity advantages over paper contracts.

Digital Signatures

Digital signatures enable one party to sign a document with a personal signature. The document receiver can look at the digital signature of the sender and determine whether the document was altered since it was signed. Digital signatures have several advantages over paper signatures, as follows:

➤ They cannot be easily forged.

➤ They make document tampering obvious.

➤ They can be verified at a distance.

➤ They can be verified by someone who has never met the signer.

➤ They are valid for copies, as well as for the original.

Digital signatures encourage electronic commerce, because it is easier for two parties to engage in business without pre-negotiating a contract. Because digital signatures can be exchanged at the time of the transaction, no previous meeting between the parties is necessary, thus making paper signatures appear more cumbersome. A third-party presence to vouch for the validity of a signature is necessary when using digital signatures. These third parties, known as *certifiers*, sign other organizations' digital signatures, enabling anyone to validate the original digital signature. The signed digital signature is known as a *certificate*. Many certifiers provide either copies of the certificate, or publish the certified data in a public place (database, Web server, and so on). Here's how it works:

1. You send your digital signature to a certifier.

2. The certifier sends you an electronic certificate.

3. You present this certificate along with your signature when sending a signed document.

4. The certificate is used to look up a copy of your electronic signature, and the copy is compared to the registered signature.

In order for this process to work, each party must trust the certifier. A growing and potentially problematic issue, which business leaders will need to reevaluate on a regular basis, is who are the best and most trustworthy certifiers? Will you trust a signature certified by the Iraqi government? How about the U.S. government? Which domestic and international private certifiers will you trust? Would you have trusted the BCCI bank? (BCCI was a worldwide bank that collapsed due to several scandals.)

Digital signatures, combined with trusted timestamp services, enable non-repudiable transactions. ***Non-repudiable transactions*** are transactions that cannot be denied after the fact. A person who signs a message cannot deny that the message was sent. If that message happened to be his or her signature on an electronic contract, then the contract is binding. Digital signatures prove the identity of a signer, and a trusted timestamp service guarantees the time of signing. Timestamp services are provided by digital notaries.

Digital Notarization

Digital documents are, by design, easily altered. Changes are simple and untraceable. Electronic commerce, however, cannot grow on a basis of alterable records. An electronic contract requires a digital audit trail that seals the document's content and provides an accurate timestamp. As more and more important documents go digital, the need to provide a digital audit trail increases. Digital notarization certifies internal document trails, making it possible for companies to use electronic forms for critical information. Providing a digital audit trail is the role of the digital notary.

Generally, the state of a particular document at a particular point in time only becomes important after several months or years have passed. What may seem unimportant at the time the action is occurring (phone records, e-mail memos, meeting minutes, personal schedules) can make the difference in a dispute at a much later date. Having records notarized as a matter of course removes any doubt about the validity of these records. Patent applications can hinge on being able to reconstruct the process used to develop an idea. A paper trail is needed to prove the time and place the idea originated, and to reconstruct the steps from conception to product. Digital notarization will become far more widespread than paper notarizations are today because of the ease and convenience of this type of notarization.

One application of digital notarizations is lab records. In the past, researchers had to keep paper records simply to provide a paper trail. A digital notary system gives researchers a way to keep electronic histories of their projects by automatically notarizing their daily records. This process provides a solid documented history of development projects. Also, digital notaries are useful for certifying financial records, contracts, and research papers. The following companies and organizations will benefit by using digital notarization:

➤ **Law enforcement agencies.** Maintaining a proper chain of evidence is crucial. Digital notaries can certify police records, as well as any evidence that can be translated into an electronic format (wiretaps, surveillance film, and so on).

➤ **Accounting firms.** Recent court awards against accounting firms have intensified the pressure on these firms to ensure the integrity of financial records.

➤ **Hospitals.** Hospitals can guarantee that patient records, lab results, and diagnosis records have not been altered.

➤ **Banks.** Banks and credit card companies maintain large volumes of electronic records, including text and graphics.

➤ **Law firms.** Law firms can efficiently sign and date many types of documents.

➤ **Wall Street.** Traders track the time of each trade made. Disputes over the time a trade was made, with the difference being only a few minutes, can potentially cost millions. Digital notaries can be used to eliminate most, if not all, disputes.

Digital notarization has several advantages over today's notary publics. A notary public verifies a document by countersigning a document and making an entry in a log. If the signature is later challenged, the notary must verify the signature. An electronic notarization can be verified in seconds, while a paper notarization may require hours or days. A digital notary system enables a company to have its electronic files notarized without having to reveal the contents of those files, and the validity of those files is then verified by an independent third party.

Digital notarization is inexpensive and far easier than paper notarization. Because of the obvious advantages, the use of digital notarization could easily become far more important than that of paper notarization. Like digital signatures, digital notarizations have several advantages over paper notarizations, as follows:

➤ They cannot be forged.

➤ They make document tampering obvious.

➤ They can be verified at a distance.

➤ They can be verified by someone who has never met the signer.

➤ They are valid for copies of a document, as well as the original.

A digital notarization is not the same thing as a digital signature, even though the underlying mathematics is similar (as described in Chapter 5). Some key differences do exist. Digital signatures verify identities of people. Digital notarization verifies when a particular document was notarized. A digital signature is a person's stamp of approval on a document—for example, a signature on a legal contract. In many cases, the author of a document is less important than the fact that a document existed at a certain point in time, thus making the digital notarization of the document a critical step in the process. If you want to sign and date an electronic document, first have the document signed, and then electronically notarize the document.

Surety Technologies, Inc. released a digital notarization program in January, 1995. As shown in figure 3.1, their system works by generating an electronic fingerprint, as follows (numbers correspond to the numbers in the figure):

1. Information derived from a document (the digital fingerprint) is sent to the notary. The actual document is not sent.

2. The notary collects together all fingerprints received in a one-second interval, and then signs the collected information.

3. Certificates are returned to each user.

4. Each certificate receives a timestamp and is stored in a local database.

5. The collected fingerprints are in turn published on the Internet and in newspapers.

The electronic fingerprint does not contain any information from your document; the fingerprint is just an identifier and confirms that it was generated from your document. This fingerprint is then sent to Surety via the Internet, or by dialing directly into their server. In order to prove that a document was actually notarized at a designated time, Surety collects all the fingerprints sent within a one second time frame and binds them together mathematically. The bound fingerprints validate that all of these fingerprints were received at one time—a difficult thing to fake. After binding the fingerprints together, information is sent back to your server. Your software issues a time-stamped certificate and stores the certificate in a database. The original document is not altered, as with most digital signature systems. The bound fingerprints are regularly published in a national newspaper, preventing anyone from forging or altering a notarization.

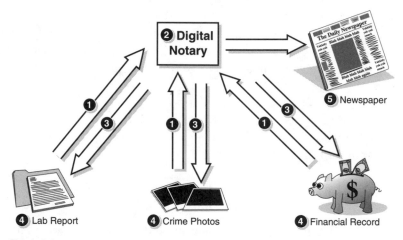

Figure 3.1

Digital notarization dates a document.

BellCore's Trusted Software Integrity System (BETSI) is another example of a notarization service—this service is currently just an experiment, designed to ensure the integrity of software obtained over the Internet via anonymous ftp. BETSI's long-term goals are to protect software users by doing the following:

➤ Making it possible to verify the identity of software providers

➤ Ensuring that software has not been modified since it was posted

For more information on BETSI, go to http://info.bellcore.com/betsi/betsi.html.

Electronic Archiving

Any company interested in widespread use of digital notarization will also want to investigate electronic archiving in order to save notarized documents. *Electronic archiving* is the process of saving and maintaining historical records in electronic format. More is involved than just backing up tapes and storing them in a safe.

A word of caution. With data formats and storage technology changing at a breakneck pace, your archives are in danger of becoming unreadable. The program needed to read a data format may become obsolete and unavailable. Also, the hardware needed to read your storage medium may be out of production. For example, how many documents does your company currently have on microfiche? Digital records stored for years do break down. An archive may be unreadable because of age. Digitally notarized documents are only useful when retrieving documents is quick and easy. Because digital documents cannot be altered without breaking the notarization, companies cannot just update the format of the stored documents—for example, you can't just take a notarized document in Word 2.0 format and change it to Word 6.0 format. Potentially, you will need to store copies of old programs just to access notarized documents.

Even keeping outdated versions of commercially available products is a challenge. Many separate programs are used throughout an organization, and keeping an inventory of all the versions of each program used over the years is a formidable task. In-house applications are especially troublesome. Rarely are previous versions of in-house applications retained. Data stored on backup tapes in proprietary format is sometimes lost. When in-house applications are updated, the in-house IS staff also makes any format changes to the data; however, format changes to notarized information are impossible without rendering the notary certificate invalid.

One solution is to export data from in-house applications into a generic format (ASCII would work for most data, because most data is text) and notarize the exported data. Save a copy of the notarized document and make certain that all versions of your in-house applications can read the exported documents. If some day you need a notarized document for a court case, for instance, you may not have time to undertake several weeks or months of programming to gain access to your notarized documents.

Electronic Payment Systems

Electronic payment systems (EPSs) come in a variety of forms. For our purposes, an EPS is any method of getting paid online. The needs of your business will determine which forms of payment you will accept. In addition, each EPS comes with its own advantages and disadvantages. For example, one weakness of many EPSs is the capability of supporting *micro payments*—payments of ten cents or less. Credit card systems are impractical because the cost of processing the transaction is greater than the actual charge. Micro payments are important in information sales, but not for hard goods; however, credit card payment systems are well-suited for hard good sales.

Here are eight requirements for the perfect EPS. The criteria are simple: the perfect EPS supports transactions between anonymous parties and does so with zero overhead cost. This criteria is designed to allow the widest possible range of business transactions, enabling businesses to deal both internationally and domestically, while reaching the widest possible customer base. No single system will have all the following characteristics. You need to evaluate actual systems against these criteria; different criteria will be more important to some than for others. The following list is not meant to imply any particular order. The perfect EPS fulfills the following requirements:

➤ **Cannot be lost, stolen, or forged.** The ultimate security. Your money is yours until you voluntarily give it up.

➤ **Has zero transaction costs.** The perfect system wouldn't cost customers or merchants anything—no sign-up fee, no minimum charge, no transaction fee. (If anyone thinks they know of a completely free EPS, there's this bridge you may be interested in....)

➤ **Is accepted worldwide.** This implies that transactions can be completed between parties that are on opposite sides of the globe just as easily as if both parties are standing in the same room. Currency issues would not be a problem, nor would there be a requirement that participants have accounts in a particular country.

➤ **Can be used for any size payment, from a penny to several billion dollars or more.** Electronic cash has the potential to create new markets for software and information. Software developers can potentially charge for individual subroutines and authors can charge by the chapter or paragraph. These markets require a payment system that can support very small amounts (a few pennies). On the flip side, major business transactions can run into the billions of dollars. A perfect system would handle both, making it unnecessary to convert between systems.

➤ **Supports credit and debit payments.** Sometimes you just want to take out an instant loan. Other times, it's more convenient to pay cash. The perfect electronic payment system would enable customers to choose (at transaction time) which type of payment they preferred.

➤ **Instantaneously transfers money between the customer and merchant.** Merchants want to get paid fast.

➤ **Provides completely anonymous, untraceable transactions.** This issue gets more press than nearly any other, and it is important, but not as important as other factors. Still, the perfect EPS would be anonymous. Merchants wanting to know the identity of their customers can collect that information other ways. Forcing customers to reveal their identity isn't an integral part of a perfect system. Some law enforcement agencies may disagree, however.

➤ **Is not subject to inflation or devaluation.** Wouldn't it be nice to know that a dollar will buy tomorrow what it buys today? No system will ever completely achieve this objective, but some private branded cash systems may come close.

Your criteria may be different. If knowing the identity of your customers is an important aspect of your business, you may only be interested in EPSs that identify the customer. The authors recommend splitting the requirement for knowing your customer from the problem of getting paid. You can always get around anonymous EPSs by requiring customers to fill out a form or sign something before accepting payment.

Types of Electronic Payment Systems

Electronic payment systems can be categorized several ways. One way is to describe the different types of electronic transactions that are possible, as discussed in the following sections. Chapter 4, "Internet Commerce Providers," provides specific examples of each system and of merchants who have chosen to use them.

E-Mail Approach

Various payment systems enable customers to use credit cards for online purchases without sending their credit card information over the Internet. The card numbers are stored away on a protected computer system and never pass over the network. You give your credit card information to the company you select to handle your transactions. The information is protected on one of their very secure computer systems, and you are given an ID. When you want to buy something online, you use your ID number to make a purchase instead of your credit card. Even if the ID number is intercepted, it cannot be used because you must approve each transaction.

Unencrypted Credit Cards

The simplest form of online payment involves sending your credit card number over the Internet with no security precautions taken—you basically take your chances. Your risk really isn't much different than when you give your credit card number over the phone when making catalog orders. In that situation, the vendor has no way to ensure that the person using the credit card is its owner. Most serious vendors on the Internet will have secure credit card systems in place in the near future. The technology will soon be available and easy to use.

Encrypted Credit Cards

Netscape, the most popular Web browser, has built encryption into its browser and Web-server software. If you are using the Netscape browser, you can make secure credit card transactions online if the participating vendor has a secure Netscape Web server. Support for Privacy Enhanced Mail (PEM) and Pretty Good Privacy (PGP) have been built into Mosaic 2.4. Now any vendor can create a secure system that accepts credit card numbers.

MasterCard and Visa are currently working on standards for secure credit card transactions on the Internet. Even with encrypted credit cards, false charges and denied charges will still be a problem. There is nothing magical about encrypting a credit card number. All the problems present with today's credit cards would be present under a system that only encrypts credit card numbers.

One of the key decisions that will need to be decided by MasterCard and Visa is whether to accept digital signatures. Digital signatures can add a level of verification not present in current credit card schemes, but would require users to obtain encryption keys before using their credit card online.

Electronic Credit Cards

Electronic credit cards rely on encryption technology from RSA Data Security, Inc. Electronic credit cards do not have the problems of false charges and denied charges regular credit cards face, because of the multiple layers of security involved that protect both the customer and the merchant. The private and public key technology requires that a thief have access to two keys (public and private) and your password to get your electronic credit card information. Security issues are discussed at length in Chapters 5 and 6.

Electronic Checks

Electronic checks involve the same level of security and general payment system set up as electronic credit cards. The difference is that instead of using an ID number, the bank issues you a whole set of numbers—similar to a checkbook minus the checks. Also, like checks, you use each number only once. The software that manages the electronic checks also provides routine tracking of the checks that you have written. These electronic checks can bounce, just like an ordinary check.

Electronic Cash

Electronic cash is the digital equivalent of dollars and cents. The technology necessary for cash transactions online is the same private and public key technology used for electronic credit cards. Banks and customers use the public and private keys so that customers can withdraw and deposit electronic cash. Electronic cash can be more convenient and flexible than traditional money, and in some forms offers the same level of anonymity as regular cash.

Privacy and the Mechanics of Getting Paid

Electronic payment systems vary in their answers to the following questions:

1. When does the merchant's account get credited?

2. When does the customer's account get debited?

3. Can the electronic cash be lost or stolen?

4. Are purchases anonymous?

5. Who is liable for forged or contested payments?

Merchants (and customers) must understand the difference between debit and credit systems, the mechanics of online and offline payments, and the privacy concerns raised by electronic cash.

Debit and Credit Payments

Debit systems work like a checking account. You put the money in and then spend it. Credit systems work like a credit card; spend first, pay later. Credit systems use digital signatures and timestamps to replace the paper trail provided with credit card slips today.

Electronic payment systems can be divided into two categories, as follows:

➤ Identified EPSs

➤ Anonymous EPSs

Identified EPSs stamp each transaction with the identity of the consumer, leaving a paper trail like an electronic credit card. *Anonymous EPSs* work the same as currency—consumers can use anonymous EPSs without identifying themselves. Figure 3.2 illustrates the various degrees of anonymity provided by different EPSs.

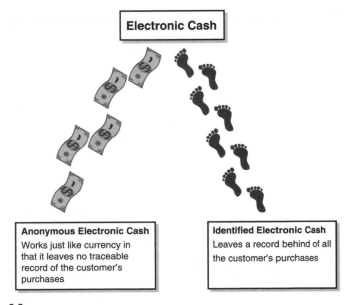

Electronic Cash

Anonymous Electronic Cash
Works just like currency in that it leaves no traceable record of the customer's purchases

Identified Electronic Cash
Leaves a record behind of all the customer's purchases

Figure 3.2
Some EPSs protect the customer's privacy.

Each of the two EPS categories is further subdivided into offline and online, resulting in the following four types of EPSs:

➤ Identified online

➤ Identified offline

➤ Anonymous online

➤ Anonymous offline

Online EPSs are either credit card or debit systems. Offline EPSs are always debit systems because the electronic cash issuer will require customers to deposit funds equal to the amount of cash they want to spend (see fig. 3.3).

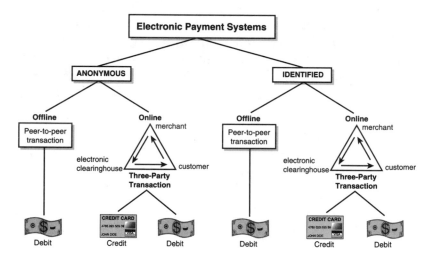

Figure 3.3

Types of electronic payment systems.

Three parties are involved with every online transaction—the customer, the merchant, and an electronic clearinghouse. The process is illustrated in figure 3.4. The customer creates a message that includes the following information:

➤ A description of the purchase

➤ The names of the customer and merchant

➤ The amount of the purchase

➤ The date and time of the purchase

The customer digitally signs the message and sends it either to the merchant or to the electronic clearinghouse (depending on the system in use). If the message is sent to the merchant, he immediately submits it to the clearinghouse for approval. In either case, the merchant receives an approval from the clearinghouse. For this example, the clearinghouse may be a bank, a credit card company, or any other company that can authorize a customer's purchase. Figure 3.4 illustrates one possible scenario (there are many ways to accomplish the actual transfer of funds).

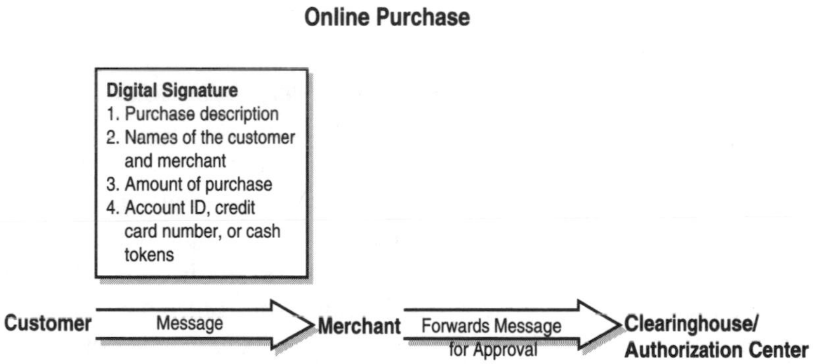

Online Purchase

Digital Signature
1. Purchase description
2. Names of the customer and merchant
3. Amount of purchase
4. Account ID, credit card number, or cash tokens

Customer → Message → Merchant → Forwards Message for Approval → Clearinghouse/ Authorization Center

Figure 3.4

Online systems: merchants receive an approval before accepting payment.

Only two parties are involved in an offline payment—the customer and the merchant. Figure 3.5 illustrates an example of one possible process for getting paid using an offline payment system. The customer buys electronic cash from an electronic cash issuer before going shopping. The electronic cash issuer gives the customer files containing the amount of cash purchased, unique numbers that identify the cash, the name of the issuing company, and the digital signature of the issuing company. A purchase is made just by transferring these files from the customer to the merchant. The merchant can then spend them or redeem them for government-backed currency.

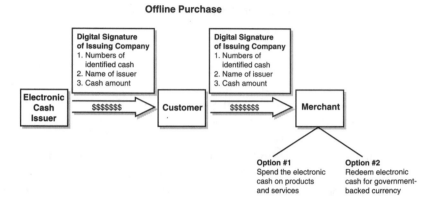

Figure 3.5

Offline transactions involve only the merchant and customer.

Legitimate consumer concerns about storing cash on personal PCs will be a major barrier to widespread adoption of offline electronic cash. Hard disk crashes and inadvertent erasures could result in loss of electronic cash. If a consumer accidentally made copies of electronic cash, he may be charged with attempted forgery. If a computer is shared with children, leaving electronic cash on the hard disk is a clear invitation to disaster. These issues require knowledge far beyond the abilities of today's average computer user. Most users will simply decide to not use a system that stores money on a PC's hard drive.

Smart cards—credit card-sized pieces of plastic with an embedded microchip that can store electronic money—are the most promising form of offline electronic cash. They avoid all the problems with storing money on a hard drive. Smart cards will be usable with PCs through special card readers. It wouldn't be surprising to see smart card readers become common accessories for home computers.

Identified Online Electronic Payment Systems

Identified online EPSs are actually just the same as paying with your credit card or a debit card. Merchants get authorization from a central computer before accepting payments, just as they do now for all credit card transactions. Both the merchant and the bank know the identity of the purchaser, along with when and where each purchase is made. Some identified online systems will immediately deduct the payment from your account, while others will simply bill your credit card.

Anonymous Online Electronic Payment Systems

A customer paying with an anonymous online EPS can remain unknown to the merchant. The merchant knows only the IP address of the customer's computer. The merchant gets authorization from the bank for each transaction to ensure the validity of the transaction, and the bank can still track all purchases made by an individual.

Merchants should not count on using IP addresses to track individual customers. Consumers accessing the Internet using systems such as CompuServe are assigned a different IP address every time they access the Internet, and most home users will not have a permanent IP address. Of course, merchants may have customers fill out forms listing the address and name for promotional purposes or to ship goods.

Identified Offline Electronic Payment Systems

Identified offline EPSs can be used in situations where it is inconvenient to contact a bank's computers. With identified offline systems, the merchant and bank know the identity of the customer. Smart cards are one form of identified offline EPSs. Software-based identified offline EPSs work by adding the customer's digital signature to the cash when it is spent.

Anonymous Offline Electronic Payment Systems

With anonymous offline EPSs, as with currency, possession is nine-tenths of the law—anonymous electronic cash has the potential to be lost or stolen. With anonymous offline EPSs, the identity of the customer remains unknown, except for the IP address of the customer's computer (which is useless to the merchant; see the preceding discussion of anonymous online EPSs). The only exception to this is when cash is double spent, as discussed in the next section.

Double Spending

Offline electronic cash stored on a PC is nothing more than a bunch of bits on your hard disk. Creating copies of electronic dollar bills is thus quite easy—no need to buy a high-priced color copier to copy cash here. By creating copies of electronic cash, anyone could start with a penny at eight in the morning and be a millionaire by noon. This is known as the ***double-spending problem***. How are people prevented from copying electronic cash and spending it twice? The answer to this question will play a key role in the success of offline electronic cash.

Not all double spending would be of malicious intent—home users, for example, may not even understand the problem, and could quite accidentally create copies of their electronic cash. System backups might have copies of electronic cash. When a system is restored using the backup, who can tell which cash has already been spent? This problem is avoidable by updating spent cash accounts on multiple systems and using RAID or mirrored disks. These techniques make it highly unlikely that a hardware failure would result in the need to restore a electronic cash database from a backup. Of course, no home user will be using these techniques, so the problem is not likely to go away.

Online electronic cash does not suffer from this problem. This type of cash is spent only once, because the electronic banks keep track of spent money and instantly subtract it from the buyer's account. If a bank tells a merchant that the requested cash has already been spent, the merchant will refuse the sale.

Relying on smart cards is a good solution for handling the double-spending problem. Instead of storing cash on your computer, it is stored on a smart card. The smart card keeps your current balance through an observer chip integrated into the card. No known way exists to alter the account balance stored on a smart card with an integrated observer chip, making the card tamper-proof. Any attempt to alter the contents voids all the cash stored on the card. Chapter 4 discusses smart card vendors in detail.

One way to discourage, but not prevent, double spending is to guarantee that anyone double spending money is easily identified. The theory is that because anyone double spending money will be caught, people won't do it. Of course, if the double spender is in South America by the time the double spending is detected, there is little that can be done. Accidental double-spending, which this scheme does not prevent, is a problem that is best handled by the backer of the electronic cash, and the person who accidentally double-spent (we're not saying it will be handled, just that it could be). Accidental double spending will not involve large sums, because it will be limited to home users and can be solved with a little education.

Both forms of offline electronic cash—identified and anonymous—do not require any special hardware, can be implemented entirely in software, and can run on any computer. With identified electronic cash, the identity of the person spending the cash is added to the cash each time it is spent. Identified offline electronic cash tracks the cash's path through the economy. When the cash is redeemed, the bank can deduce some interesting statistics. The bank knows what each person purchased, where it was purchased, when it was purchased, and the cost, as well as the amount of time each person held the cash before spending it.

Anonymous electronic cash is also modified with each transaction. Information is attached to anonymous electronic cash, which enables a bank to identify a double spender. If a person does not double spend, the identity of the person cannot be deduced, because the bank is unable to reconstruct the path the cash took through the economy.

Both of these strategies leave one question unanswered: Who is liable for double-spent cash? Merchants have no way of knowing if previously spent electronic cash is being used to make a purchase. If a merchant tries to redeem double-spent cash, will he or she be paid? If not, a strong incentive exists to pass the buck (literally) rather than redeem it. If a bank refuses to accept cash that has been double spent, what is to prevent someone from spending the cash somewhere else? Make sure you have answers to these questions before accepting offline cash at your digital storefront.

The EPS Infrastructure

EDI and credit cards are responsible for the creation of an infrastructure well-suited for supporting EPSs. Worldwide credit card companies, automated teller machines (ATMs), and electronic clearinghouses are already in place and ready to participate in the new electronic commerce. Networks linking banks, businesses, and clearinghouses are worldwide in scope. Extending these networks to the home is now as easy as purchasing a modem.

The cost of operating these networks can give you some idea of the cost of supporting worldwide electronic cash transactions. Merchants pay 2-3 percent, plus 20 cents per transaction, for credit card purchases. Customers pay 13-21 percent interest on unpaid balances. Checks cost a few pennies each, with penalties for overdrawn accounts. A similar cost structure will emerge for EPSs. The cheapest transactions are those that most closely resemble cash purchases, with costs escalating for automatic clearing of checks, and the highest costs associated with credit purchases.

The ability of credit card purchasers to accept payment in virtually any currency, and to resolve accounts on a global scale, gives them an automatic advantage when it comes to processing orders on the Internet. Other schemes that require a U.S. domestic checking account, or that put the burden of exchanging currency on the merchant, are less attractive.

Systems that rely on an automated clearinghouse may be at a disadvantage on the Internet, however. Although transactions cost only 15 cents each, payments are limited to U.S. banks, at least in the near term. This is because the U.S. Federal Reserve actually transfers money among participating banks.

Banks are not the only ones likely to issue electronic cash, although they do have one key advantage. Online companies today handle billing for their information providers. This role could be expanded to play a significant part in paying for information sales. Other companies will also issue electronic cash. Still, only banks are currently allowed to participate in fractional banking systems. The fractional system enables banks to create more electronic cash than they have assets to back. Other institutions issuing electronic cash will back their currency with assets equal in value to the cash in circulation. This should enable banks to earn more revenue using customers' money, while that money stays in the form of electronic cash.

EPS Software

Merchants need to integrate merchant software into their systems for each payment type they decide to accept. Offering a wide variety of payment types will take significant resources to program and test the various software packages. Compatibility problems may arise among multiple vendors' software. If you are outsourcing your server, investigate the types of payments your service provider can support. Select one that supports the payment types you desire.

Customers may need to acquire software for each payment system they want to use. At the current time, the customer software for every system can be easily downloaded for free from the Internet. Some systems also require a secure Web browser.

Electronic Cash Paper Trails

Purchase orders, confirmation numbers, bills, and receipts are common pieces of paper making up an audit trail. An entire transaction can be reconstructed using the pieces of paper issued by companies. Online payment systems also require an audit trail. The traditional pieces of paper have electronic equivalents. Make sure you understand the audit trail for each type of electronic cash you accept. Some EPSs store an audit trail with the actual cash; others rely on clearinghouses. Give considerable thought to the new forms and financial records your company may need when making the leap into the online world. If your company requires purchase orders, then choose a system that lends itself to the creation of purchase orders. Because purchase orders are a form of contract potentially requiring a digital signature, most offline systems would not be acceptable for a company that requires purchase orders. Digital signatures cannot be verified in an offline transaction.

Summary

This chapter introduced the new technologies that are expanding the realm of electronic commerce to the Internet and small businesses. Each of the key components of commerce (contracts, signatures, notaries, payment systems, and audit trails) are supported in the new electronic commerce. Furthermore, these technologies are cheap and easy to use. Merchants should understand all of these technologies, but should pay particular attention to the payment system selected. Electronic payment systems are evolving rapidly, so a set of criteria was presented that any merchant can use to evaluate any payment system that may come along.

The next chapter, "Internet Commerce Providers," surveys several actual payment systems that are either currently available or in beta testing. The advantages, disadvantages, and risks of each system are discussed.

Chapter 4

Internet Commerce Providers

New electronic payment systems can move electronic cash along multiple channels largely outside the established network of banks, checks, and paper currency overseen by the Federal Reserve. Merchants and their customers will be able to send their money more cheaply, conveniently, and quickly than through the traditional banking system.

This chapter examines in detail several of the electronic payment systems that are available over the Internet. Some electronic payment systems enable businesses to deal with each other directly, instead of through electronic clearinghouses. Some systems utilize credit cards, while others involve using the digital equivalent of real cash—strings of bits and bytes that can be exchanged for goods and services. Electronic cash is similar to its tangible counterpart in that it is anonymous, works person-to-person, and does not have credit limits. Because electronic cash is software, it can be programmed to do things that paper money will never do. For example, electronic money can be earmarked for certain kinds of payments. Companies and banks are jumping into the market with both feet, and whoever gets there first will likely set the standards for electronic cash.

A variety of companies worldwide are releasing electronic payment systems (EPSs) based on the approaches outlined in Chapter 3, "The Electronic Commerce Revolution." Each of the systems has its own advantages and disadvantages. This chapter explores some of the early market leaders. New companies are announcing plans every week, so don't take this list as exhaustive.

It will be interesting to see how the emerging industry will handle payment problems. Presently, merchants are liable for fraudulent credit-card transactions, which are difficult to prove regardless of whether they are made online or offline. Also, customers currently have no recourse under existing law for disputed debit transactions.

DigiCash

DigiCash's most highly advertised product, ecash, is designed for secure payments from any personal computer to any other workstation, over e-mail or the Internet. In the past, DigiCash (http://www.digicash.com) has pioneered cash for chip cards (smart cards) and electronic wallets (software that manages electronic cash), always with a tamper-resistant chip for storing the value. One smart card system was for automatic highway toll collection. Figure 4.1 shows the DigiCash home page.

DigiCash started a pilot project in October, 1994, using digital money online, which was continuing when this book went to press. Consumers are part of a DigiCash marketplace, a collection of companies that are participating in the trial and which accept ecash, using ecash to do business with companies such as Encyclopaedia Britiannica, Inc., *Wired* magazine, and several smaller companies. The digital money used in this trial run is called the Cyberbuck. Cyberbucks used in the trial cannot be exchanged for real money, but valuable goods and services can be purchased with it. A number of merchants have set up cybershops and are participating in the pilot.

Figure 4.1

DigiCash is currently piloting an online anonymous debit electronic payment system.

While the pilot has been extended, Mark Twain Banks (http://www.marktwain.com), has begun to use real Cyberbucks, which can be exchanged for real currency (see fig. 4.2). Mark Twain Banks is the first U.S. bank to issue and accept Cyberbucks. Several companies are already signing up to accept Cyberbucks, including BizNet Technologies (http://www.bnt.com), Sun Microsystems (http://www.sun.com), and The Well (http://www.well.com).

Figure 4.2

Mark Twain Banks home page.

Software Requirements

Because DigiCash is a peer-to-peer system, both the merchant and customer use the same ecash software, which is freely available. Most merchants need the text-based version of the software, so they can integrate it into their internal servers. The software works on all major platforms (MS Windows, Macintosh, and Unix). The graphical user interface displays the amount of money transacted in cash.

Target Market

Cyberbucks are especially useful for small-scale impulse purchases like newspaper articles, stock quotes, software manuals, and so on because there is no transaction charge. Fund transfers are also easily accomplished with DigiCash.

How to Make a Transaction

Both the consumer and merchant need software from DigiCash before they can use Cyberbucks. The consumer must have an account with a participating bank—DigiCash does not issue electronic cash. They provide software that enables banks to issue electronic cash. Cyberbucks can be used over e-mail or the Internet. The steps needed to complete a transaction are as follows:

1. The customer downloads a free copy of the encryption software developed by DigiCash from any Web site that accepts the company's electronic money.

2. The customer establishes an account with a participating DigiCash bank, such as Mark Twain Banks, and is assigned a digital signature. The digital signature contains a random seed, which will be used to generate Cyberbuck serial numbers later on.

3. The customer deposits money, using either a credit card or personal check, into a participating DigiCash bank.

4. The customer makes an electronic withdrawal from the bank account.

5. The bank checks the customer's signature with the bank's signature.

6. If the signatures match, the customer's computer issues a series of encrypted serial numbers representing dollar bills and coins. The serial numbers are stored in electronic envelopes and sent to the bank. The bank signs the envelopes without knowing the actual serial numbers. The signed envelopes are returned to the customer, who then removes the envelope. All of this happens automatically whenever a customer withdraws money from an account. This scheme prevents the bank or merchant from tracing the Cyberbuck back to the customer.

7. The customer stores the Cyberbucks on his or her computer. The customer can guard against computer crashes by writing down the random seed generated when the account is opened.

8. The customer purchases a product online at a shop accepting ecash.

9. The merchant verifies the validity of the Cyberbuck by contacting the issuing bank.

10. The electronic currency is deposited directly into the merchant's ecash account.

11. The merchant instantly provides the goods or services requested, if possible—the Cyberbuck is the value involved with the transaction and has the bank's seal of approval.

Using Cyberbucks is no harder than using most other electronic payment systems, and offers the advantage of low cost and privacy for the customer.

Getting Paid

The merchant gets paid by redeeming each Cyberbuck at the issuing bank, which transfers the money into the merchant's account over the Internet. Merchants pay a U.S. $5–25 monthly fee, plus a 2–3% charge, when exchanging Cyberbucks for real money. There is no minimum charge.

Security and Privacy

Ecash is as anonymous as paper cash. The software enables the issuing bank to certify an electronic note without tracing to whom it was issued. Money is withdrawn from an account using a password known only to the customer—not even the bank knows the password. The anonymity is one-sided in favor of the customer. The merchant is identified by the bank when clearing a transaction; Cyberbucks do not guarantee customer privacy, however, because merchants can easily keep track of where they send their wares.

Businesses Using DigiCash

Full support is given to new online shops using ecash. Some of the cybershops currently participating in the pilot include *Wired* magazine, SUNY Plattsburgh's DigiCash College Store, Computermaster, Inc., and Bytown Electronic Marketplace.

Outlook

The current version of ecash requires a network connection; however, a version for e-mail will be available in the near future. The long term goal is to create the digital equivalent of cash that is totally anonymous and universally accepted, but it may prove very difficult given government concerns about money laundering, gambling, and other financial crimes.

Because ecash is purely a debit system, transactions are likely to be significantly less expensive than credit-card clearing.

DigiCash does not intend to start exchanging between Cyberbucks and other currencies, even though DigiCash is running an ecash bank in the trial. What will likely happen is that DigiCash will charge banks some type of licensing fee for its software. DigiCash currently sells its software with a non-exclusive licensing policy, allowing multiple parties to issue ecash with their own competitive, pricing structure.

CyberCash

CyberCash was founded in August, 1994, and serves as a secure conduit through which payments are transported between buyers and their banks. The system is set up so that buyers do not have to set up special accounts with a bank or with CyberCash (http://www.cybercash.com). Figure 4.3 shows the CyberCash home page.

Figure 4.3

CyberCash is currently an online anonymous credit electronic payment system.

CyberCash teamed up with encryption experts Enterprise Integration Technologies, Trusted Information Systems, and RSA Data Security to create a way to encode credit card numbers. Currently, CyberCash is working with Wells Fargo on a system to encrypt credit card data.

CyberCash charges a fixed fee per transaction, with no percentage add-on. For credit card authorization, the charge is five cents, to which the credit card processor adds its customary fee, often two percent plus 20 cents. The CyberCash charge for a debit transaction is 30 cents, with no processing fee. The cost of debit transactions will probably be lower in the future, when volume will be higher

Software Requirements

Both merchants and consumers receive free CyberCash software, so they both can conduct money transactions on the Internet. Merchants also receive a free software library to build and parse CyberCash messages.

The CyberCash system operates on top of any general security system, such as SSL or Secure HTTP. At the time of this printing, CyberCash beta software is currently available free-of-charge and can be downloaded from the company's WWW server at http://www.cybercash.com.

Target Market

Unlike DigiCash, CyberCash is not set up to accept nickel-and-dime transactions, because the flat per-transaction charges would be greater than the actual payments. CyberCash is better suited for home banking and catalog sales.

How to Make a Transaction

CyberCash's Secure Internet Payment Service™ enables merchants to operate a digital store, and makes customer anonymity possible. Merchants can safely process credit card transactions, get immediate online authorization, and usually settle the transactions with the bank or processor by the next business day. Consumers get an automated secure transmission of their credit card, as well as privacy protection. Steps in a typical CyberCash transaction are as follows:

1. The customer downloads the free, graphical CyberCash interface.

2. The customer selects the CyberCash icon when they are ready to make a purchase on a merchant storefront.

3. The selection automatically notifies the merchant to send an online invoice to the customer.

4. The customer fills in his name and credit-card information on the order blank. As shown in figure 4.4, the customer can

select from a variety of payment options when using
CyberCash.

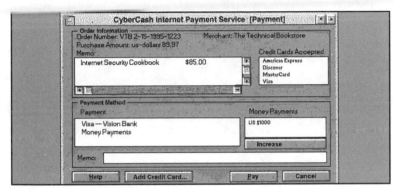

Figure 4.4

The customer selects type of payment from the CyberCash Internet
Payment Service dialog box.

5. The customer's password-protected information is
   automatically encrypted and sent over the Internet to the
   merchant.

6. The merchant, who cannot see the customer's credit card,
   sends the necessary information to CyberCash to process
   the payment request.

7. CyberCash performs error checking and forwards all the
   information to the normal, trusted credit card authorization
   and settlement networks. CyberCash retains no information
   related to the merchandise being ordered.

8. If the transaction clears, CyberCash returns a credit card
   authorization receipt to the merchant. Figure 4.5 shows the
   information sent to a merchant.

9. In less than a minute, the merchant finalizes the transaction
   with the consumer and ships the product.

CyberCash is attractive because no special accounts with
CyberCash must be set up by either the customer or merchant—
only the normal accounts with credit card companies are
required. Because consumers are already familiar with credit
cards, CyberCash should be accepted by customers.

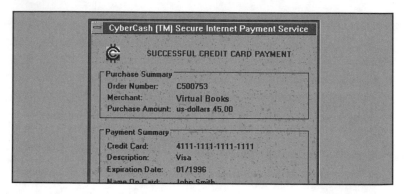

Figure 4.5
An electronic receipt is sent to the customer at the completion of a successful payment.

Becoming a CyberCash Merchant

To become a CyberCash merchant, you must be authorized to accept credit cards from a bank or other agent, and have your own server and a storefront on the Internet. You must apply to a bank or other agent directly to be authorized to accept credit cards. Be warned that getting authorization to accept credit card numbers in card-not-present situations is not automatic. Credit card companies are wary of fly-by-night operations issuing fraudulent credit card charges.

Getting Paid

Debit money transactions appear in the merchant's account after a one-day clearing period. Credit card transactions are cleared and settled by a credit card processor.

The main advantage to the merchant is that payment is guaranteed before any product is shipped, unlike some other systems. In theory, merchants can use the CyberCash system to sell any product online that they could offline—they are not restricted to soft goods and services (software, information), and there are no upper limits on transaction amounts.

Security and Privacy

The client software includes RSA public-key encryption, using a full 768-bit RSA key, as well as a 56-bit DES key, to encrypt messages. The user's private key is encrypted and stored on his hard drive. The user unlocks the private key with a password when the software is started. The customer's bank receives detailed information on each transaction, but a customer can remain anonymous to the merchant except for the IP address.

The CyberCash client can be installed as a viewer in a Web browser (the process is different for each browser). CyberCash can be set up to work with a firewall, by installing the CyberCash proxy software on a proxy server.

Businesses Using CyberCash

Some of the banks that offer Secure Internet Payment Service™ are Wells Fargo Bank, American Express, Mellon Bank, and First USA.

Merchants accepting CyberCash-protected credit card payments include Hot Wired, Working Assets Long Distance, CD-R Products, Silver Cloud Sports, Inc., Virtual Vineyards, and others.

Outlook

The cumbersome feature of CyberCash is the inconvenience of having to enter a credit card slip for each transaction. When this book went to press, no mechanism existed for establishing a subscription so that you only had to enter your credit information one time, rather than for each transaction.

The soon-to-be-released CyberCash Money Payments Service™ will make it possible for anyone using the Internet to make a payment to anyone else with an e-mail address. This debit version of CyberCash will make funds transfer, bill paying, and peer-to-peer payment even more efficient.

Another soon-to-be-released product, CyberCash MiniPayments™, works like coins—it will make small payments on the Internet possible for items such as publications and database searches.

Open Market

Open Market (http://www.openmarket.com) processes orders and accepts credit card payments in real-time (see fig. 4.6). Open Market offers both products and services for digital storefronts. You can either run your own storefront using Open Market software, or have Open Market host your storefront for you.

Figure 4.6
Open Market is an online anonymous credit electronic payment system.

Open Market's series of tools for establishing a business on the Web is called Merchant Solution. Merchant Builder encompasses several products, including StoreBuilder™ and TransactionLink™. StoreBuilder™ generates and manages Web site content. TransactionLink™ makes electronic commerce possible, and Secure WebServer™ provides the security necessary for online transactions.

Software Requirements

Customers can use any Web browser, but a secure Web browser is more advantageous. A secure Web browser adds the extra protection of encryption.

Target Market

Open Market can handle any kind of transaction—from pennies to tens of thousands of dollars. Open Market is suitable for information-based products and *hard goods* (physical products such as clothes, appliances, and so on).

How to Make a Transaction

After opening an account, a buyer uses an online shopping cart to gather goods and services from independent Open Market participating merchants. The steps in a typical Open Market transaction are as follows:

1. When a customer opens an account with Open Market, Open Market collects the following information: name, access name, password, e-mail address, and credit card or other payment information.

2. The customer selects a payment URL when he or she is ready to make a purchase.

3. Details on what is for sale and the price are sent to the Open Market payment server for authentication.

4. The payment server employs the appropriate authentication method, depending upon the transaction profile. A small transaction may only require a user name/password. A larger charge may require the use of a hand-held authenticator, which can resemble a credit card.

5. If a credit card is used, the credit card clearing network is contacted to obtain authorization.

6. The merchant is sent an authorization URL and releases the product.

7. The customer can review all transactions by accessing the online Smart Statement—a summary of recent purchases.

The online shopping cart is easy to use, and provides customers with a way to review a purchase before making the final commitment. By offering both a service and products that enable a merchant to run his own server, Open Market should appeal to a broad range of merchants.

Becoming an Open Market Merchant

Merchants must set up an account with Open Market. The merchant start-up fee is only $10.

Getting Paid

Merchants can choose their method of payment, or offer multiple methods. Open Market supports multiple currencies and non-standard payment schemes like frequent flyer miles. For credit card processing, the costs are 3 percent, plus 20 cents per transaction, plus setup fees.

Security and Privacy

Secure WebServer™ supports customers with both SSL and SHTTP security protocols and unsecure browsers, so that all shoppers can access an online store. Open Market keeps detailed transaction records, but maintains the customer's privacy. The only information the merchant has is the customer's IP address.

Businesses Using Open Market

Open Market's Commercial Sites Index include American National Telecom, Inc., Apparel Exchange, Cirrus Logic, Inc., Consumer World, Continental Business Systems, Inc., and many others. You can search the 126 businesses and organizations listed in the Commercial Sites Index by keyword.

Outlook

Open Market has advantages for both consumers and merchants. Open Market is a flexible system that provides customer service, subscription billing, and business-to-business accounting, something none of the other current payment systems are doing. The system can be set up to accumulate small transactions and submit them as one large transaction, which reduces the cost associated with small transactions. With Open Market, transactions can be categorized so that the appropriate security measures are used for each transaction. One problem is that, like CyberCash, the customer must interact with the payment screen for every transaction.

Currently, Open Market is developing an online business community, converting a proprietary online information service into an open pay-per-page service targeted to specific customers, and creating a service that includes the automatic fingerprinting of reports to protect the publisher against unauthorized use.

First Virtual

First Virtual (http://www.fv.com) is a financial services company and the first electronic merchant banker in operation designed to handle online information sales and other soft goods (see fig. 4.7). First Virtual has been offering Internet payments since October, 1994. The company has two features that separate it from other payment systems—it does not use encryption, and it is a try-before-you-buy system. Instead of using encryption, First Virtual arranges things so that no private information passes over the Internet. First Virtual's try-before-you-buy system means that merchants do not get paid until after they deliver the product.

Figure 4.7
First Virtual is an online anonymous credit electronic payment system.

The company is virtual in its organizational structure—the key players all work in different states, and phone-response and Internet-server maintenance are contracted out to companies in yet other states.

Software Requirements

First Virtual was created using existing technology, and is fully operational without customers having to purchase or install additional software or equipment to use the payment system. Customers can use e-mail or any Web browser to pay. First Virtual provides merchants with free software, which connects merchant servers to First Virtual.

Target Market

First Virtual handles low to moderately priced information sales, but if the merchant is willing to take the risk, it can also handle large transactions or hard goods. Because the merchant does not get paid until after shipping the goods, the merchant is risking not getting paid. First Virtual will eliminate customers that abuse this privilege, but merchants may still want to limit their exposure.

How to Make a Transaction

First Virtual requires customers to set up an account before using their services. For each purchase, the customer is sent an e-mail asking for confirmation before the company pays the merchant. The steps involved in using First Virtual are as follows:

1. The customer registers an account by calling First Virtual's automated telephone center, and then providing basic account information and a credit card number.

2. The customer selects an online product for purchase.

3. The merchant displays a form and asks for the customer's password.

4. The merchant sends the transaction request and customer password to First Virtual.

5. First Virtual contacts the buyer via e-mail and provides the merchant's business name, the price of the item, and a description of the item.

6. First Virtual sends an e-mail message to the customer, asking for payment confirmation (if the buyer does not reply, First Virtual repeats the message within a few days).

7. The customer confirms or denies the purchase.

8. An e-mail confirmation is sent to the customer from First Virtual, indicating that a sale has or has not been made.

9. Payment is made by direct deposit into the merchant's established checking account.

Many customers will be resistant to First Virtual due to the number of e-mail messages that must be dealt with. The need to have a checking account and the inability to get paid before shipping goods means that this scheme will be attractive to a limited number of merchants.

Becoming a First Virtual Merchant

To become a First Virtual merchant, you should do the following:

1. Have a private e-mail address and a United States checking account.

2. Apply for a First Virtual Account.

3. Activate the account for selling by mailing a voided check to First Virtual.

4. Set up information in the First Virtual InfoHaus (First Virtual's public-access information warehouse) or on a WWW or FTP site.

Merchants may also establish a presence on the InfoHaus, where First Virtual will automatically take care of information delivery, accounting, billing, collections, and payout. No programming or HTML knowledge is required in order to use the InfoHaus.

When using the First Virtual system, the seller accepts all the risk of non-payment; First Virtual accepts none. Consider First Virtual only if the following conditions generally apply:

➤ Small amounts of money are involved.

➤ Buyers are likely to confirm their transactions.

➤ A few failed payments will not create financial hardship.

➤ Immediate use of funds is not necessary.

Getting Paid

The merchant is never guaranteed payment, because the system is based on the try-before-you-buy approach—the customer gets the product before he has to pay for it. A merchant gets a delayed payment through an automated clearing house transfer to its bank account.

Merchants costs are a $10 initial registration fee to First Virtual, a 29-cent transaction fee, and a two-percent commission on each sale. Sellers also pay a $1 processing fee each time an aggregated deposit is made to their account. Every week, merchants supply sales lists to First Virtual. First Virtual processes the lists, and then sends e-mail to the customer confirming the orders.

Security and Privacy

Encryption is not necessary with First Virtual, because sensitive information never has to travel over the Internet. Instead, customer credit card information is provided over a private telephone line. Customers use account ID numbers, which may safely travel in ordinary Internet e-mail. Even if the ID number is intercepted, it is useless because each purchase must be confirmed by the customer. This scheme protects the consumer, but could leave the merchant exposed, because they would ship goods before realizing a fraudulent ID has been used.

First Virtual receives detailed information on each transaction, but the customer can remain anonymous to the merchant except for his or her IP address. Merchants cannot rely on IP addresses to uniquely identify a customer—many customers will be using systems that dynamically allocate an IP address each time the customer accesses the Internet. Most users of CompuServe, America Online, and Prodigy (and others) fall into this category.

Businesses Using First Virtual

Merchants include Apple, Reuters, and National Public Radio, who are all selling information. In addition, *The Washington Weekly* can be purchased using First Virtual's system.

Outlook

The costs and risks to consumers are minimal, but the passwords and barrage of e-mail for each purchase is inconvenient. The one-time cost for consumers to register with First Virtual is $2. There is an additional $2 fee when First Virtual is asked to update or change their financial information. Merchants pay more to use the system and take all the risk of fraudulent orders and pay-ments. First Virtual will monitor the system and cut off users who abuse the system, by refusing to pay after receiving products.

CheckFree

CheckFree (http://www.checkfree.com) is one of the largest electronic commerce companies serving consumers, businesses, and financial institutions, and is extending its success with businesses to the online consumer (see fig. 4.8).

Using a wallet metaphor, CheckFree hopes to give customers confidence when buying online by starting with something familiar. The CheckFree software resembles a wallet, and thus uses terminology based on a wallet.

Software Requirements

CheckFree Wallet is a small stand-alone application that enables consumers to use any major Web browser for shopping and purchasing goods, services, or information from online mer-chants. The wallet has been available since mid-1995.

Figure 4.8

The CheckFree home page.

Target Market

The CheckFree Wallet is appropriate for both information-based products and hard goods. Anything that would be practical to sell using a credit card is a good match for CheckFree Wallet.

How to Make a Transaction

The first time you use CheckFree Wallet, you fill out billing and credit card information and establish a password. You only have to enter this information one time; thereafter, when you want to make a purchase, CheckFree Wallet takes care of the entire transaction using your credit card. Figure 4.9 shows the path of an electronic transaction with CheckFree Wallet from the customer's PC to the bank.

CheckFree provides a real-world example of the CheckFree Wallet in use on its Web site. Here is a real-world illustration:

1. Chris wants to send a bottle of wine to a client. She goes to Virtual Vineyards on the Web, and chooses a bottle of wine.

2. She selects her items for purchase, fills out the shipping address dialog box, and chooses CheckFree Wallet as the method of payment.

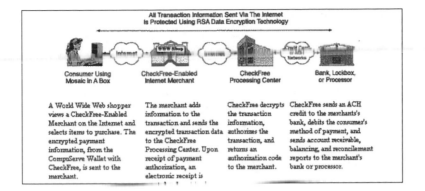

All Transaction Information Sent Via The Internet Is Protected Using RSA Data Encryption Technology

Consumer Using Mosaic In A Box	CheckFree-Enabled Internet Merchant	CheckFree Processing Center	Bank, Lockbox, or Processor
A World Wide Web shopper views a CheckFree-Enabled Merchant on the Internet and selects items to purchase. The encrypted payment information, from the CompuServe Wallet with CheckFree, is sent to the merchant.	The merchant adds information to the transaction and sends the encrypted transaction data to the CheckFree Processing Center. Upon receipt of payment authorization, an electronic receipt is	CheckFree decrypts the transaction information, authorizes the transaction, and returns an authorization code to the merchant.	CheckFree sends an ACH credit to the merchants's bank, debits the consumer's method of payment, and sends account receivable, balancing, and reconcilement reports to the merchant's bank or processor.

Figure 4.9

The path of an electronic transaction with CheckFree Wallet.

3. Chris enters her personal password to gain access to CheckFree Wallet.

4. She selects Visa as her method of payment. At the click of a mouse, all of the purchase and credit card information is digitally encrypted and sent to Virtual Vineyards. From there, the encrypted information is electronically signed and sent to CheckFree for processing.

5. Seconds later, Virtual Vineyards presents Chris with a final summary screen, which details the transaction confirmation number, purchase amount, and credit card approval code.

6. At the same time Chris is reviewing the final purchase information, Virtual Vineyards' order entry system receives the purchase data and processes the order for shipment to Chris.

CheckFree Wallet is easy to use for both customers and merchant, but does require customers to identify themselves.

Getting Paid

Merchants pay regular credit card transaction processing fees.

Security and Privacy

All credit card information is protected by a 768-bit, dual-key encryption system licensed by RSA Data Security, Inc. Because CheckFree Wallet is approved by the U.S. government for export, it is not limited to use just in the United States, but can include more global markets. CheckFree transactions are not anonymous, because only credit card transactions are supported.

Businesses Using CheckFree Wallet

CompuServe and CheckFree recently combined services to offer a secure online payment system for shopping on the Web. CompuServe is including CheckFree's payment technology with Mosaic In A Box for Windows 95—CompuServe's Internet access solution.

Outlook

Future plans include expanding CheckFree Wallet for purchases by check and electronic cash. CheckFree and CyberCash entered into an agreement to cooperatively develop and market products and services in July of 1995. This agreement enabled consumers to safely conduct payment transactions in real time over the Internet using credit cards, debit cards, checks, or cash.

NetCash

Anyone can spend or accept NetCash (http://netcash.com) via e-mail or the Web. Electronic payment coupons—NetCash—are used to buy information products. NetCash coupons are nothing more than a 16-character string. The customer spends these coupons by sending a merchant the correct string using a WWW form or an e-mail message. Figure 4.10 shows the NetCash home page.

NetCash coupons are designed to handle small transactions and to be used like pocket change. Because small transactions are supported, both tangible products and electronic information can be sold. NetCash has been up and running since 1994.

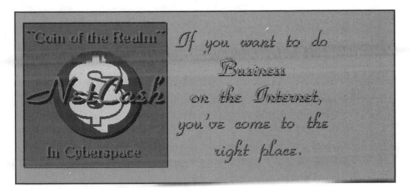

Figure 4.10
NetCash is an online anonymous debit electronic payment system.

Software Requirements

There are no special software requirements for either the customer or merchant. Any Web browser or e-mail account can
accept or send NetCash. A secure Web browser or the use of PGP
is recommended, but not required. Pretty Good Privacy (PGP) is a
secure e-mail system available for free on the Internet. PGP
encrypts your e-mail using the same technologies used in a
secure Web browser.

Target Market

Information products under $100 are the primary market; how-
ever, hard goods and more expensive items can be purchased
using NetCash. Customers are expected to prefer other payment
methods for large purchases due to the costs incurred by the
customer when using NetCash. For example, with credit card-
based systems, the merchant pays the 2 percent charge.

How to Make a Transaction

Internet shoppers need a U.S checking account in order to get
NetCash coupons. Once a shopper is registered, he or she can buy
electronic coupons marked with serial numbers from NetCash for
their face value, plus a two-percent commission with a $1 mini-
mum. This is the same charge most credit card companies have

for cash advances. A customer can also mail a check or money order—the fee is still two percent, but with no minimum. The steps involved with using NetCash are as follows:

1. The customer completes the NetCash Request Form (basic information and their checking account number) and returns it to NetBank.

2. NetBank processes the request form and sends a response message within minutes containing a NetCash "pending" coupon that can be used at any time.

3. The customer selects a participating merchant's product or service for purchase and sends the "pending" coupon via e-mail or through a process established on the merchant's WWW site.

4. If the customer does not have exact change, an e-mail message is sent to NetBank requesting change for an existing coupon. NetBank then sends the new coupons back to the customer.

5. The merchant accepts the "pending" coupon and recognizes the new status of the coupon—a check is waiting for clearance.

6. Once the check clears, the "pending" status of the coupon is changed to "valid" and the merchant is paid.

Some merchants do not accept "pending" coupons. A check needs to be cleared before making purchases from those merchant sites.

Becoming a NetCash Merchant

Merchants pay no application fees or startup charges. They simply complete the NetBank Merchant Service Agreement, send it to NetBank, and a merchant account is established. The process takes one or two business days.

Getting Paid

NetCash issues "pending" coupons immediately upon receiving a NetCash request, as a courtesy to its customers. The cash value of a coupon is contingent on the customer's bank honoring the check and remitting payment to NetBank. The merchant redeems the coupon at the NetCash NetBank and NetCash takes two percent off the top of total receipts as its fee. It can take anywhere from a week to ten days for a merchant to receive payment.

Merchants can spend NetCash collected from customers or issue refunds in NetCash, but must pay a fee when converting NetCash back into U.S. dollars. Converting NetCash coupons back to U.S. dollars involves sending a deposit transaction to NetBank; the cash is then deposited directly into your account. Periodically, NetBank totals deposits for each account and sends a reimbursement check.

Security and Privacy

NetCash relies on the security provided by a Web browser or e-mail program to protect messages sent over the Internet. NetBank merchants and customers are only protected if they use a secure Web browser or e-mail system. NetCash protects customers and merchants because private information, such as account numbers, are never sent over the Internet.

Customers can maintain anonymity when making transactions except for their IP address. As discussed previously, merchants should not track purchases by IP number, thinking that they are tracking individual customers.

Businesses Using NetCash

NetCash customers include *Boardwatch* magazine, software companies, and music video stores.

Outlook

Imagine a world where merchants accepting traveler's checks can only give change using traveler's checks. Merchants would have to keep running down to the corner bank to get a traveler's check in the exact amount needed for each transaction. This is the situation with NetCash. Merchant servers will need to contact NetCash for change with nearly every transaction. Customers will end up with a variety of denominations on their hard drive. While this is a hassle, it is not difficult. One extra exchange of messages with NetBank is required for each transaction.

NetCash has been up and running longer than most other payment systems despite its minimal security and low-cost transactions. Because of the delay in getting paid, the system is only somewhat attractive to merchants. The extra e-mail message required to get exact change may discourage widespread use among customers.

NetChex

NetChex (http://www.netchex.com) is a virtual checking account (see fig. 4.11). Customers authorize the generation of checks on their behalf. NetChex becomes an extension of the customers existing checking account, and can be used with existing checking, credit card, and debit card accounts. Merchants receive actual paper checks via overnight or second day air, and customers use NetChex to write checks electronically to make online purchases or pay bills. Both the customer and the merchant must have NetChex accounts before using NetChex.

NetChex offers several unique security features, including dynamic generation of keys, hardware-based identification, automatic disabling of tampered accounts, limits on the number of checks that a customer is authorized to create, photo IDs required for account creation, and e-mail confirmations of every purchase for both the customer and merchant. NetChex provides one of the most complete security systems for online payment.

Software Requirements

Customers must install client software provided by NetChex. This software is available for free on the Internet. One of NetChex's security features is that a copy of the client software can only be installed on a single machine. The serial ROM number unique to each computer is needed to install the software. NetChex can optionally provide a duplicate install key, which will enable installation on a second computer. This requirement provides a hardware-based aspect to the security, making it extremely difficult to forge a user's private key.

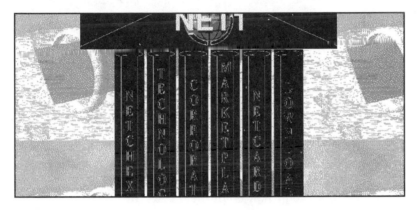

Figure 4.11

NetChex is an online identified debit electronic payment system.

The merchant needs no special software.

Target Market

NetChex is appropriate for both products and services, as well as bill paying: utility bills, cable bills, telephone bills, and so on.

How to Make a Transaction

To use NetChex, a customer must have a U.S bank account. NetChex is free to customers—they do not pay a service fee for writing checks or any other membership fees. The steps involved with using NetChex are as follows:

1. The customer downloads and completes the NetChex Member Application. The customer must provide personal and banking information, a copy of a photo ID with a

current address, and a copy of a voided check. The customer faxes or mails the application to NetChex. This information never passes over the Internet.

2.   NetChex takes about 24 hours to approve the check and contact you by telephone with the proper unlock codes to install the full version of the Client Software.

3.   The customer can then write a check against a NetChex account.

4.   NetChex receives the authorized check from the customer and notifies the merchant via e-mail of its receipt and validation.

5.   The customer also receives confirmation of the transaction, which includes the merchant code, date, amount, customer name, and other pertinent data.

6.   NetChex generates a check and mails it to the merchant. Within 24 hours, the check is deposited into the merchant's bank. No money is withheld from the check.

Becoming a NetChex Merchant

Merchants must get a NetChex account before accepting NetChex payments. Merchants should follow these steps to get a NetChex account:

1.   Download an application from the Web and complete all the necessary information.

2.   You must include a copy of a photo ID of the primary signer on the account and attach a voided check from the checking account that will receive NetChex deposits. Indicate how you would like your bank to receive your checks: first class mail, second day, or next day. Fax or mail the application to NetChex.

3.   Within 24 hours, your application should be approved and you will be notified by telephone as soon as the application process is completed.

Getting Paid

Merchants receive payment within 24 hours. The merchant is charged between 3–5 percent of the face value for each transaction, in addition to a monthly service charge of $10.00. NetChex bills merchants once a month, but does not automatically withhold any money from customer checks. The merchant can have NetChex automatically generate a check payable to NetChex once a month.

Security and Privacy

NetChex uses integrated hardware keys to create dynamic signature key generation, uniquely identifying the computer user originating the Internet transaction. Unlike other payment systems, the user's key is dynamically generated for each transaction. The key is generated using information from the previous transaction such as payee, amount, and date, as well as other information shared during the sign-up process.

This process ensures that even if someone does manage to decode a transaction, the next transaction will be equally difficult to decode. With non-dynamic key systems, decoding a single transaction will provide the hacker with the private key, which the hacker can then use to easily decode other messages. Authorized transactions can only be generated from the customer's computer that NetChex authorized during the sign-up process. This feature, combined with dynamic key generation, makes it unlikely in the extreme that someone will crack a NetChex transaction.

Because the merchant receives a check drawn against the customer's account, the merchant will know the identity of its customers. NetChex can also track each transaction, and disables the client software and the account of the user if any attempt is made to copy the NetChex client software to another computer.

Outlook

NetChex is expensive for merchants, charging 3–5 percent instead of the normal 2–3 percent for credit cards (this charge should decrease in the near future). NetChex does enable merchants to reach a wider domestic audience than pure credit card-based systems. Merchants don't need to store credit card information on their servers, reducing potential liability concerns. Merchants also assume the risk of bounced checks and don't receive immediate payment in any case. Although NetChex has some interesting security features, the authors feel that a totally Net-based check scheme will dominate.

Smart Cards

Smart cards look like credit cards, but they contain microchips programmed with the amount of electronic cash currently on the card. Smart cards may turn out to be the electronic cash currency that will get the most customer acceptance—they are ideal for small money transactions, as well as being portable, secure, versatile, and programmable. Smart cards are not restricted to the Internet, and are easy to use in a variety of situations: at a pay phone, vending machine, or grocery store, for example. Special hardware will allow smart cards to be plugged into your PC, making financial transactions over the Internet possible.

Stored data is locked on the card until you present a password that unlocks the card. Encryption keys are written into the silicon, so they cannot be copied. Flash memory accounts for the cards' capability to maintain information without being powered. The initial investment required of merchants wishing to accept smart cards is steep; however, merchants could benefit in the long run by cutting down on money handling costs and services involved in credit card transactions.

The transition to smart cards in the U.S. could happen several ways. The least likely way is that merchants all accept a single standard, go out and buy the hardware, and start accepting general purpose smart cards. More likely scenarios are evolving, from debit cards to smart cards and the proliferation of special-ized smart cards. Special-purpose smart cards for vending machines and telephones are already being used in the U.S. As special-purpose cards become more widespread, the infrastruc-ture to support smart cards will be built. The transition from special-purpose smart cards to general-purpose smart cards would be only one small extra step. As a merchant, you need to keep track of the advances made by smart cards over the next few years, so that you can make intelligent decisions on when to start accepting them.

Mondex

Launched by NatWest, Mondex cards (http://www.mondex.com) are capable of storing up to five currencies electronically (see fig. 4.12). These cards are designed to replicate the core feature of cash and to be a real alternative to traditional notes and coins. The cash is transferred instantly between individuals without involving a third party.

Figure 4.12
Mondex is an offline anonymous debit electronic payment system.

A Mondex card is a normal plastic card with a small microcom-puter chip embedded into it, allowing cash to be stored electroni-cally. Customers can use the card wherever the Mondex sign is displayed. The transaction is simply a transfer of value just like paying with ordinary cash.

Cash is transferred and loaded onto the cards over the telephone lines. Mondex expects this to become the main way of making deposits and withdrawals in the next ten years. Mondex uses the ISO standard—the global standard for integrated circuit cards.

Each card carries a 16-digit identity number stored on the chip registered at the card-providing bank, so lost cards, if found can be identified and returned to their owners. If the card is not recovered, however, all cash on the card is lost. You are out the money, but you can lock the card so someone else cannot spend it. Banks will offer a return reward system, so people are motivated to return lost or stolen cards.

Software Requirements

Your PC will need a smart card reader before using Mondex smart cards. The software that links the hardware to your Windows programs is not yet available. Contact Mondex directly for more information on availability. All of the authentication and funds transfer is handled by the hardware; the software just connects the hardware to your communications program. No need exists for a PIN or authorization at the point of sale. Merchants who want to accept Mondex smart cards over the Internet need to contact Mondex for the latest software and hardware.

Target Market

Large and small purchases are possible because Mondex does not charge per transaction. Customers can spend as little or as much money as is on their card. Mondex is designed to be international in scope. Payments can be made in person, over the phone, or over the Internet. Mondex is especially appropriate for retailers— tills can be set to receive only, making pilfering a thing of the past. In addition, retailers using Mondex tills will be able to automatically balance tills (*tills* is merchant lingo for "cash registers").

How to Make a Transaction

Two Mondex cards are needed for each transaction—both the customer and the merchant must have a card. The Mondex wallet enables person-to-person payments between cardholders. Cardholders can lend a friend five dollars without contacting a third party. Using a telephone, person-to-person payments and withdrawals can be made worldwide. On a trip and need some extra cash? Just go to the nearest ATM or Mondex-equipped telephone.

Customers can check their card balance by inserting the card into a specially-designed balance reader. A typical Internet Mondex transaction might be the following:

1. While in an online mall, the customer selects an item for purchase.

2. The merchant confirms the selection.

3. When asked, the customer inserts the Mondex card into a card reader that attaches to the serial port of their computer.

4. The computer confirms that there is another valid Mondex device at the other end of the link.

5. Upon confirmation, the value of the purchase is transferred in the currency you request from your card to the vendor.

6. You immediately receive your purchase if it can be sent electronically. Physical goods are promptly shipped.

Mondex cards are useful in non-networked situations, so customers need not decide ahead of time how much money they want to spend on the Web. Money loaded onto a card could always be used throughout a normal day, providing a customer with flexibility. Though Mondex cards represent a new technology, this flexibility could help speed their acceptance.

Getting Paid

Mondex transactions transfer value instantaneously. There is no waiting for authorizations or signatures at the point of sale. Merchants can exchange Mondex cash for government currency at any time. There is no per-transaction charge for Mondex.

Security and Privacy

Mondex smart cards are completely anonymous. There is no requirement that either party identify themselves. In practice, customers will know the identity of merchants.

Mondex cardholders can generate financial statements using their Mondex card. Neither the bank nor the merchant can trace a customers financial transactions—only cardholders have access to the statement entries on their cards. In addition, Mondex cards can be locked to prevent unauthorized access.

Each card has a unique code, which enables banks to return lost or stolen cards.

Outlook

Smart card systems have enough benefits over other online payment systems to make their eventual use nearly inevitable. Customers using Mondex for their day-to-day shopping will be motivated to get a Mondex reader for their PC in order to use Mondex online. The authors expect widespread use in retailing to precede widespread use online.

Mondex has advantages over check and credit card systems. While checks are limited to domestic customers and merchants, Mondex is designed to be a global payment system. Mondex has integrated multicurrency—it is designed to operate in any participating currency. Credit card transactions are more expensive than Mondex transactions, have the possibility of fraud, and expose the merchant to potential liability. Because Mondex transactions represent an instantaneous transfer of value, these problems are all avoided.

The single largest barrier to widespread adoption is the hardware required. Convincing companies to buy and install smart card readers will take several years (at least). Smart card companies will need to cooperate to ensure that a single hardware reader will handle all smart cards, much as credit card readers today can handle Visa, MasterCard, and so forth.

The short term outlook for Mondex is fair, while the long-term potential is good. Mondex will not become widely used until more merchants have the hardware needed to accept these cards, but merchants aren't going to install the hardware until customers demand it. Over the long term, credit card readers will be enhanced to accept smart cards, making Mondex a viable strategy for merchants. Smart cards are already in widespread use in some other countries.

IC One

IC One (http://burgoyne.com/pages/kjbarnes/iconebsg.html) is developing a line of specialized smart cards, including one that will hold electronic money. Other smart card applications being developed include the following:

➤ Smart telephone cards

➤ Ticketless travel

➤ Medical records storage

➤ Electronic keys

The same IC One card can be used for all of these applications. The goal for the IC One card is to enable people to store all of their credit card accounts, checking accounts, and merchant-specific accounts on a single card. IC One is in the final development stages of the IC One card, so detailed information on cost and availability is not yet available.

Summary

Each form of payment you use today—cash, checks, credit cards, and traveler's checks—will have an online equivalent. You have explored the offerings from various companies in this chapter, including at least one company for each of these payment types. Online payments will have even more variety than is available today. This chapter provides some insight into these other types of payment systems.

The number of online payment systems continues to grow at an astounding rate. As a merchant, being able to clearly understand the cost and risks associated with each payment system is extremely important. The key characteristics to consider when evaluating electronic payment systems are the transaction cost, your liability, and the amount of security provided. Most merchants will accept a variety of payment systems, so you need to carefully consider any incompatibilities of the various software packages. Over the next year, the authors expect most merchants to use credit card and check-based systems. DigiCash's Cyberbucks and smart cards will take longer to gain widespread acceptance. Older systems, based on exchanging e-mail, will start to look antiquated and cumbersome as new systems are developed.

The next chapter, "Cryptography Basics," provides more detailed information on the underlying encryption technology used by many electronic payment systems and all secure Web browsers. The concepts of authentication, verification, and public key cryptography are presented in detailed terms for non-security experts.

Part II

Web Technology

Chapter 5

Cryptography Basics

This chapter introduces the key technology that provides privacy and authentication. Using Pretty Good Privacy (PGP) as an example, the authors show how public key encryption is the cornerstone of electronic commerce. This chapter examines the concepts of public key encryption, privacy, authentication, and digital signatures. You'll also get a brief introduction to the company at the center of these developments, RSA Data Security. Although this chapter is a bit technical at times, the authors feel that understanding encryption technology, along with its limitations, is worth the effort.

When exchanging money and important documents over the Internet, you don't want people eavesdropping on your business transactions. By encrypting your messages, you can prevent unauthorized access to your personal and business information. *Encryption* is the process of scrambling a message, so it is unreadable by everyone except the person who has the proper key to decrypt the message. Consequently, encryption can protect your data while it travels over the Internet, as well as prevent your data from unauthorized users trying to invade your system. Because encryption scrambles your data, even if someone manages to break into your system, or manages to intercept a message sent over the Internet, your information cannot be read by intruders. In this chapter, you will become familiar with the following cryptography topics:

➤ Encryption

➤ Privacy and authentication

➤ PGP (Pretty Good Privacy)

➤ Public key encryption

➤ Public key management

➤ Private key management

➤ Digital signatures

➤ RSA

➤ Security—more or less

Encryption

A variety of encryption packages are available in both hardware and software forms. The simplest form of encryption is to simply exchange one character for another. Puzzles based on this concept are available in many Sunday newspapers. Obviously, an encryption scheme that can be cracked over danish and coffee is not very secure. Nevertheless, advanced encryption schemes rely on this same basic concept of substituting one set of characters for another. Instead of substituting one character for another, modern encryption schemes essentially substitute one string of a hundred words for another string of a hundred words. The idea is to make it nearly impossible to guess the substitution pattern. Only with the world's biggest computers working around the clock trying every possibility can someone crack today's encryption schemes.

Businesses benefit from good encryption packages, because they make it possible for credit card information and other important documents to travel securely over the network, sparing businesses the expense of a private leased-line network.

Consider the case of L3Comm, a moderate-sized business with many small offices across the U.S. L3Comm has several choices for connecting these offices together—private leased lines, frame relay connections, long distance phone calls, and the Internet. Leased lines and long distance phone calls are prohibitively expensive, and, until recently, the Internet was insecure. Frame relay connections are a relatively recent advancement.

In the past, major corporations that could afford to lease private lines from the phone companies have had a tremendous advantage in connecting remote offices. Not anymore. With the advent of modern encryption techniques, the smallest companies can encrypt their messages before sending them over the Internet, making the Internet a practical alternative. As a result, encryption technology is changing the Internet from a purely public arena into a collection of private networks.

The Internet itself is not secure. You cannot control the route your messages will take when they travel the Internet. Commercial data thieves exist and are ready to intercept your messages. Businesses must operate on the assumption that all information that travels over the Internet is vulnerable to interception. All users of the Internet are responsible for their own security. Businesses wanting to have a private conversation with their customers must arrange for end-to-end encryption of messages.

End-to-end encryption encrypts messages before sending them and offers the best overall protection; however, your encryption program is only as safe as your encryption keys. If someone gets a copy of your private key, you have a security problem. Anyone with your private key can read messages sent to you and impersonate you on the Internet. The encryption schemes discussed in this chapter are only part of an overall security system that should involve written policies and procedures, constant monitoring, and pre-planned responses in case of a break-in.

Privacy and Authentication

Businesses have other concerns besides protecting their data from unauthorized access. If a legal dispute arises three months from now, how can a business prove that purchase orders, documents, and credit card numbers were sent by a particular person and that nothing has been changed? Businesses need to know who their customers are and need to ensure that none of their messages are altered while traveling the Internet.

Authentication is a clever use of encryption technology to guarantee the validity of a message. With *digital signatures*, a type of authentication, a sender of a message cannot later deny having created the message, and can be legally held to the terms and conditions agreed to in the message. Digital signatures are covered in more detail later in this chapter.

Don't confuse authentication and privacy. *Privacy* is a sender issue, ensuring that messages can only be read by intended recipient. *Authentication* verifies that the person sending you a message is not an impostor and that your message has not been altered; therefore, authentication is a concern of the message recipient. Businesses and individuals doing business on the Internet need to be concerned with both privacy and authentication.

Air Fluff Food

In the following fictitious scenario, a customer, Kate, wants to order a new popcorn popper from Air Fluff Food, a kitchen appliance vendor shown in figure 5.1.

Kate, a Web surfer, wants to place an order using Air Fluff Food's new Web page. Air Fluff is still using credit cards, so Kate needs to send her credit card information to Air Fluff. When Air Fluff verifies the credit card information, they will mail Kate the latest in snack preparation technology.

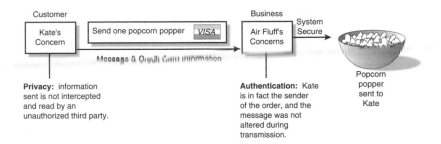

Figure 5.1

Privacy and authentication are concerns during an online transaction.

What are the privacy and authentication issues surrounding this transaction? Kate needs to send her credit card information securely to Air Fluff, knowing that only Air Fluff will be able to read her credit card number (privacy). Air Fluff needs to know that it really is Kate sending the message and that the message has not been altered en route (authentication).

Security—No Guarantees

No security technology is perfect—for every lock, there is a locksmith. Security guarantees especially do not exist for information passing over the Internet. Luckily, absolute security isn't required when dealing with electronic payment systems. The goal is to deter all but the most dedicated professionals from even trying, and to make the cost of breaking your security higher than the payoff of doing so.

If you can prevent dedicated professionals from decoding your information until after the information is no longer useful, you have accomplished your number-one security goal. This level of security is achievable, and is, in fact, available today with a program called PGP. By understanding what makes some encryption methods more or less secure, you can better understand the risks involved with different electronic payment schemes.

PGP

PGP (Pretty Good Privacy) is a program that makes it possible to authentically and confidentially send electronic mail and files. PGP uses a combination of encryption techniques to provide military-level security. This program was the brainchild of Phil Zimmerman, who made the program freely available (for individual use only, businesses pay a small fee) via the Internet, bulletin boards, and commercial networks such as CompuServe, at what turned out to be a considerable personal cost.

Despite the fact that the basic encryption techniques used by PGP are well-understood and available worldwide, the U.S. government considers PGP and programs like PGP to be a non-exportable product. While it is not illegal to use PGP within the U.S., it is illegal to carry PGP out of the country. While no one to date has been prosecuted for carrying a laptop with PGP installed out of the country, the law is currently written so that this is a crime (this law was being reviewed at the time this book was written). This law has caused problems for Phil Zimmerman. Despite an ongoing federal investigation, PGP is alive and well, and is currently the most widely used general purpose package for e-mail security. PGP is available in several international versions, so you do not need to export PGP in order to exchange encrypted messages with international clients.

Because PGP is extremely secure and not controlled by any governmental or standards organization, the program is attractive to businesses and individuals that need or want secure transmission capability over the Internet. PGP has no "back doors" that enable privileged users to break into your system or read your messages. The entire source code for PGP is available, free of charge, on the Internet.

PGP is available commercially for a small fee from ViaCrypt. The current version of ViaCrypt's PGP is 2.7. If you are installing or using PGP, make sure you have this version. PGP version 3.0 will be released soon, and backward compatibility with previous versions (before 2.7) is not guaranteed.

Businesses are required to purchase the commercial version of
PGP. Buying a commercial version of PGP entitles you to technical support. Contact ViaCrypt Products at viacrypt@acm.org

Public Key Encryption

The heart of PGP is public key encryption. *Public key encryption*
uses a pair of matched keys, one public and one private, to
provide end-to-end privacy and authentication. Before using PGP
(or any public key system), a user must generate a pair of keys.
PGP can generate a set of keys in a few seconds. Once generated,
a public/private key pair are forever linked. One is useless without the other—a message encrypted with a public key can *only* be
decrypted with the matching private key. A message encrypted
using a public key *cannot* be decrypted using the public key. This
process is counter-intuitive for most people (see fig. 5.2). Many
people's intuition is that a message encrypted using a key should
be able to be decrypted using that key. This is not true for public
key encryption.

Message encrypted with a public key can only be decrypted with a matching private key.

Message encrypted with a public key **CANNOT** be decrypted with a public key.

Figure 5.2
Public key encryption uses paired keys.

Similarly, a message encrypted with a private key can only be decrypted using the matching public key.

The only difference between a public key and a private key is that the public key is distributed on the Internet and private keys are kept locked up. In practice, for performance reasons, the software that generates the key pair will select one key as the private key so that decryption speed is minimized. If a private key is lost, the matching public key is useless.

If a private key is lost or stolen, the matching public key is no longer secure and can no longer be trusted. As soon as you realize that your private key is compromised, you must immediately communicate this fact to anyone holding a copy of your public key. Anyone with access to your private key can assume your identity and read and respond to all messages addressed to you.

Combining Encryption Techniques

In practice, public key cryptography is combined with other encryption techniques, such as Data Encryption Standard (DES), when encrypting files or messages to guarantee privacy. DES is a widely used U.S. government standard that uses a single key type of encryption. The advantage of combining types of encryption is speed—for example, encrypting files using DES is roughly 100 times faster than encrypting a file using public key cryptography. This speed advantage is important because it enables the use of large keys, providing enhanced security.

A new IDEA key is generated for each message. The message is encrypted using the IDEA key. The IDEA key is then encrypted using the public key of the recipient, as shown in figure 5.3.

The recipient first decrypts the IDEA key and then decrypts the message, as shown in figure 5.4.

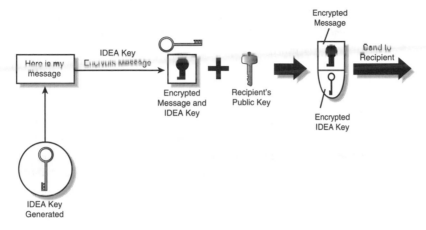

Figure 5.3

Public key encryption is combined with other encryption techniques

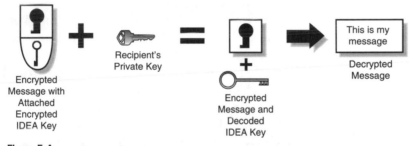

Figure 5.4

Using the IDEA key together with public key encryption.

Limitations of Single Key Encryption

Before the advent of public key encryption, if you wanted to exchange encrypted messages with someone, you had to give him a copy of the key you used to encrypt the message. Sending this key using e-mail is no good because a hacker could eavesdrop, get a copy of your key, and use it to encrypt subsequent messages. You had to find some other way of coordinating the exchange of keys before sending encrypted mail. This exchange could involve postal mail, phone conversations, or an exchange of diskettes. Another drawback is that to prevent another person from using your key to read all of your encrypted data, you have to use a different key for each session. This makes managing all of your keys difficult.

The alternative of using a different key for every person you communicate with is impractical. Public key encryption changed all this. You can pass out copies of your public key while keeping your private key locked up. You no longer need to trust a person in order to exchange encrypted messages with him or her. A person with access to your public key cannot use it to harm you in any way. He cannot intercept and read messages sent to you, nor can he read encrypted data stored on your machine.

Public key encryption has been around since 1977. Only recently, with the explosion of the Internet, has public key encryption become commercially important. Even though public key encryption is new to many companies, you can rest assured that no one is about to figure out a magic way of breaking public key encryption schemes. The methods available to crackers to decode encrypted messages are well-understood, and they all take significant computer resources. Although it is possible to decode a message by guessing all the possible keys, long key lengths (716 bits or more) make this an impractical method. While it is theoretically possible, even with very long keys, to guess the key on the first attempt, this is very improbable. The important fact to remember is that long keys, on average, take longer to decode than short keys.

Public Key Management

A small community has grown up around PGP. Before a public/private key system is useful, people must have access to public keys from a secure, trusted source. There is no way to avoid trusting, to some degree, the source of public keys, whether you get the key directly from the other individual or from an authorized third party.

Servers are available on the Internet that keep databases of public keys. These servers are well-guarded and designed to provide a secure, trusted source of public keys to businesses and individuals. Public keys would be useless if a hacker could freely alter them. The public keys need to be easily available, but secure from any changes.

Having a third party collect and store public keys enables businesses and individuals to communicate without first having to coordinate an exchange of keys. Both parties wanting to exchange information can create a pair of keys at any time, and store the public key with a third party. When a message is received, the correct public key is retrieved from the third party, as shown in figure 5.5. The originator and recipient never need to directly contact each other to exchange public keys.

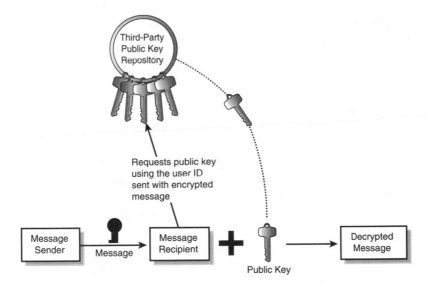

Figure 5.5
Storing public keys with a third-party public key repository.

Public keys stored on a public key ring (*public key rings* are just databases for public keys) are stamped with certificates, which guarantee that the key has not changed. A certificate functions like the stamp of a notary public. A notary public witnesses a signature and provides a stamp that verifies the validity of the signature. Similarly, a certifier receives a user name/public key pair, and then issues a certificate that verifies that the user name and public key are a valid pair. Certificates are publicly issued (distributed on the Internet) by certifiers, generally large organizations. When retrieving a public key, check the certificates it has. If the key is certified by an organization you trust, you can accept the public key as valid. Because of the widespread availability of the certificates, no one can change a certificate after it has been issued. A public key is guaranteed to be usable if it is stamped with one or more publicly available certificates. The certificate guarantees that the public key and the person's name stored with that key belong to the same person.

There are a number of ways you can distribute your public key. You can make it available on your Web page, leave it in a PGP public-key repository, or send your public key to everyone with whom you correspond.

The availability of public keys from a trusted third party is the basis for *spontaneous transactions* (transactions that require no previous contact between the parties). For example, a person can encrypt a credit card number and send it along with his name to a business. The customer uses the business's public key to encrypt the message. The customer can use the business's name to look up its public key from a trusted certifying authority. By default, no special permissions are required to access a public key. Because the customer trusts the certifying authority, no previous contact with the business is required, but the customer is still assured that only the target business can read the message. The customer only needs to trust a single certifying authority for this scheme to work, instead of having to trust many individual businesses. Other electronic payment systems that use encryption work in a similar manner.

Private Key Management

Public key management is handled by parties outside of your organization. You are responsible for managing your own private keys. Most successful attacks against public key cryptography are actually attacks against poorly protected private keys. Having a complete system in place to protect private keys is far more important than other factors, such as having a long key (discussed in the next section).

Private key management for individuals is easy. For example, PGP automatically creates and manages a private key ring. Just keep a backup copy of your private key ring at an off-site location. Private key management for organizations is trickier.

Businesses will need to develop new policies and procedures for the management of private keys. Most businesses already have policies regarding passwords. Common policies specify minimum password lengths and the life span of a password. These policies are easily enforced within an organization by special settings on the servers. If a password is forgotten, a new one is generated. Administrators usually do not have access to employee passwords.

Private Key Management versus Password Management

Private key management is very different from password management. Passwords, something you know, are easy to create, distribute, and change. Private keys, something you own, are not as easy to create or replace. Replacing a private key involves creating a new public and private key pair, distributing the public key to a repository, distributing the private key to the user, and marking the old public key as old. More importantly, messages encrypted with the old public key are forever gone after the loss of the matching private key. Any company storing encrypted data on its computers must have an off-site backup of its private keys.

Some organizations will try to apply policies regarding passwords used to log on to passphrases, which are used to protect private keys. These kinds of policies are a waste of company resources. Although some policies will remain the same, especially policies concerning the minimum length of a passphrase, policies regarding passphrases should be developed without regard to old policies.

Responding to Break-ins

Most applications that use public key encryption encrypt private keys using a passphrase (a *passphrase* is like a password, only longer). Passphrases prevent adversaries who have a copy of your private key from using it to break into your system or impersonate you over the Internet. Private keys are useless without access to the passphrase. Don't confuse a passphrase protecting a private key with a password used to log on to a system. Changing the passphrase protecting a private key does nothing to protect your data. Each copy of a private key is protected by its own passphrase. Changing the passphrase on your copy will have no effect on a copy stolen by a hacker. The hacker's attempts to guess the passphrase protecting a stolen copy of your private key will not be affected if you change the passphrase on your own copy of the private key.

If a hacker has a copy of your private key, and manages to break the encryption protecting it, the hacker can read and respond to messages sent to you and assume your identity. The only response to a hacker getting copies of your private keys is to generate new key pairs, resign, and reissue all public keys affected. Although you should re-encrypt all data on your system using the new keys (to try and minimize future damage), you must assume that the data has been stolen.

Administrators, as a rule, usually have not had access to passwords. Information protected by passwords is safe from administrators (at least from administrators without total access to the system). Now, because of the need to store backup copies of private keys, administrators will have access to all private keys and therefore have access to all data. The possibility of fraud and abuse make this unacceptable to many organizations. Solutions to this concern involve tight control of backup copies of private keys, such as a locked safe not accessible by the administrator.

Administrators in companies using public key encryption-based electronic payment systems must protect against lost keys and forgotten passwords. Storing copies of private keys in a locked safe is one option. An administrator responsible for creating and distributing all of the key pairs within an organization can easily create a backup copy protected with a known passphrase. An administrator with access to all of an organization's private and public keys is also capable of reading all of the organization's encrypted data.

Detecting Break-Ins

Recognizing an attempted break-in is also harder with a public key encryption system. With passwords, simply tracking unsuccessful attempts to log on is often sufficient to recognize a break-in attempt. Repeated unsuccessful attempts to guess a password signals an attempted break-in. If a hacker cracks a private key, he or she can immediately gain access to all resources protected by that public key, so a more sophisticated monitoring system is necessary. Clues to a successful break-in are accounts being used at unusual times of the day, unusual patterns in resource usage, or a surge in activity in a particular part of the system.

For example, a hacker with a copy of your private key may attempt to copy large amounts of files from your system. This surge in file copying is a possible sign of an intruder; however, there are often very legitimate reasons someone within your organization may be copying large amounts of files, so detecting an actual break-in may be difficult.

Digital Signatures

A *digital signature* is an encrypted attachment to a message. The message itself does not have to be encrypted in order for it to be signed. The digital signature is simply an additional attachment to the message, and does not change the message, as shown in figure 5.6.

Digital signatures are used to authenticate a message. They verify that senders are who they claim to be and that a message has not been altered since being digitally signed.

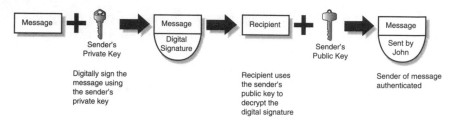

Figure 5.6

A digital signature is a small, encrypted attachment to a message.

Digital signatures are fundamental technology needed to implement an electronic payment system, and are an application of public/private key encryption. Just as credit cards rely on written signatures, electronic cash relies on digital signatures.

Digital signatures are created using the private key of the sender and the message to be signed. Because only the sender has access to his or her private key, only the sender can create an unique digital signature. Anyone can check the signature. Verify a digital signature by decrypting the signature using the sender's public key and comparing the result to what would be expected for that particular message. The sender's private key remains private, yet any business or individual can verify the digital signature.

The digital signature does not hide any information. Because anyone can decrypt the signature, the information stored in the digital signature is freely available. That's exactly the point of signatures, because having a signature that no one can read isn't helpful when trying to authenticate a message.

Digital signatures, unlike written signatures, guarantee that a note has not been changed since it was signed. A digital signature does not prevent the message from being changed, but it does make the fact that a message was changed evident. Anyone can recognize an altered digitally signed message. The secret behind this ability is in the contents of the signature.

Remember, a digital signature is something encrypted with the sender's private key. The "something" that gets encrypted isn't a random choice, nor is it the same for all messages. The "something" is generated fresh for each message to be signed. Let's take a closer look at how this "something" is generated.

Here's what happens. A mathematical function is applied to the message being signed. The output of this mathematical function is encrypted and becomes the digital signature. If the message is changed, the output of the mathematical function changes as well. By comparing the contents of the digital signature with what would be expected for a particular message, you can tell if a message has been changed since it was signed.

The process of creating a digital signature is as follows:

1. Create a message.

2. Create a hash code for the message. A *hash code* is a short sequence of bits generated by applying some mathematical function to the message. The actual mathematical function used is not important as long as everyone knows the function.

3. The hash code is encrypted using the private key of the sender. The encrypted hash code is the digital signature.

4. The signature is sent along with the message.

5. The recipient removes the digital signature and decrypts it using the sender's public key.

6. The recipient generates a hash code from the original message and compares this hash code with the result of decrypting the signature. If they match, the message is accepted as unaltered.

Digital signatures are usually attached to the message being sent, but not always. Digital signatures that are stored independent of the signed message are useful in some circumstances. Some messages need to be signed by multiple people. If all signatures were attached to the message, the order of the people signing becomes important—the second person receives the message after being signed by the first, the third after the second, and so on. Each person is signing and verifying not only the original message, but the previous signatures as well. Detached signatures avoid this complexity. All detached signatures refer only to the original message.

Detached signatures are also useful when keeping a log of all signed messages sent and received. Considerable space is saved by saving only the signatures and not the whole message. Use detached signatures when sending executable programs. If a program is infected with a virus it gets changed, so a signature can protect against viruses.

PGP supports detached signatures, which can be saved independently of the signed message.

RSA Data Security

RSA (named after the three MIT professors, Ron Rivest, Adi Shamir, and Len Adelman, who pioneered the public key cryptosystem) builds the most popular public key encryption system. RSA is quickly becoming the defacto standard for public key encryption software. The PGP public key encryption software is licensed from RSA Data Security of Redwood City, California. RSA's technology is licensed by virtually every major database and network developer. RSA's customers include Lotus, Oracle, CompuServe, AT&T, Novell, and other leading firms. This soft-ware is built into Macintosh System 7.5, Windows 95, and the SunScreen security package from Sun.

RSA Data Security, Inc. actually has four primary products, as follows:

➤ RSA Secure

➤ MailSafe

➤ Bsafe

➤ Tipem

RSA Secure enables Windows users to manually or automatically encrypt files. MailSafe encrypts and digitally signs e-mail. Bsafe is a toolkit for software developers who want to add security to their programs. Tipem is a toolkit for developers who want to add security to messaging programs.

RSA holds the patent on public key encryption, so if you're developing your own software programs, your search for competitive vendors should be short—there aren't any. Fortunately, RSA is keeping its licensing fees low, enabling an explosion in electronic commerce. For more information on RSA, its products, and cryptography in general, visit RSA's Web site at http://www.rsa.com or call (415) 595-7703.

RSA's technology is being incorporated into World Wide Web servers and will form the basis of secure transactions using the Web. Both methods of securing transactions over the Web—Secure Sockets Layer Protocol (SSL) and Secure HyperText Transfer Protocol (SHTTP)—are based on RSA's encryption software. Although SSL and SHTTP are based on RSA software, they are not compatible—for example, you cannot encrypt a Web page using SSL and read the Web page using SHTTP. Terisa, a firm partly owned by RSA, has committed to creating versions of SSL and SHTTP that will be compatible. Terisa was founded by RSA and EIT (Enterprise Integration Technologies Corp.) to provide software developer toolkits for developing secure Web applications.

Security—More or Less

Not all software that incorporates RSA's encryption software can work together. Just because two software programs use public key encryption does not mean that they can trade encrypted messages. Firms that license RSA's software make several decisions that affect the ability of programs to work together. The most important of these decisions is the size of the keys. Each firm that licenses RSA's software can choose a different key size.

In order to exchange encrypted messages, two programs have to be able to use the same key length. The larger your key size, the more security you have—for example, PGP 2.6.2 licenses software from RSA and lets the user choose a key size up to 2047 bits. Lotus Notes also incorporates RSA software, but uses a 128-bit key (North American version of Lotus Notes). Messages encrypted using Notes' system can be decrypted in a day by anyone with access to 50 Pentium computers. Messages encrypted using PGP's scheme are secure from any non-government agency. Even the government would have to really want to break your messages before it would be worth devoting the resources needed to decode a PGP message.

Government Regulation

The U.S. government classifies public key encryption as munitions, and restricts the length of the key that can be used in any exported software. Most firms avoid supporting two versions of their software, one for domestic use and one for international use. Most firms release only a single version of their software using a short key length, which complies with the current export laws. By controlling the key length of exported software, the U.S. government has been able to weaken the encryption used in software released domestically.

Estimating Minimum Security Requirements

Companies building or using encryption-based electronic payment systems need to be sensitive to the amount of security provided by the public key encryption software they are using. Transactions do not need to be crack-proof (there is no such thing as crack-proof anyway). Information only needs to remain secure while it is still useful to a hacker. If it takes three days to clear a transaction, then protecting the data for five or six days is probably enough. If your typical transaction size is under $100, then almost any encryption scheme will cost hackers more to decode than it is worth. The exception to this rule is credit card numbers. If you're sending credit card numbers over the Internet, then you will want to use the strongest encryption available, because credit card numbers are useful long after the particular transaction has been completed. The cost of decrypting a credit card number is greater than the benefit derived if the credit card number was encrypted using a key length of 128 bits or more, so insist on at least a 128-bit key if you are using credit cards online.

The idea that information has a useful life span and only needs to be protected a little longer than its useful life span is a difficult one for many people to accept. Even though most of us make trade-offs between convenience and security every day, we expect perfect security when it comes to computers. Perfect security is an emotionally appealing goal that is never reached in practice. Online merchants need to be sensitive to people's expectations, while balancing the actual costs and benefits of different security measures.

Companies and individuals using encryption-based electronic payment systems need to balance convenience and potential liability concerns with the desire for greater security. For companies doing business domestically only, the decision is an easy one. It is just as easy to use a large key as it is to use a small key, so use a large key. When doing business internationally, only use a large key if there is software available in the other country that can decode the message.

Bank Loan Example

Here is an example of two organizations using public key encryption to provide privacy and authentication during a transaction. A bank wants to check the credit history of a loan applicant. The credit bureau needs to know that it really is a bank requesting the information (authenticity) and that no one else can read the request (privacy). The bank digitally signs the request message using the bank's private key, and then encrypts the message using the credit bureau's public key. Once the message is encrypted, only the credit bureau's private key can decrypt the message. The credit bureau decrypts the message using its private key, and then checks the digital signature to verify that it came from the bank and that the message was not altered in transit (see fig. 5.7).

Before sending the credit history of the loan applicant back to the bank, the credit bureau signs the message using the bureau's private key, and then encrypts the message using the bank's public key. The bank decrypts the message using the bank's private key, and then checks the signature using the credit bureau's public key.

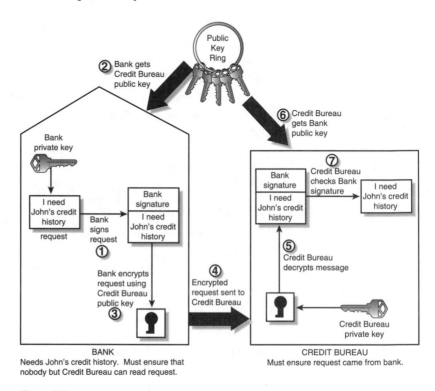

Figure 5.7

Using public key encryption to provide privacy and authentication.

Four keys are involved in this example—a public and private key for the bank, and a public and private key for the credit bureau. Both the bank and the credit bureau need access to the other's public key. In this example, when two companies regularly do business with each other, they probably arranged to exchange keys directly. If an individual were requesting his own credit record, the credit bureau would probably get his key from a third-party public key repository.

Summary

RSA, synonymous with public key cryptography, is quickly becoming the standard for authentication. Other techniques remain popular for pure privacy because of the export restrictions placed on RSA technology. RSA is a patented, export-restricted technique of providing authentication and privacy over the Internet. In practice, products that incorporate RSA technology, such as PGP, combine RSA with other encryption techniques to provide an enhanced level of security.

Authentication based on public key cryptography forms the basis for digital signatures. Digital signatures, unlike their written counterparts, can be used to verify both the contents of a message and the identity of the sender.

Public key encryption systems are difficult to break using brute force methods. Ron Rivest, one of the original creators of RSA, estimates a cost of $8.2 million to crack a 512-bit key. The weakest link in many implementations of public key cryptography is the management of private keys. Private keys must be kept secure; yet, they must be available for use. Private key management is considerably more involved than password management, and businesses and individuals need to develop new policies and procedures for managing them.

This chapter has covered public key encryption and how it can be used to provide authentication and privacy. Chapter 6, "Web Server Capabilities," explores the ways that public key encryption is being used in secure Web servers and browsers. An overview of the SSL and SHTTP standards is also presented. In addition to authentication and privacy, actual Web servers must provide a way to control access to various parts of the server. The chapter also shows how to configure access control for the shttpd server from NCSA, an example of a secure Web server.

Chapter 6

Web Server Capabilities

Although the Web is known for its flashy graphics and the capability to link information sources together, Web servers are also capable of transferring files, performing searches, and more. When setting up a Web-based electronic commerce site, you should keep in mind all the capabilities a Web server provides. Because the Web is the premiere way to interact with individual Internet users, companies are busy extending their current Web servers to support electronic commerce. The authors definitely recommend using a secure Web server—one that supports public key cryptography and digital signatures—for electronic commerce. These secure Web servers are based on older Web servers, which could not encrypt or sign documents, so it is important to understand the capabilities of these servers. This chapter provides a brief overview of Web browsers and Web servers. This very limited introduction will do the following:

➤ Provide you with the background to understand the discussion of secure Web servers in the next chapter

➤ Alert you to the functions available in Web servers today

➤ Review methods of protecting a Web server

> ➤ Look at some basic HTML concepts

> ➤ Discuss some non-security related advances in Web technology coming soon

If you've already set up a Web server, then this chapter should be a review. You should be forewarned that the security issues outlined here are not the only issues facing a Web server administrator. Whole books have been written on the topic of security, and a complete discussion is beyond the scope of this book. A Web server used for electronic commerce needs to use the best security that can be afforded.

Web Servers

A Web server's basic function is to send HyperText Markup Language (HTML) documents (and associated graphics) to Web browsers. *HTML documents* are simple text documents that are formatted by a Web browser into the flashy screens for which the Web is known. Web servers aren't limited to serving HTML documents, however; they also are capable of retrieving information from nearly any source on the Web. Web servers can perform searches using gopher (gopher helps you locate resources using menu selection tool) or WAIS (Wide Area Information Servers—help you search indexed material using keywords or phrases), and can transport files using FTP (File Transfer Protocol—the Internet's basic file transfer mechanism). These servers also provide you with the maximum flexibility in information format and source. You do not need to worry that by setting up a Web server, you are limiting access to other forms of information.

The Web server responds to requests from Web browsers. The basic conversation between a Web server and browser is shown in figure 6.1. Here are the steps involved:

1. When a user clicks on a hyperlink in his Web browser, the browser sends a request for the HTML document referenced by the hyperlink.

2. The server receives the request, decides if it is a legal request, and delivers the HTML document.

3. The Web browser parses the HTML document to look for references to graphics, displays the HTML page, and starts requesting the graphics fields, one at a time.

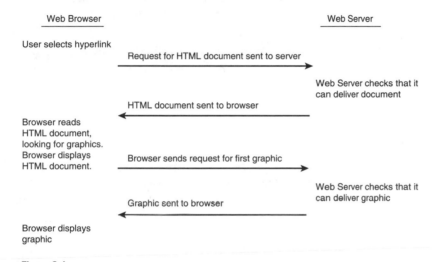

Figure 6.1
A Web browser retrieving a page from a Web server.

Some Web browsers make you wait to receive all graphics before you can select another hyperlink. Other browsers let you select a new hyperlink before all graphics have been retrieved.

Netscape was the first to let users see graphics as they are being downloaded, and move on to another page while the graphics are still being retrieved. This feature is a huge time-saver for users—you should make sure that your server can support this feature. Not all secure servers will be able to support this feature, however, due to the way they digitally sign documents.

Each user request for an HTML document is handled independently of all other user requests. No state information is remembered between requests. The Web browser doesn't remember that it just retrieved a document from a server, and the server doesn't remember that it just sent a document to a user. Each request is handled as an independent entity. This fact has implications for secure Web servers, limiting the types of transactions that can be supported. A typical transaction, for example, involves multiple messages between the server and browser (purchase request, confirmation, and download of information). Both the server and browser need to link all the messages transferred during the transaction. This requires both the server and the browser to remember that they are talking to one another. It should therefore come as no surprise that most of the proposals for Web security include some method of maintaining state information.

CGI Programs

Common Gateway Interface (CGI) programs are not new to Web servers. If you have experience with other forms of Internet servers (FTP, WAIS, and so forth), then you are probably familiar with CGI programs. *CGI programs* are stand-alone programs, written in any programming language you prefer (Perl is a popular language for CGI programs), which the Web server executes in response to a Web browser request. You can configure a Web server, for each document or directory, to run a CGI program instead of simply delivering a file.

CGI programs are general-purpose programs—there is no limit to what they can do (theoretically). If you were so inclined, you could have a CGI program balance your checkbook every time a request was received by your server. CGI programs are generally used to do the following:

➤ Connect Web servers to other systems

➤ Dynamically generate HTML documents

➤ Process forms

➤ Handle "clickable" images

When a server receives a request for a document, it checks its configuration to see if it should run a CGI program instead. The CGI program can get information from the server about the current request. The CGI program's output is used as the response to the user's request. For example, a user ordering something on the Web will fill out a form (name, address, item ordered, and so on) and submit it to the merchant. A CGI program is needed to process the form. The server launches the CGI program, which knows how to process the form and passes the value of the fields on the form (along with other useful information) to the CGI program. The program processes the form and sends a document back to the user. Before sending the document to the user, the server looks through the document to see whether the document needs to be modified in any way. Under some circumstances, the server may change the document before sending it to the user. Some examples of this are covered in the next chapter.

CGI programs are considered a potentially severe security leak. You should limit a user's ability to run CGI programs. A CGI program could be used to wipe out your disk, or gain access to protected areas of the server. To reduce problems, restrict the directories allowed to run CGI programs. Each platform will have a different way of implementing this security, and that topic is beyond the scope of this book.

Server-Side Includes

Server-side includes are character sequences that convey a special meaning to a Web server. Whenever a Web server sees a server-side include, it can do the following:

➤ Replace the server-side include with some other character sequence

➤ Take some action, such as changing the way a file is parsed

➤ Execute a CGI program (or shell script)

Server-side includes enable you to create generic HTML files. You don't have to include server-specific information directly in your HTML files; instead, use a server-side include to instruct the server to dynamically insert information just before sending the HTML file to a user. For example, server-specific information could include file paths or server name. Typical information that is added on-the-fly using a server-side include is the current date, file modification date, and file sizes.

Server-side includes are a potential performance nightmare, because they greatly increase the amount of computation needed to process a request. *Parsing* documents—the process of searching through the document looking for specific character sequences—is a CPU-intensive task. When server-side includes are enabled, the server must look through every document before sending it to a user. This overhead can add up quickly on a heavily used server. Server-side includes are also a potential security leak due to their capability of executing programs. You should strictly limit the types of server-side includes users can insert into their HTML code.

The ability to execute random programs provides a huge hole in your security scheme. You should turn off server-side includes in users' home directories and any other directories you do not trust. Of the remaining directories, decide which ones are highly trusted. These highly trusted directories should be the only ones allowed to use server-side includes to execute programs. Configuring server-side includes is different for each platform, and is beyond the scope of this book. Check the documentation for your Web server for details.

Protecting Your Web Server

For your purposes, a *nonsecure* Web server is any server that does not support public key encryption-based authentication and privacy. These servers are not completely insecure and wide open to attack, however; in fact, current servers come with a number of ways to protect themselves from attack. They just don't offer much to protect information received from or sent to users. The same techniques that are used to protect a nonsecure Web server are used to protect a secure Web server, which will inherit the security features of the nonsecure server upon which it is based. Current servers enable you to control access to documents and directories, authenticate users, and control execution options by directory or user.

Controlling physical access to the server is always step one in any security plan. Passwords are useless if someone can read directly from the server's hard drive. Large organizations will have computer rooms with locked doors, and smaller companies will need to evaluate the security threat posed by their employees. Leaving a Web server that holds credit card information and cash unprotected may seem no different from leaving the cash drawer unlocked. Even if you regularly leave the cash drawer unlocked, you can tell if someone is stealing, but how will you know if someone is stealing electronic cash from your Web server? A locked closet is cheap and effective ($20 for a lock on a door), and well within the price range of even the smallest companies.

User authentication can be determined by a user id/password or by the Internet address of the user. Unix administrators beware— the user id/passwords used by the Web server are completely independent of any other accounts maintained on the system. You will need to change accounts in multiple places when removing or adding a user. This will double the effort required to maintain passwords.

Once you have determined the id of the user, you can allow or deny access on a per-document or directory basis. If you run a site inside a university, you could deny access to students during peak hours (or allow only student access during peak hours). As an example, let's examine the NCSA httpd Web server to see how these tasks can be accomplished.

Access to a directory is controlled by placing an .htaccess file in the directory. The .htaccess file is checked by the server before delivering a document. To limit access based on user id/passwords, use an .htaccess file such as the following:

```
AuthUserFile /password/.psword
AuthGroupFile /dev/null
AuthName LimitAccessByPassword
AuthType Basic

<Limit GET>
require user jdoe
</Limit>
```

Note that the actual password is stored in another file, which can be placed in a protected directory. This example requires a user id/password whenever a user attempts a *GET action*, which is Web lingo for a user trying to get a Web page from your server. The only valid user id for the preceding example is jdoe.

The second line of the example indicates that no groups are used. Groups are a convenient way to manage access for large numbers of users. If you have 30 students in a class, and they are the only ones who should have access to a particular directory, you should create a group file for them instead of listing each student individually in the .htaccess file. You can reuse a group file in multiple .htaccess files; for instance, if a student drops the course, you only need to remove one name from the group file, rather than from every .htaccess file.

Password files are created using the htpasswd program. To add a user id/password to a password file, type the following:

```
htpasswd -c /password/.psword jdoe
```

and enter the password twice when instructed. The -c tells htpasswd to create a new user id, rather than change an existing one. You can add multiple user id/passwords by repeating this procedure.

The following shows how to limit access based on Internet address. This example prevents anyone logged on in the statecol.edu domain from accessing the directory.

```
AuthUserFile /dev/null
AuthGroupFile /dev/null
AuthName LimitLocalUsers
AuthType Basic

<Limit GET>
order allow,deny
allow from all
deny from .statecol.edu
</Limit>
```

User id/password authentication is open to eavesdropping attacks—hackers could monitor your communications and steal user id/passwords. User id/passwords are not encrypted. Even though you may feel that the risks from eavesdropping attacks are overblown, it's better to be safe than sorry. Given sufficient motivation, like the possibility of getting several million dollars, eavesdropping attacks could become more common.

Even if you employ each of the recommended methods to control access to your server, described in the following list, you should still not store critical information on externally visible Web servers:

➤ Require user id/passwords.

➤ Disable server-side includes in non-trusted directories.

➤ Protect user directories.

➤ Prevent anyone from overriding your settings.

➤ Use a file system with built-in security features (such as NTFS) if your operating system supports it. (If not, consider getting one that does!)

In particular, you should never store credit card information or digital cash on an external server. Hackers are far more likely to get information directly from the hard drive on your Web server than to record conversations over the Internet. It is recommended that you avoid storing credit card information unencrypted (even on internal, physically protected servers). If necessary, purchase one of the security toolkits available from Terisa systems (http://www.terisa.com, profiled in Chapter 5), and have your IS staff or a consultant integrate it into your systems. A small organization without the resources to write its own programs or hire a consultant should move sensitive information from the Web server to another workstation on a daily basis. This will at least limit the potential loss from an attack.

Secure Sockets Layer Protocol (SSL) only protects data while it is traveling over the Internet. Most attacks against Internet servers involve getting data off the server's hard disk. Thus, SSL does not protect against these kind of attacks. Merchants should not rely on SSL alone to provide encryption protection for their servers.

Web Browsers

Web browsers run on the user's workstation and provide the graphic interface of the Web. Web browsers vary greatly in their ability to understand different versions of HTML. HTML 2.0 is supported by nearly every browser, but Netscape also supports HTML 3.0, as well as some proprietary enhancements such as dynamic updating. Only Netscape and Spyglass-Enhanced Mosaic support tables. In addition to parsing and displaying HTML files, Web browsers all can be extended with viewers.

When a Web browser sees a file that it cannot handle with its built-in capabilities, it checks its configuration to see if it has a viewer that can handle the file. Common viewers include JPEG, sound drivers, and movie players. This extendible nature of Web browsers enables them to grow. Viewers are available for virtually every platform and file type. As soon as a new file type becomes popular, someone makes a viewer that can handle that type of file. Figure 6.2 shows the architecture of a Web browser.

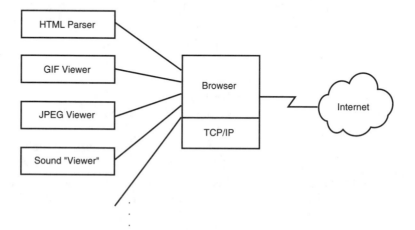

Figure 6.2
Web browser architecture.

The authors recommend the Netscape browser (available at
http://www.netscape.com) for Web surfers—Netscape continues
to offer the widest range of features and standards. One of the
various Mosaic browsers (available through many, many servers)
would be a second choice. You should avoid services that require
the use of a proprietary interface (or make it difficult to use your
browser of choice). It's impossible for any one company to keep
up with the bewildering pace of improvement in Web software
today. By marrying yourself to one program, you will definitely
fall behind in the function/feature race, and this will end up
costing you money. One of the realities of doing business on the
Web is the need to keep up—to offer features that will keep
customers coming back for more. Part of this is being able to test
out (and use) the newest browsers.

HTML Overview

HyperText Markup Language (HTML) files comprise the underlying technology that makes the Web possible. HTML documents
are regular ASCII files with special character sequences called
tags. Because these documents are the heart of any Web server, if
you want to run a Web server or create a digital storefront, you
will have to understand HTML—it isn't a static standard, but is
evolving rapidly, making it difficult to stay on top of all the
possibilities. HTML's rapid evolution has resulted in multiple
standards. Make sure that your server supports at least HTML v2
and that your vendor has committed to supporting HTML v3,
along with future enhancements.

Although it is possible to create HTML documents using a text
editor, the authors recommend using a graphical editor capable
of generating HTML documents. A graphical editor can hide
much of the detail of HTML, enabling you to concentrate on the
look and feel of your Web page. When you are more comfortable,
you can delve into all the messy details of HTML. Microsoft has
published an Internet Assistant for Word for Windows 6.0a that
enables Word to save files in HTML format. This enables you to
use all of Word's formatting features to generate an HTML

document. The Word Internet Assistant is available free through CompuServe (Go MSWORD, download WORDIA.EXE). WordPerfect has released a similar tool. It can't be long before other desktop publishing tools develop their own HTML formatters.

HTML is changing so quickly that you will probably want to hand-edit your files to include features not supported by your editor. Even if you don't ever intend to hand-edit HTML files, understanding the terminology is a basic skill required to run a Web server.

The following is an example of a simple HTML file created for the Acme company:

```
<title>Acme HTML</title>
<h1>Acme Welcome</h1>
<em>Hello</em>, <p>
Welcome to Acme's world of HTML.<p>
<a href=http://www.acme.com/anotherdoc.html >Acme hyperlink
</a>
```

This text is formatted for the screen by a Web browser (or any other program than can understand HTML). Text inside the angle brackets, known as tags, are instructions to the formatter. Except for the paragraph tag <p>, tags come in pairs. For example, <b> and </b> are the tags instructing the formatter to bold all text that appears between the two tags (ignoring any nested tags). The HTML file in the example uses the following tags:

➤ <title>—Specifies the title of the HTML document. This text is often displayed in the title bar of the browser window.

➤ <h1>—A top level header. Most browsers will use a larger font size and/or bold first level headings.

➤ <em>—Emphasize all text until the corresponding </em> is encountered (emphasized text is usually italicized).

➤ <a ...>—Anchor tag. Specifies a hyperlink to another document.

The exact fonts to be used in the first level heading are not specified. This is consistent with the spirit of HTML, which holds that the author should specify a text's meaning rather than its physical attributes. If a section of text is a header, make it a header—don't make it "bold italic 14-point Times Roman." H1 is a logical style, whereas "Times Roman 14" is a physical style. A *logical style* specifies the intent of the author, while a *physical style* specifies an exact look. Stick to the use of logical styles rather than defining the actual font you want used. The advantage of logical styles is that you specify the meaning of H1 in one place. If you decide that all H1s should be centered, you do not need to go back and change every H1 tag; instead, you just change the definition of H1.

The following text:

```
<a href=http://www.acme.com/anotherdoc.html >Acme hyperlink
➡</a>
```

is a hyperlink. When a Web browser formats this text for the screen, the words "Acme hyperlink" will be highlighted. When the user clicks on the text, the Web browser retrieves the document anotherdoc.html.

The following text:

```
http://www.acme.com/anotherdoc.html
```

is known as an URL, which links the current document to other documents on the Web. An URL is the actual address of a document or location within a document. URLs have this format:

```
protocol://server/path.
```

In the example, http is the protocol, www.acme.com is the server, and anotherdoc.html is the path. Paths follow the Unix naming conventions (the slashes are backward for Windows users). Legal values for protocol include the following:

➤ http—retrieve a hypertext document

➤ ftp—retrieve a file using FTP

➤ file—view a file on the local disk

➤ WAIS—get a file from a WAIS server

➤ news—get an article from a Usenet newsgroup

➤ telnet—make a telnet connection

Web servers also have the capability of doing searches using archie (a tool that will search indexes of files on Internet servers) and gopher. Clearly, the World Wide Web is a superset of everything else on the Internet. In Chapter 7, "Secure Web Servers," two additional security protocols are discussed—SHTTP (Secure HTTP) and SSL (Secure Sockets Layer Protocol).

The World Wide Web just wouldn't be great without all the graphics. You can include a graphic in your HTML file by putting the following in your HTML document:

```
<img src=URL>
```

Replace "URL" with the correct URL for your image. The file extension you give your graphics fields is important. Web browsers look at the extensions to see if they can accept the image format. Follow the standard conventions when creating image files—for example, use .gif for all GIF files and .jpg for JPEG files. The standard file extensions are as follows:

➤ .gif—GIF graphic files

➤ .jpg or jpeg—JPEG graphic files

➤ .txt—Plain ASCII text

➤ .html—HTML documents

➤ .ps—PostScript files

➤ .aiff—AIFF sound files

➤ .au—AU sound files

➤ .mov—Quicktime movies

➤ .mpg or .mpeg—MPEG movies

➤ .xbm—XBM bitmaps

Other HTML tags exist that enable you to add comments to your HTML file, add blank lines, form lists, and more. The intent is not to teach you HTML here, however—whole books have been written on the subject. Just make sure you understand the basic concepts. HTML files contain tags that tell a browser how to format a document. An anchor tag contains a hyperlink to another document. A linked document can be on the same server or on a server halfway around the world. Web browsers ignore tags they don't understand.

A good reference for learning HTML is *A Beginner's Guide to HTML* at http://www.ncsa.uiuc.edu/general/internet/www/htmlprimer.html. You should also check out Macmillan's HTML Workshop at http://www.mcp.com/3362026762376/general/workshop/.

Understanding Forms

If the Web only *presented* information, it wouldn't be very useful. Forms allow Web servers to collect information from users. The following HTML form tag:

```
<form action="http://www.acme.com/newform" method="POST">
➡form definition </form>
```

specifies a fill-out form within an HTML document. This example uses the following attributes:

➤ `action` specifies the URL to which the form will be sent. If no action is specified, then the form is sent to the current URL.

➤ `method` specifies the way the form will be sent to the server. Two methods are supported, GET and POST, but you should only use POST. GET is obsolete for all practical purposes. The main difference between GET and POST is that the CGI program that processes the form can be passed more information using the POST method.

With forms, you can create an HTML document describing a product with photos and descriptions, and have an order form to fill out at the bottom of the page. You can place more than one form on a page. To differentiate different forms from each other and from the rest of the page, place a horizontal line before and after each form, as follows:

```
<hr>
<form action="http://www.acme.com/newform" method="POST">
➥form definition </form>
<hr>
```

The form definition can contain any tag except another form. There are three special tags for use inside forms:

➤ input—a simple input field on a form. Input has no closing tag.

```
<input type="text" name="textfield" value="Default
➥Value" size=20 maxlength=40>
```

An input tag can have any of the following types:

➤ text—a text entry field, the default.

➤ checkbox—a checkbox toggles on/off when the user clicks on it.

➤ radio—radio buttons with the same name are grouped together. Only one radio button within a group can be selected.

➤ password—a text field that displays asterisks for every character typed.

➤ submit—a push button that causes the browser to send the contents of the form to the URL specified. All forms must have a submit tag.

➤ reset—clears all fields within the form.

name is used to identify the value entered in this input field. The browser pairs up the name and value when POSTing the form to the server. name is required for all input types except submit and reset.

For text fields, value is the default value for the field. For checkboxes and radio buttons, value is the value given to the button when it is selected. For submit and react, value is the label on the push button.

size specifies the physical size in characters of a text field. It is only used with text fields. Multiple line entry fields can be specified using size=width,height.

maxlength is the maximum number of characters that a user can enter into a text field.

➤ select—use select to create lists that the user can select from. The list can be either a menu or a list box.

```
<select name="menu-example" size=1>
<option> First menu item
<option> Second menu item
<option> Third menu item
</select>
```

Use size=2 to create a listbox. The only valid tag inside select is option. Each option is an entry on a menu or a value on a list. You can also specify multiple when creating a listbox. This creates a multiple selection listbox. To specify a default selection, add a selected attribute to one (or more, if multiple is specified) option tags.

➤ textarea—create a multiline text entry field.

```
<textarea name="address" rows=4 cols=30></textarea>
```

Any text between inside a textarea tag is formatted exactly as entered, line feeds and all.

A Web server will have a CGI program set up to handle incoming forms. The server will pass the contents of the form to the program (different servers accomplish this in different ways). You should usually respond to the user with some form of acknowledgment—have your CGI program generate an HTML document to send to the user. As you will see in the next chapter, this response is a crucial step when users are spending money. You will want to use the capability of a secure server to digitally sign responses to forms.

Java

Sun Microsystems has announced a new programming language called Java. One projected use of Java is as an extension to HTML, which promises to make HTML documents passé. Java enables Webmasters to include whole executable programs in their Web pages. Java is more than just another HTML extension—it has the potential to dominate the Web. When a Java-compatible browser downloads a document with an embedded Java program, it installs and executes the program instantly. Java-capable browsers will be available for all platforms in relatively short order (some are available already). This will make Java the first truly architecturally neutral programming language. Any company setting up a Web server today should find a good Java programmer (or more likely, train one) to help develop their Web site.

Don't expect all of your customers to use a Java browser. Java represents a major security leak for users. Consider the fact that users are downloading and executing programs. Most users are still accessing the Web from work, and are not allowed to download executable programs from the Internet, even if they were personally open to the idea. Windows-based users have no effective security to prevent a Java program from deleting their hard disk, or worse.

For companies doing business on the Web, the possibilities are endless. Want to distribute a new file type? Your customers no longer need to separately download and install a special viewer. If you have the latest video compression technique, you no longer need to climb the "client software distribution" mountain. In the past, no file format would gain wide acceptance until nearly everybody had the capability to use that type of file. This generally meant getting your file format adopted as a standard or distributed by one of the major software houses—no more! You send them the viewer right along with the document. If your technique is great, the word will spread and you'll have a hit—all without ever needing to push for standards or invest huge sums to distribute your software.

Java solves two major headaches for software developers: platform independence and software distribution. Developing software that will install and work on Mac, Windows, and Unix is a major accomplishment—very few commercially successful programs have climbed this mountain. Java solves the problem quite nicely with no additional effort required on the part of the application developer (the author recommends still testing a program on a variety of platforms just to be sure). The same program can be executed on any platform that has a Java-capable browser. Java programs are general purpose programs with few exceptions (Sun has inserted some limitations, however, in an attempt to prevent Java viruses).

Ever have problems supporting *backleveled* client software (older versions of software that users haven't upgraded)? With Java, you can instantly update the client software, making backlevel compatibility a thing of the past. Want to change the format of a data file to speed transmission over the Internet? Just do it. Send along the latest Java program to read the new format—no need to mess up your program.

Of course, Java will present programmers with some interesting challenges. Programs will need to be small so that they can be transmitted quickly, but powerful and fast so that they are an enjoyable experience for end users.

The example commonly used to illustrate Java's potential is a stock ticker. Let's say you want to keep updated on the happenings on Wall Street while surfing the Net. Some brokerage house could make a Java program that automatically connects to their server every few minutes and downloads the latest round of ticker tape. They might offer a subscription or charge for each connection. The Java ticker program could run continuously along the bottom of the screen. The brokerage house could even build in a way to analyze stock prices and place orders automatically. When a second version of the program, which reads international stock exchanges, is ready, the brokerage house places it on their server. Customers will automatically download, install, and start using the latest version the next time they connect—no disks to mail, and no separate setup program to run.

Sun has made Java available free of charge. Servers and browsers will be pressed to add Java compatibility to their browsers. In April 1995, Netscape committed to including Java in a future release of the Netscape browser.

Summary

Because Web browsers and servers are flexible, powerful tools for distributing information, many companies are doing business on the Web using credit cards. Secure Web servers and browsers are thus being released to provide the support for encryption-based electronic payment systems and electronic commerce. These secure Web servers add encryption to the security capabilities of previous Web servers. Secure Web servers inherit the ability to control access to directories and files from previous Web servers. Therefore, understanding the capabilities and history of Web servers is an important stepping stone to understanding secure Web servers. With secure Web servers, the administrator gets a few extra jobs, but doesn't lose any of the old ones.

Web servers can distribute information using any of the protocols available over the Internet, including FTP, Usenet, and Telnet. The information available through the Web is a superset of the information available through other methods; the Web is expected to quickly absorb these other methods of information distribution.

The Web can also be used to collect information through the use of forms. Forms support all of the common methods of collecting information, including entry fields, radio buttons, and check boxes. Information collected using forms today is, almost always, sent over the Internet unencrypted. Electronic commerce will require a higher level of privacy. Nonetheless, the weakest link in the security field is and will continue to be controlling access to the server itself. Administrators need to carefully analyze the capabilities allowed each user that can access the server. The author recommends never storing important financial or personnel data in an unencrypted form. Programming toolkits are now available to enable any company to use security to protect all information on their servers. Failure to use the available technology will surely translate into a more vulnerable system.

Chapter 7 discusses two applications of public key encryption that are being integrated into Web servers—SSL and SHTTP. The chapter also provides an overview of common hacker attacks and how SSL and SHTTP can help foil them. In addition, the secure version of the Mosaic Web server—shttpd—is covered in some detail, as an example of an encryption-capable server.

Chapter 7

Secure Web Servers

HTTP-based Web servers support user id/password authentication and some basic security mechanisms. They do not provide secure channels of communication, but instead enable eavesdroppers to steal user ids and passwords. Other information, such as credit card numbers and order forms, are also vulnerable. There is a growing need for secure communication channels and encryption-based authentication to support online transactions. For this reason, two approaches have been proposed: Secure Sockets Layer Protocol and Secure HyperText Transfer Protocol. *Secure Sockets Layer Protocol* (SSL) provides for secure communications channels and authentication. *Secure HyperText Transfer Protocol* (SHTTP) provides a basis for secure communications, authentication, digital signatures, and encryption.

Servers that support SSL, SHTTP, or other (future) public key encryption-based schemes are a necessary part of any digital storefront. The encryption incorporated into the server is the perfect complement for any of the electronic payment systems outlined in Chapter 4, "Internet Commerce Providers." The combination of server-based encryption and an online payment system enables you to exchange encrypted order forms, confirmations, and so on with a customer and accept payment—all through the Web. Server-based encryption is useful even when using a payment system that is not encryption-based, such as First Virtual, enabling a merchant to provide privacy to customers. In a similar manner, while not needing or using the encryption from the server, digital cash schemes such as DigiCash's Cyberbucks should be used with a server that supports encryption to provide security for non-payment messages.

This chapter assumes that you are familiar with the basic capabilities of non-secure Web servers and HTML. You should have a conceptual understanding of digital signatures, encryption, and authentication—these topics were covered in Chapters 4 and 5. In this chapter, an overview of SSL is provided, and you are shown how to set up and use an SHTTP server, and how to integrate digital cash into your operations. Even if you have decided to outsource the administration of your Web server, you should read this chapter to understand the capabilities of the secure Web servers.

Secure Sockets Layer Protocol

The Secure Sockets Layer Protocol is a non-proprietary communications protocol designed to provide privacy over the Internet. SSL can be used to authenticate Internet servers and clients, but is not restricted to use with Web browsers and servers. This protocol is also independent of the application being run (Web, FTP, telnet, and so forth). Clients and servers running SSL negotiate all security-related matters before transferring any application information (such as a Web page). SSL provides a reliable, private, authenticated communications channel between Internet clients and servers. SSL does not support digital signatures of Web pages. Because SSL does not support data encryption after the data has been transferred, SSL cannot be used as a basis for encryption-based electronic payment systems.

SSL Handshaking and Information Exchange

SSL divides communication into a handshake phase and an information exchange phase. An SSL handshake phase begins with an exchange of HELLO messages. The client HELLO contains a challenge that will be used to authenticate the server later on, and also includes a list of the encryption techniques it supports. If the client finds a session id (provided by the server in a previous communication) for use with this server, it sends it in the HELLO message. The server HELLO message contains a random number generated by the server for each conversation. You will see later how this random number prevents certain kinds of hacker attacks. The server edits the list of encryption techniques, removing any that it does not support. This edited list is returned to the client as part of the server HELLO message. If the server finds a matching session id, it sends a session id OK flag in its HELLO message. If the client and server do not have a common session id, then this is a new connection. Figure 7.1 shows an exchange of HELLO messages between a client and server.

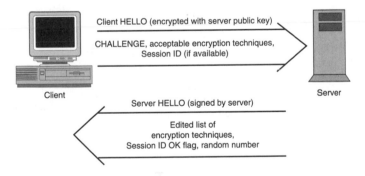

Figure 7.1
SSL conversations begin with an exchange of HELLO messages.

If this is a new connection between the client and server, a new master key is generated and exchanged. The client always generates master keys. The client sends the master key to the server encrypted with the server's public key. The master key is not used for bulk information transfer; it is used to generate four session keys—two each for the client and server. The client and server each have a separate key for use with incoming (read) and outgoing (write) messages. If this is not a new connection, then the server and client both use the previously exchanged session keys.

The server now sends a VERIFY message to the client. The verify message is the challenge sent in the client HELLO message signed using the server's private key. Because only the server has access to the private key, the client is assured of the server's identity.

The server can now optionally verify the identity of the client. The server sends a request to the client. The client must encrypt the correct response using the client write session key.

The handshake portion of the conversation is ended when the client and server exchange FINISHED messages. The client FINISHED message contains the random number sent by the server encrypted using the client write key. The server FINISHED message contains a new session identifier, encrypted using the server write key. Figure 7.2 shows an entire SSL handshake phase.

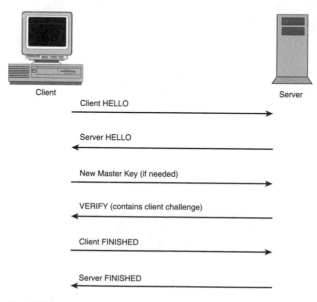

Figure 7.2

An SSL handshake session precedes any exchange of information.

After completion of the handshake, the client and server exchange information using the session keys. The handshake session is repeated for every message sent between the server and client. This prevents a hacker from decoding one message and using it to decode other messages.

The SSL protocol only supports secure communication channels; it does not support complete end-to-end encryption. This protocol is useful for demonstrating some concepts common to all encryption schemes—the exchange of keys followed by an exchange of information. SSL is not an appropriate protocol on which to base a digital storefront. If any company other than Netscape had developed SSL, then it would probably have never been an issue. Netscape, however, has incorporated the protocol into its servers and browsers, so you are likely to come across it as you evaluate different Web platforms.

SSL Requirements and Facts

SSL is designed so that Web surfers do not need to take any special action before being able to take advantage of this encryption technique. Even though SSL is based on public key encryption, users do not need to create and register their own key pairs. Some key facts about the SSL protocol are as follows:

➤ A server must have a certified public key for SSL to work. Clients do not have to have public keys.

➤ SSL uses RSA public key technology.

➤ U.S. export laws restrict the key length of international versions of encryption software to 40 bits. A 40-bit key takes about one day to crack (with sufficient computing power), and provides acceptable protection for the transmission of credit card numbers, but should not be used for highly sensitive information or very large transactions. Domestic implementations should have a key length of at least 128 bits.

➤ SSL does not support the signing of application level information. Therefore, SSL does not support *nonrepudiable transactions* (transactions that neither party can deny happened after the fact). After an SSL message exchange is complete, there is no way to prove that it happened.

Netscape has built a server and browser that implement the SSL protocol. A record of an encrypted conversation between a client running the Netscape browser and a server running the Netscape server was posted on the Internet as a challenge. It took about eight days of effort to decode the message. A group of people combined resources to decode a second challenge in 32 hours. These challenges do not represent a flaw in SSL or private key cryptography, however. Cryptologists have long known that a 40-bit key is breakable, given enough computing resources. The effort required to solve these challenges is exactly within the range predicted by cryptologists.

U.S. export law restricts key lengths to 40 bits. A 40-bit RC4 key can be broken in about a week with 40 Pentium workstations. Domestic keys with lengths of 128 bits or more are considered too large to be decoded. A 40-bit RSA key can be broken trivially.

The goal of the SSL protocol, and network security in general, is not to provide unbreakable protection—the goal is to make decoding messages cost more than the information is worth. If you make crackers spend more money decoding your messages than they can hope to get back, then they are less likely to even try to penetrate your system. The next sections look at some common hacker attacks and how SSL thwarts these attacks.

Cracking Messages Encrypted with SSL

Current techniques enable hackers to decode individual messages. After a hacker decodes an individual message, he or she can easily decode any other message encrypted with the same key. The following section discuss three different methods of attacking an SSL client or server.

Clear Text Attack

A *clear text attack* is any attempt to decode a message that is based on knowing the partial contents of the message. Decoding a message is fairly easy when you can guess much of its contents. For years, code breaking has relied on knowing what patterns to look for in a message. Web browsers commonly use the word "get," which is the command sent by a browser to a server to retrieve a new Web page. A hacker trying to decode a message between a Web browser and server can use this pattern to generate a database containing the word "get" encrypted with all possible key values. After this database is built, decoding Web messages is quick and easy. An actual Web message containing the word "get" is compared against the database. If a match is found, then the key used to encrypt the test case is the same key used to encrypt the message.

SSL defeats a clear text attack by using large key lengths. The Netscape SSL implementation actually uses a 128-bit key for domestic and international versions. When exchanging keys, the international version sends 88 bits unencrypted and 40 bits encrypted (this strategy is allowed by U.S. export laws). A 128-bit key is too large to be attacked with a clear text attack—it would take a computer larger than the known universe to store the test database. This means that a clear text attack is not feasible.

Brute Force Attack

For anyone without alternate access to the keys used to encrypt a message (such as paying off an administrator), the only feasible way to decode a message encrypted using SSL is using the brute force attack. This applies to any other RSA public key-based security method, such as SHTTP (see "Secure HyperText Transfer Protocol" later in this chapter), with 128-bit or larger keys. A *brute force attack* is a process of trial and error by which keys are tested at random for their capability to decode the message. The cost (the dollars and cents needed to buy the hardware required) of a brute force attack is increased as the number of possible keys increases. As the power of computers increases, making it easier to use large keys, the cost of a brute force attack becomes prohibitive—therefore, the more powerful the computer, the greater the security of network communications.

Replay Attack

A *replay attack* occurs when a hacker records a conversation between a client and server, and later connects to the server and replays the recorded conversation. SSL defeats this attack by attaching to the message the unique random number generated by the server for that message. This random number makes every message exchange different from every other message exchange. Because the random number generated by the server is different from that of the original message, the server recognizes and defeats a replay attack. The effectiveness of this method depends on generating a truly random number, which is difficult to do with software-generated random numbers. If it is easy to guess the random number, then a replay attack could be successful.

In computer lingo, the random number generated by the server to prevent playback attacks is known as a *nonce*. The nonce is generated by one party, and the other party must encrypt the nonce using the agreed-upon session key.

Impostors

The Internet is a collection of unprotected servers. A hacker can potentially intercept all messages between a client and server by fooling the client into believing he is the real server. SSL claims to prevent this type of attack with the use of *server certificates* (discussed in more detail in Chapter 5, "Cryptography Basics"). The server always sends its server certificate information to the client so that the client can authenticate the server. The client is further assured by requiring the server to digitally sign a challenge using the server's private key. Even if an impostor can transmit the correct certificate information, he cannot sign a document using the server's private key.

Network security is a complicated subject that requires ongoing evaluation of your systems and procedures. More in-depth information is contained in the book, *Actually Useful Internet Security Techniques*, by Larry J. Hughes (New Riders, 1995). This book covers each of the attacks mentioned here in more detail, and suggests other techniques for protecting your information.

Secure HyperText Transfer Protocol

Secure HyperText Transfer Protocol (SHTTP) is designed to enable secure, spontaneous transactions over the Internet. *Spontaneous transactions* require no previous coordination between the parties involved. Buying a newspaper at a newsstand is a spontaneous transaction—no ID or paperwork is required. Transactions over the Internet need to be every bit as simple and secure as buying a newspaper. SHTTP provides the encryption and authentication required for Internet transactions. Both the Web browser and the Web server must support the SHTTP protocol before authentication, encryption, or digital signatures work. SHTTP enables the following:

➤ Browsers to encrypt information being sent to a server

➤ Browsers to digitally sign requests

➤ Browsers to authenticate the identity of a server

➤ Servers to encrypt replies to browsers

➤ Servers to digitally sign replies

➤ Servers to authenticate the identity of browsers

Unlike SSL, SHTTP supports the signing of application-level information. For example, a server that supports SHTTP can digitally sign a Web page, whereas a server supporting only SSL could not. Thus, SHTTP supports nonrepudiable transactions—this is the major advantage of SHTTP over SSL. SHTTP is a set of additions to the HTML language. Because SHTTP is based on HTML, its use is restricted to Web applications. Because of SHTTP's ability to support digital signatures, it's expected to become the most widely used security standard on the Web.

Not all transactions require the same level of security. You probably don't have any protection for your home page, for example, which enables people to visit your electronic storefront without identifying themselves. When a visitor becomes a customer, however, both the business and customer want some form of security. SHTTP is designed to provide the flexibility needed for varying degrees of security, while protecting both the customer and the business.

The customer and business may have different concerns during a transaction. A customer who orders a computer from a catalog on a Web server needs to know that the server belongs to a legitimate computer retailer rather than a fly-by-night outfit that has no intention of delivering the goods. A customer must be able to authenticate the identity of both the server being accessed and the catalog being used.

After verifying the identity of the server and validity of the catalog, the customer transmits shipping and billing information to the retailer. The business will want to protect the identity of its customers from its competitors. The customer needs to protect sensitive billing information and to have confirmation of the sale. Both the business and customer will want to prevent anyone but the actual customer from reading the confirmation.

If a company sets up special rates for frequent customers, it must know the identity of everyone accessing its server. The identity of the user is needed to allow or deny access to special areas of the server.

SHTTP specifies the protocol used by the customer and business computers when exchanging information. Merchants can use SHTTP to provide authentication, privacy, or digital signatures, but it does not specify how these are to be provided. This will allow the protocol to change as security features are added to

Web servers. For example, SHTTP enables a business to force a customer to identify himself before being allowed to access a protected page. The exact mechanism is not specified. The customer must identify himself, but is not forced by the protocol into using public-key encryption. In fact, SHTTP does not specify any implementation details—it only specifies what is to happen, not how.

The customer's secure Web browser and the business' SHTTP server must be able to negotiate a common method of authenticating users and encrypting and signing documents. Different browsers and servers implement security using different techniques. Because SHTTP does not specify the type of implementation to be used, not all SHTTP browsers can access all SHTTP servers. A server might request a client-generated encryption key for use when returning information, for example, but the client might be unable to generate an acceptable key. In this case, although both the browser and server are using SHTTP, they cannot communicate. Nonsecure Web browsers such as Mosaic can access nonprotected parts of an SHTTP server, however.

SHTTP tells Web browsers and Web servers how to negotiate a common method of security, but does not limit the number of ways security might be provided. This approach is especially important for international businesses. U.S. law restricts the exportation of certain encryption technologies; therefore, if an international version of the software is not available, your international customers might use a different set of encryption algorithms than your domestic customers. Luckily, the encryption algorithms are well-known worldwide, and a compatible international version the software you need should be available.

This approach also enables an SHTTP document to work on different SHTTP servers that support varying encryption algorithms. Future advances in cryptography, therefore, can be incorporated into servers and browsers without causing backward compatibility problems. Most browser and server developers use toolkits provided by Terisa when designing their software, so incompatibilities should be minimized. Example implementations of an SHTTP Web server and browser are available from NCSA.

Terisa, a joint venture of leading security companies, is producing toolkits for software developers. These toolkits will be used by companies that develop Web server software, such as Netscape. In the near future, Web servers will support both SSL and SHTTP. Businesses setting up shop on the Internet are not customers of Terisa, but should make sure that the Web software running on their server incorporates the technology licensed by Terisa.

Secure NCSA httpd

Secure NCSA httpd is a reference implementation of the SHTTP protocol, meant as an example to developers of other SHTTP servers. Secure NCSA httpd adds encryption-based authentication, digital signatures, and encryption to the existing NCSA httpd Web server. This section illustrates the capabilities of an SHTTP server. Remember, as outlined in Chapter 6, "Web Server Capabilities," there is more to providing security than encryption—you must provide physical security for the server and protect the server from net-based attacks, many of which have nothing to do with the Web server software. Other servers have different configurations and capabilities.

SHTTP specifies the tags that can be added to an HTML document. You do not need to add all these tags directly to your HTML files—the Secure NCSA server automatically includes some of the necessary information for you. You should be aware, however, of tags that cause the server to alter the HTML file. An understanding of the actual communication between the server and browser is useful when troubleshooting.

Webmasters control the security features of the Secure NCSA httpd through the use of HTML properties, local security configuration files, server-side includes (explained in Chapter 6), and SHTTP header directives. Secure Mosaic is needed to manage the server's public/private keys. All SHTTP servers must have a certified public key.

Secure NCSA httpd uses public-key cryptography to digitally sign documents. The Secure NCSA httpd signs outbound documents using the server's private key. The server's certificate information is sent along with the signature so that the secure browser can verify the server's digital signature. *Digital signatures*—the digital equivalent of a handwritten signature (explained in Chapter 5)—received from customers are verified using the customer's public key.

Secure NCSA httpd can encrypt outbound documents using either public/private keys or shared session keys. Inbound encrypted documents can be decrypted in a similar manner. When the server is set up to use public-key encryption, messages can be encrypted in both directions without the customer having a public key of his own. This important capability frees customers from having to obtain and manage their own public and private keys, a considerable hurdle for many customers. Figure 7.3 shows how this is accomplished. The server asks the client to generate a shared key, encrypt it with the server's public key, and deliver it to the server. The shared session key is used to encrypt any documents sent between the server and browser.

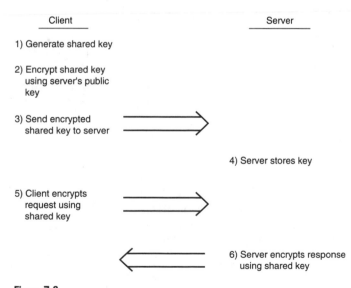

Client   Server

1) Generate shared key

2) Encrypt shared key
using server's public
key

3) Send encrypted
shared key to server

4) Server stores key

5) Client encrypts
request using
shared key

6) Server encrypts response
using shared key

Figure 7.3

Secure NCSA httpd and Secure Mosaic can exchange encrypted information without a Mosaic public key.

SHTTP assumes that all servers have at least one public/private key pair with an accompanying certificate. The current implementation of Secure NCSA httpd supports the use of a single private key. The private key is stored on the server in an encrypted database. The database is protected by a password known only to the Webmaster for your site.

The password you choose should follow all the normal guidelines, as follows:

➤ Should be at least eight characters long

➤ Should include both alpha and numeric characters

➤ Should be difficult to guess

In addition, you must store a copy of your public and private keys, along with the password, in a locked safe. These guidelines are only a necessary first step in safeguarding your private key.

The Webmaster at your site needs to know the password to start the server, so your Webmaster should be a trusted person. Through his or her access to the company's private keys, the Webmaster has access to all encrypted data sent through your Web server. The same private key used by Secure NCSA httpd can be used by Secure Mosaic to read any encrypted documents.

Encryption and signing are controlled on a per-document basis. Each HTML document can have an associated local configuration file that specifies the security behavior of the server. CGI programs—general purpose programs that can be used as custom extensions to your Web server (as explained in Chapter 6)—can insert special message headers in their output. For each document, the server can be instructed to either sign, encrypt, sign and encrypt, or neither sign nor encrypt.

Secure NCSA httpd provides several new environment variables for use with CGI programs, which use these variables to learn about the status of incoming requests. These programs can tell if a request is either signed, encrypted, signed and encrypted, or neither signed nor encrypted, as well as identify the browser making the request.

Controlling Client Behavior

Secure browsers, when accessing an SHTTP link, scan the properties specified in the link and react accordingly. SHTTP adds several properties to a hyperlink that tells the browser if any encryption and/or signature is required. This works great for links between pages within your server. You set up your hyperlinks to specify the correct combination of signing and encrypting.

What happens when an external server embeds a link to one of your protected pages? Can it change the URL so less security is required? The answer is no. A local configuration file on your server tells the server what security enhancements to require.

The access method used by the browser must match the requirements set in the local configuration file. The properties specified in the SHTTP link enable the server to control the behavior of secure browsers. Non-secure browsers will ignore the special SHTTP properties or return an error. In any case, non-secure browsers cannot access secured pages. The following examples show the exact properties that must be specified for each desired behavior.

Encryption without Signature

The SHTTP URL instructs browsers to encrypt their transmissions to the server. Instead of specifying http://, specify shttp:// for the protocol. Before a browser can encrypt the request, it needs the public key of the server. To retrieve the public key, the browser needs the distinguished name (DN) of the server, along with the server certificate information. The *distinguished name* of a server is a unique name worldwide registered for that server.

Distinguished names have four parts: a common name (CN), an organization unit (OU), an organization name (O), and a country code (C). The following distinguished name:

CN=John Doe, OU=Marketing, O=Acme Corp., C=US

is for John Doe, who works in marketing for the Acme Corp. based in the U.S. Both servers and people can have distinguished names. Servers usually have common names, however, which clearly identify them as a server rather than as a person. For example, the common name of a server might be Mail Server, which would, in most people's minds, identify this entity as a server and not a person. This format (CN=, OU=, O=, C=) is the X.500 naming standard, the unused, or at least underused, "CCITT-approved" worldwide standard for names in the Internet. You must register your organization name before using the country code. Doing so guarantees the uniqueness of your organization name; the certifying agency usually handles this step for you.

All SHTTP hyperlinks must specify a DN. The DN and certificate information arc used to look up the public key in a public key server. You include your server name and certificate information in the hyperlink so that browsers can look up your public key. The following shows an HTML file that tells the client to encrypt requests:

```
<head>
<!-- #certs name="Acme"-->
<CRYPTOPTS name="cryptography-options"
SHTTP-Privacy-Domains:orig-required=PKCS-7;recv-
➥required=PKCS-7;
SHTTP-Key-Exchange-Algorithm: orig-required=RSA;recv-
➥required=RSA;
SHTTP-Signature-Algorithm: orig-required=RSA;recv-
➥required=RSA;
SHTTP-Message-Digest-Algorithm: orig-required=MD5;recv-
➥required=MD5;
Your-Key-Pattern:'signing-key', <dn-spec>:='/
➥'*','*',TRUSTED_CERT_AGENCY,'*'/'>
```

```
</CRYPTOPTS>
</head>
<body>
<a href="shttp://www.acme.com/"
DN=<!-- #dn name="Acme"-->
CRYPTOPTS="cryptography-options">
A secure hyperlink
</a>
</body>
```

Because you have left server-side includes enabled (you did, right?), the server will examine the preceding code and take the following actions. When the server encounters the following server-side include:

```
<!--#certs name="Acme"-->
```

it inserts the certificate information for the specified distinguished name. This information is sent to the Web browser as part of the HTML page.

When the user selects an SHTTP link that specifies encryption, as follows:

```
<a href="shttp://www.acme.com/" >
```

the public key associated with the certificate information is retrieved. The public key is used to encrypt a one-time session key, which is generated by the browser. A new one-time session key is generated for each hyperlink accessed. All information sent to the server is encrypted using the one-time session key. The session key is then encrypted using the public key of the server and sent with the information. A one-time session key is used because it takes less CPU power than encrypting everything using a public key. Pretty Good Privacy (PGP), an e-mail system with built-in encryption (explained in Chapter 4), uses the same technique when sending messages.

Note the position of the cryptographic options block (CRYPTOPTS). In this case, the CRYPTOPTS block is not part of the hyperlink. This block is part of the header information, and fully specifies the encryption techniques that the browser must use when communicating with the server. The CRYPTOPTS block also specifies the implementations that are supported by the server, and is given a name—in this case, "Acme"—that is used throughout the HTML document. Anytime a hyperlink wants to use the options specified in the CRYPTOPTS block, it need only specify the name of the CRYPTOPTS block and not each individual option.

Encryption with Signature

The following HTML document shows how to instruct a browser to encrypt and sign a request. The CRYPTOPTS block tells the browser to sign and encrypt requests sent to the server.

```
<head>
<!-- #certs name="Acme"-->
</head>
<body>
<a href="shttp://www.acme.com/"
DN=<!-- #dn name="Acme"-->
CRYPTOPTS="SHTTP-Privacy-Enhancements:orig-
required=sign,encrypt;recv-required=sign,encrypt;
SHTTP-Message-Digest-Algorithm: orig-required=MD5;recv-
➡required=MD5;">
A signed and encrypted hyperlink.
</a>The browser will sign and encrypt the request for shttp:/
➡/www.acme.com/.
</body>
```

Secure Mosaic will present the user with a Secure Submit button before sending an encrypted or signed request. By selecting the Secure Submit button, in this case, Secure NCSA Mosaic will digitally sign a message following the same pattern used by PGP. The secure submit button is automatically generated by Secure Mosaic whenever an SHTTP hyperlink is selected by the user.

Thus, in the preceding example, when the user selects the hyperlink <a href="shttp://www.acme.com/" ...>, Secure Mosaic presents the Secure Sibmit button.

Chapter 5, "Cryptography Basics," explains in detail the digital signature process. Secure Mosaic, by default, uses the MD5 hash function to generate the contents of the digital signature. The output of the MD5 hash function (a *hash function* generates a string of bits that has a mathematical relationship to the message) is encrypted using the user's private key. The signature is attached to the message. A session key is generated and used to encrypt both the message and the signature. The server's public key is used to encrypt the session key. The encrypted message and signature, the encrypted session key, and the user's certificate information is sent to the server.

The user needs to have created and certified a public key before signing a document. This may represent a significant hurdle for some users. Be careful when asking for signatures—not all clients will be able to provide them. The alternative is the familiar user id/password.

Signature without Encryption

You may want to restrict access to your server based on the identity of the user. You need to use some form of authentication to verify the identity of the user. You have two options for authenticating users under SHTTP, as follows:

➤ digital signatures

➤ user id/passwords

The following CRYPTOPTS entry:

```
CRYTPOPTS=SHTTP-Privacy-Enhancements: recv-required=sign"
```

tells the browser that replies should be digitally signed, but not encrypted. The signature is used to authenticate the user.

Digital signatures require no prior contact between the customer and business, but they do require the user to generate and store public and private keys. User ids and passwords will be more familiar to users, but require the prearrangement of accounts. Passwords are a type of shared secret—both the customer and business must keep a copy of the secret password. Shared encryption keys are another form of shared secret.

An offline exchange of shared secrets is called an *out-of-band key exchange*. Out-of-band key exchanges are prearranged exchanges of user id/password combinations or shared encryption keys. The following shows an HTML file that depends on out-of-band key exchanges.

```
<head>
<!-- #certs name="Acme"-->
</head>
<body>
<form action="shttp://www.acme.com/"
DN=<!-- #dn name="Acme"-->
CRYPTOPTS="SHTTP-Privacy-Enhancements:orig-
➥required=sign,encrypt;recv-required=auth,encrypt>
A form requiring an out-of-band key exchange.
<p>
An input field which should be encrypted:
<input size=30 name="secretfield">
<p>
<input type="submit" value="Submit">
</form>
</body>
```

There is no code in the HTML file that tells the server to exchange keys with the browser. This means that some other method of exchanging keys has been arranged. By definition, these offline exchanges are out-of-band exchanges. The key difference is the line "recv-required=auth,encrypt." If you wanted to force an in-band exchange of keys, you would change "auth" (asking for user id/password) to "sign" (requesting a digital signature).

In-band exchanges are also possible. The following shows a hyperlink that generates an in-band key. The nonce value has been randomly generated by the server before sending this file to the client.

```
<a href="shttp://www.acme.com/inband.html
DN=<!-- #dn name="Acme"-->
CRYPTOPTS="<!--#s-key alg="des-esc"-->
nonce:snonce">
In band hyperlink
</a>
```

In-band exchanges are used to exchange shared encryption keys just before using them. You might set up a server to use an in-band exchange of shared encryption keys to boost the perfor-mance of your server. A secure Web server will spend much of its time encrypting and decrypting information. Any improvement in the speed of encrypting and decrypting information, therefore, can have significant impact on overall performance and capacity. Shared encryption keys are much faster than public keys, so you should minimize the use of encryption using public keys.

The alternative to public key encryption is *shared key encryption*. By maximizing the use of shared keys, speed and capacity are increased. Public key cryptography is still a critical ingredient in any Internet-based shared key encryption scheme—in-band exchanges of shared keys are impossible without public keys. Because you can't eliminate the use of public keys, a good strat-egy is not to use public keys to encrypt all the information you send out. The only information that must be encrypted using public key cryptography is the shared encryption keys used for the rest of the session. In fact, encrypting and exchanging shared encryption keys is the primary use of public key cryptography today. Once a shared encryption key has been exchanged, it is used for the remainder of the session.

You can't use shared keys to encrypt and exchange shared keys for the following reasons:

➤ How would you exchange the original shared keys?

➤ If you had already exchanged shared keys, why exchange another set?

Because of these problems, public keys are needed to exchange shared keys. Facilitating the exchange of shared keys is actually the primary role public key encryption plays in most security schemes.

As a dedicated student of HTML, your immediate reaction to the use of a shared key during a session is likely, "There is no such thing as a session when talking about the WWW." This is true. Each HTML document request/response is completely independent of any other request/response. How then do a server and browser coordinate the use of shared keys across many request/responses? SHTTP uses nonces, which are created by the server during an in-band exchange of keys. The nonces are sent to the client with the keys. The client then includes the nonce in any encrypted message sent to the server. The server uses the nonce to look up the correct shared key and decrypt the information.

Think of nonces as unique numbers generated by the server when an in-band exchange of keys is required. As with SSL, nonces are unique random numbers inserted into a message exchange to defeat playback attacks.

Secure NCSA httpd enables Webmasters to specify the use of in-band exchanged shared keys. Managing server behavior is covered later in this chapter in the "Managing Server Behavior" section.

Secure Mosaic comes with the capability to manage shared secrets, which are stored in a local database. The shared secret database is used by both Secure Mosaic and Secure NCSA httpd. The following CRYPTOPTS entry:

```
CRYPROPTS="SHTTP-Privacy-Enhancements: recv-required=auth"
```

instructs the browser to search the local database for passwords. A list of options is presented to the user. The user selects the correct shared secret and the browser sends it to the server. In this example, the user selects the correct user id for the target server. The server checks the password against those stored in its local database. If no match is found, access is denied.

Use the keyword "auth" to force users to sign and encrypt using shared secrets. Use the keyword "sign" to force users to sign and encrypt using public key cryptography.

Encrypting Images

Most Web browsers retrieve images after retrieving the HTML document. If the images must be protected, the links to these images can specify the use of in-band keys to encrypt and sign the images. A merchant could have many reasons for wanting to protect images. For example, the following shows how to force the server to generate an in-band key for each image to be transferred:

```
<img src="shttp://www.acme.com/secureimg.gif"
DN=<!-- #dn name="Acme"-->
CRYPTOPTS="<!--#s-key alg="des-esc"-->
SHTTP-Privacy-Enhancements:recv-required=encrypt;
nonce:snonce">
```

In this example, the browser does not have to use public key cryptography to exchange a one-time session key. The following CRYPTOPTS entry:

```
CRYPTOPTS="<!--s-key alg="des-ecb" -->
SHTTP-Privacy-Enhancements:recv-required=encrypt"
```

causes the server to generate a shared key for the browser to use when requesting the images.

Forcing the Use of Trusted Certificates

You may want to restrict the certificates you accept as valid. As the number of certifying authorities grows, this option will become more important. By specifying the certificates you will accept, you are forcing customers to have their public keys certified by one of the certifying agencies you accept. You restrict the certificates you will accept by inserting regular expressions into the CRYPTOPTS block for a hyperlink. When the user selects a hyperlink containing a regular expression, Secure Mosaic presents a list box with only those keys that are certified by acceptable certifying authorities.

The primary certifying authorities in operation today are Apple, for its eWorld product, and Verisign, an RSA spin-off. Future business demands will determine whether more CAs are created.

Managing Server Behavior

Secure NCSA httpd behavior is controlled by settings in configuration files, environment variables used by CGI programs, and embedded tags in HTML documents. Secure NCSA httpd uses multiple configuration files. Other servers may use a single configuration file, but the basic concepts are similar.

Restricting Access to Documents and Directories

Secure NCSA httpd uses local security configuration files to control access to documents and directories. To control access to a file—such as the restricted.html file—a file called .restricted.html is placed in the same directory. The name of the local security file is the same as the file it protects except for the leading dot. The server searches for dot files before processing a request. The following shows a portion of a dot file. The required SHTTP entry tells the server to honor a request for an HTML file only if SHTTP is used:

```
AuthType SHTTP
SHTTPAuthAccept encrypt
<limit GET>
require shttp
</limit>
```

The default behavior of Secure NCSA httpd is to honor all requests. If you want to restrict access to a document, you must create a corresponding local security file. The information in the local security file must match the information in the hyperlink used to access a document. If a hyperlink instructs the browser to encrypt but not sign requests, and the local security file tells the server to accept only signed requests, then the server will return an error when the browser attempts to access the document.

Changing the security required to access a document entails changing the settings in the local security file and updating all hyperlinks to the document. Updating the links can be a time-consuming, error-prone process. There are no automatic tools available to automatically update the security enhancements used with hyperlinks. This means each change must be entered by hand, introducing the possibility of typos and missed changes. Because of the cost of changing the security settings of a document, SHTTP documents must be planned and tested carefully.

Local security files can be used to force the use of privacy enhancements or to control access to documents and directories. Local security files can be used to encrypt and sign the output of CGI programs, as well as static HTML documents. The following local security file entry:

```
SHTTPPrivacyEnhancements sign,encrypt
```

tells the server to sign and encrypt the corresponding HTML document (or CGI program output) before sending it to a user. The SHTTPPrivacyEnhancements setting uses the same keywords as the SHTTP-Privacy-Enhancements variable used in SHTTP CRYPTOPTS blocks. Use "sign" to force the server to electronically sign outbound documents, "encrypt" to encrypt outbound documents, and "auth" to authenticate the outbound document using a shared secret.

To prevent non-SHTTP requests from accessing a file or directory, use the "require shttp" entry. When the server sees the require shttp entry in a local security file, all non-SHTTP requests for a document will be denied. The server will return an error instead. You can further restrict the type of requests by using the SHTTPAuthAccept entry. The SHTTPAuthAccept entry lists the acceptable types of privacy enhancements that must be present before the server will honor a request. Legal values for the SHTTPAuthAccept entry are sign, auth, and encrypt.

The settings in local security files can be overridden by CGI programs. This feature enables you to alter the security features used on a per request basis. For example, privacy enhancements may be skipped altogether for requests from in-house employees.

Modifying the Behavior of CGI Programs

Common gateway interface (CGI) programs, as explained in Chapter 5, are used to build links from your Web server to other systems in your organization. Strictly speaking, CGI programs are not part of the server—they are written specifically for your storefront to alter the behavior of the Web server. From an administrative perspective, CGI programs are an integral part of the server. These programs are also used to dynamically generate HTML documents. You can configure the server to run a CGI program when a request for a specific document is received. The output of the CGI program is interpreted by the server, and the results are passed to the browser.

CGI programs are a major security risk. Improperly coded CGI programs open a huge door through which any cracker can easily penetrate your system. If you're thinking of saving a few bucks by having your in-house programming staff code the CGI programs, make sure you get extensive training and have their work thoroughly checked.

Secure NCSA httpd adds some environment variables that can be accessed by CGI programs. These variables allow the CGI program to obtain the cryptographic status of a request (signed, encrypted, both, or none), along with the keys used to sign or encrypt the request. For example, if a CGI program needs to know if a request is encrypted using a user id and password, it first checks the value of the SHTTP_PROCESS variable. If the value of SHTTP_PROCESS is AUTHENTICATE, then the CGI program checks the SHTTP_AUTH_USER variable to retrieve the user id and password sent by the browser. Table 7.1 summarizes the environment variables available to a CGI program.

Table 7.1   SHTTP Environment Variables for CGI Programs

Environment Variable Name	Description
SHTTP_AUTH_USER	Returns the name of a shared secret sent by the browser when the server requests the user for authentication. The name of the shared secret can be a user id/password or the name of a shared key.
SHTTP_HEADER_DATA	Returns the complete header block sent by the browser.
SHTTP_NONCE_ECHO	A colon separated list of nonces returned by the browser.
SHTTP_PROCESS	Indicates which privacy enhancements, if any, were used by the browser.
SHTTP_SIGNER	The distinguished name of the signer in X.500 format.
SHTTP_SIGNER_CERT_CHAIN	Certificate chain of signer.
SHTTP_CERT_CHAIN_LEN	Length of the certificate chain.
SHTTP_VERSION	The SHTTP version used by the browser.

CGI programs can also affect the behavior of the server by including certain character sequences in their output. These character sequences are listed in the next section, "Server-Side Includes."

These programs can also override the settings in a local security file by including a privacy enhancements block in their output. The server checks for the following character sequence:

```
Privacy-Enhancements=
```

in the header block of the CGI output. Sign, auth, and encrypt are acceptable values. If a local security file specifies encrypt, but the CGI program specifies sign, the document is signed but not encrypted.

CGI programs can also cause the server to include information in the document being sent to a user. By adding the following:

```
Content-type:text/x-parsed-html
```

to the header block of any output, a CGI program causes the server to parse the HTML document looking for server-side includes.

Server-Side Includes

Server-side includes for the Secure NCSA httpd server work exactly as they do for the non-secure server. *Server-side includes* are special character sequences inserted into an HTML document. When the server comes across a character sequence it understands, it takes the appropriate action. For the Secure NCSA httpd server, these actions can be inserting the certificate information of the server, inserting the distinguished name of the server, or inserting an in-band shared key.

Inserting the Public Key Certificate Information

The following server-side include:

```
<!--#certs name="Acme"-->
```

causes the server to include the certificate information for the named server. The browser will need the certificate information when retrieving the public key for your server. Because the current implementation of the server uses only a single name, the value of the name= variable is ignored. Future releases will allow for multiple certificates, so it is a good idea to include the proper name right from the start. Certificate information is normally inserted into the header of an HTML document.

Inserting the Distinguished Name

The following server-side include:

```
<!--#dn name="Acme"-->
```

causes the server to include the distinguished name of the server. The DN is inserted wherever the DN server-side include is encountered. The browser will need the certificate information when retrieving the public key for your server. Because the current implementation of the server uses only a single name, the value of the name= variable is ignored. This means that each Secure NCSA server can have only a single distinguished name. This can be a serious restriction in some environments, driving up the cost by forcing the purchase of additional machines when a single machine could easily handle the load.

Secure NCSA servers can only have a single distinguished name. This is different from most non-secure servers, which allow multiple names per server. This can force you to buy extra hardware, even when a single computer could easily carry the load.

Future releases will allow for multiple distinguished names, so it is a good idea to include the proper name right from the start.

Distinguished names are normally inserted into hyperlinks. For example, the following hyperlink:

```
<a href="shttp://www.L3Comm.com/" DN="<!--#dn name="L3Comm"
➥-->">
text
</a>
```

will be expanded by the server before being sent to a user, as follows:

```
<a href="shttp://www.L3Comm.com/" DN="CN=L3COMM,
OU=Publishing, O=L3Comm, C=US">
text
</a>
```

In-Band Key Exchange

The following server-side include:

```
<!--#s-key alg="des-ecb"-->
```

instructs the server to replace the server-side include with a shared key. The server generates a shared key and inserts it in place of the server-side include. This include is useful for generating keys for in-band exchange. You place this server-side include in a hyperlink, and then encrypt the page before being sent to the user. The following, for example, causes a shared key to be generated and associated with the nonce value 23456789:

```
<a href="shttp://www.L3Comm.com//homepage.html"
DN="CN=L3COMM, OU=Publishing, O=L3Comm, C=US"
CRYPTOPTS="Nonce: 23456789
<!--#s-key alg="des-ecb"-->">
link text
</a>
```

The presence of the nonce value tells the browser to send this value to the server when attempting to access this hyperlink. The browser will encrypt the request using the shared key.

The server uses the nonce value to determine which shared key to use when decrypting this request.

Creating SHTTP Documents

There may be a time lag before HTML editors support the new SHTTP tags—therefore, you might need to manually create or edit your HTML files to add privacy enhancements. Web software changes rapidly, so you may only need to wait a few months before new tags are supported by HTML editors. The tags outlined in this section should enable you to meet your security needs. The basic points to remember are as follows:

➤ Every server must have a public key. This in turn means that every server must have a distinguished name.

➤ Every SHTTP request needs at least the URL and distinguished name of the server.

➤ The default behavior or clients, in the absence of any instructions in the hyperlink or header block, is to encrypt but not sign requests.

➤ The default behavior of servers is to neither sign nor encrypt responses.

➤ Privacy enhancements are specified both in the header block and in hyperlinks.

SHTTP is likely to undergo more changes—you should consult the documentation that comes with your SHTTP server. The examples given in the preceding sections are for the Secure NCSA httpd server (version x.y on platform Z) only.

Customer Access Methods

You should pay particular attention to how customers will access your secure server. Even though you may design your pages to be accessed in a particular order, you cannot control the order of the pages accessed by customers. You can't assume that customers will visit your home page before attempting to access other pages on your server. With non-secure servers, this fact is incorporated into the design of each HTML page. When you add the complexity of secure pages, session keys, and public keys, this becomes more difficult. Simply returning an error when a nonsecure access attempt is made will confuse many customers. They may believe that your server is down or that you are no longer in business. You should consider a CGI program that returns an explanation, telling the customer why his or her access attempt has been denied and the correct way to access your system.

In addition to the normal ways customers have of accessing your Web server (searches, lists of links, published guides, and so forth), SHTTP adds one more way users may access your server—through the public key ring holding your server's public key.

Using SHTTP—An Example

The previous sections have covered the main SHTTP constructs in isolation. This section combines them together in a coherent example. Other examples should be included with your server software. In this example, the business uses the capability of Secure Mosaic and Secure NCSA httpd to encrypt and sign credit card transactions.

Let's use the Safe Insurance business example to illustrate the use of SHTTP. Safe Insurance (a fictitious company—any resemblance to a real company is purely coincidental) wants to sell car insurance direct to customers through their Web server. Customers will need to access the server, fill out information concerning their car, and order from a list of available policies. Safe Insurance must evaluate each policy request before responding to customers. Each policy application must be accompanied by an upfront payment. Safe Insurance offers discounts to current policy holders with safe driving records.

In this example, a customer accesses Safe Insurance's home page using Secure Mosaic by following a secure hyperlink listed in a public Internet resource listing. When the customer selects the following secure hyperlink:

```
<a href="shttp://www.safe_insurance.com/welcome.html"
➥DN="CN=safe-server, OU=marketing, O=Safe Insurance, CN=US">
Safe Insurance
</a>
```

the secure browser will use the distinguished name to retrieve the public key for Safe Insurance from some Internet directory. The transport method specified is shttp instead of http. Because no CRYPTOPTS is specified, the browser encrypts but does not sign the request for the Safe Insurance home page.

The administrator has set up the home page to be signed, but not encrypted. The home page is signed so that the customer knows he has reached the correct server. There is no sensitive information provided on the home page, so no encryption is necessary. The administrator tells the server to sign, but not encrypt, by placing a local security file called .welcome.html in the same directory as the file welcome.html. The file .welcome.html has the following entry:

```
SHTTPPrivacyEnhancements sign.
```

The Safe Insurance home page is received by the browser and the signature is verified. The home page lists different types of insurance that can be ordered from Safe Insurance. When the user selects the following car insurance link:

```
<a href="shttp://www.safe_insurance.com/car_order.html"
DN="CN=safe-server, OU=marketing, O=Safe Insurance, CN=US">
➥Safe Insurance
</a>
```

the browser once again encrypts the request using Safe Insurance's public key. The Safe Insurance server sends the order form in the clear. No local security file is needed.

The user fills out his personal information, including his credit card number, and selects the Send button. The hyperlink corresponding to the Send button is as follows:

```
<form action="shttp://www.safe_insurance.com/
➥underwriting.html"
DN="CN=safe-server, OU=marketing, O=Safe Insurance, CN=US"
CRYPTOPTS="SHTTP-Privacy-Enhancements: recv-required=sign,
➥encrypt">
```

The browser will sign and encrypt this information before sending it to the server. The browser signs the request, generates a shared key, encrypts the request and signature using the shared key, encrypts the shared key using the servers public key, and sends it all off to the server. The browser also sends the user's public key certificate information so that the server can verify the user's digital signature.

When the server receives the policy request, it runs the CGI program underwriting.html. Typically, this program would forward the policy request information to another Safe Insurance database system to have the request reviewed by an underwriter. The CGI program must also respond to the user with a confirmation of receipt. In this example, the confirmation is only an acknowledgment of receipt, not an acceptance of the policy application. This confirmation is a legal document that Safe Insurance does not want its competitors to read. The response should be both signed and encrypted before being sent to the customer.

The CGI program can find out the identity of the customer by accessing the SHTTP-SIGNER environment variable. This identity is compared against current policy holders to see if any discounts are possible. The CGI program instructs the server to sign and encrypt the response by including the following character sequence in the header of the HTML file created:

```
Content-type:text/x-parsed-html
Privacy-Enhancements= sign,encrypt
```

An in-band key exchange is started by inserting the following:

```
<!--#s-key alg="des-ecb" -->
```

The server will parse the HTML file, sign the file using the server private key, generate an in-band shared key, encrypt the confirmation using the shared key, encrypt the shared key using the customer's previously supplied public key, and send the response to the customer.

The customer's browser will reverse the operations and verify the confirmation. The user should save the confirmation—insurance companies in some states are required to respond within a set amount of time.

Integrating Electronic Payment Systems

This simple example shows how to use the security features of SHTTP to provide a simple online ordering system. If Safe Insurance accepted some form of electronic cash as payment, that payment would be sent along with the policy application. Let's see how the scenario changes when one of the electronic payment systems is used.

The first decision faced by Safe Insurance concerns what forms of electronic payment are desirable. Insurance is a *soft good* (as opposed to hard goods like cars and computers)—there is nothing to ship to the customer; soft goods can be delivered online. Safe Insurance may decide to send a policy in the mail, but even this step should not be necessary. Insurance is relatively expensive, so concerns about small payments are not a concern. Insurance does involve regular payments over a period of time, so an electronic system that supports automatic monthly billing is desirable. Digicash's Ecash is a poor fit, because of the hassle of returning the up-front payment if the application is rejected and the lack of support for automatic monthly billing. A better choice would thus be a credit system with support for monthly billing. Credit can easily be issued to the customer's credit card should the application be rejected.

Safe Insurance decides they can reach more customers by accepting multiple forms of credit-based payment. The policy application form should be altered to offer a variety of payment options. The exact sequence of actions would depend on the option chosen by the customer.

Even though Safe Insurance is integrating electronic cash into its online catalog, it need not offer only one payment option. It can still offer encrypted credit cards as an additional payment option.

If Safe Insurance decides to integrate the Open Market system (Open Market is discussed in Chapter 4), the policy application form would be changed to forward payment information to the Open Market payment server. After some security checks, the payment server instructs the customer browser to access Safe Insurance's server using an authorization URL. Safe Insurance's server must be capable of recognizing an authorization URL and taking special action, typically running a second CGI program. Because the Open market system transfers encryption keys and passwords, the customer should use a secure browser such as Secure Mosaic.

Each payment system accepted by Safe Insurance will—almost always—involve some application programming. The server must be able to recognize and differentiate between payment methods, and respond with the appropriate action.

Secure Server Products

The first secure Web server products are already available. Netscape and Open Market offer servers with built-in support for electronic commerce. When evaluating Web servers for your site, pay attention to the add-on products available. Special products to support order processing (including automatic clearing of funds) can save considerable time when setting up your server. Make sure that the add-on products support the payment types you want to accept and that they work from behind a firewall.

Netscape Servers

Netscape offers a full range of server products to choose from, including the following:

> **Netscape Commerce Server**—Secure server supporting electronic commerce.

> **Netscape Communications Server**—Similar to the Commerce server, but without some security features.

> **Netscape News Server**—Features support electronic publishing.

> **Netscape Proxy Server**—enables other servers to work from behind a firewall.

Netscape servers are available for Unix and Windows NT.

Netscape Commerce Server and Netscape Proxy servers support SSL. Netscape has committed to including SHTTP support in future releases, and is making their servers available for a free trial of 60 days (Netscape is currently the most popular Web server, and can be reached at http://www.netscape.com). Not all of their servers incorporate encryption technology. You can purchase the Netscape Communications Server, which lacks the support for SSL. Figure 7.4 shows the Netscape home page.

Open Market Secure WebServer

The Open Market Secure WebServer supports both the SHTTP and SSL protocols. It is available for the following platforms:

> SunOS

> Sun Solaris

> Digital Unix

> BSD/386

> IBM AIX

> SGI IRIX

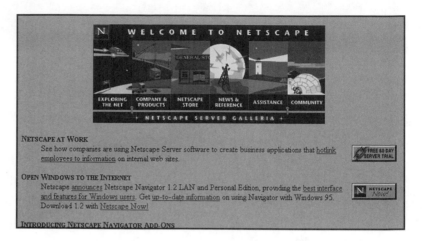

Figure 7.4

The Netscape home page.

The Open Market Secure WebServer is available in both domestic and international versions, with the international version using shorter key lengths. It is compatible with any secure Web browser.

Open Market is providing the entire infrastructure needed for electronic commerce, rather than simply supporting encryption schemes. Their Integrated Commerce Service offers a way for businesses to take orders, accept payment, and manage customer service. Customers who want to use Open Market's Integrated Commerce Service must purchase their Transaction Link product. Transaction Link connects the merchant server to the Open Market order verification servers.

Figure 7.5 shows the Open Market home page.

Figure 7.5

The Open Market home page.

Chapter 4, "*Internet Commerce Providers*," covers the Open Market offering in detail. Open Market can be reached at http://www.openmarket.com/.

Summary

SHTTP provides the basic privacy and security needed for electronic commerce. In addition to the secure communications channels claimed to be provided by SSL, SHTTP provides for digital signatures and other forms of network authentication.

Even though some online payment systems come with their own special software that provides encryption, a company can still gain value by using a secure Web server. The capabilities of a secure Web server such as Secure NCSA httpd can be used to reach more customers than a nonsecure server. Any electronic payment system compatible with a nonsecure Web server should be compatible with a secure Web server. Nothing is lost by moving to a secure Web server (everything else being equal). Even if you decide to outsource your Web server to a time-sharing company, you should make sure that a secure Web server is being used.

Hacker attacks can be mounted against any secure server. While it is theoretically possible to guess a key, the cost of doing so is too large for casual hackers. Only large organizations have the resources to decode encrypted messages that are encrypted using large keys (at least 128 bits in length, but 700 bits or more is best) in a reasonable amount of time. The cost of decoding a message is likely to increase as the power of computers increase, making it impossible for even large organizations to decode encrypted messages (assuming governments don't outlaw strong encryption). A more likely avenue of attack is through the people operating the business. Customers must trust the businesses they patronize. Even today, customer credit card numbers are routinely processed by low-paid clerks, who may be sorely tempted to steal a few numbers for themselves or for sale. No amount of technology can maintain the security of credit card numbers if the people processing the orders cannot be trusted. The security of a system is determined by its weakest link, which is usually the people processing orders or administering the system. While technology can provide the basis for secure transactions, real security depends on a complete system of policies and the people who implement them.

The next chapter, "Alternate Technologies for Electronic Commerce," examines Lotus Notes as an alternate platform for digital storefronts. Although everyone building a storefront will want to build a Web site, other technologies can be used to reach other audiences. These audiences will be smaller and more specialized than a Web audience, but may be highly desirable for some businesses.

Chapter 8

Alternate Technologies for Electronic Commerce

Throughout this book, the authors have assumed that you will be using the World Wide Web for your digital storefront. Because Web browsers are widely distributed, providing you with a ready market of users, it is recommended that you use the Web as part of your digital storefront strategy. The Web doesn't have to be your only distribution channel, however. The authors want to encourage you to broaden your thinking; an alternate platform that doesn't get much press in Internet books—Lotus Notes—will thus be discussed.

In this chapter, the authors aren't worried about building Notes applications for internal use, but instead focus on using Notes as an alternate distribution channel. In many cases, Notes can help you reach audiences that do not have access to the Web. Notes was the first major product to incorporate RSA's encryption technology, and has a built-in search engine and application builder, making Notes appropriate for business-to-business information sales. In this chapter, you will learn when Notes is appropriate, what type of audience you can reach, and how to go about setting up a Notes storefront. This chapter does not cover the step-by-step technical details of setting up a Notes server, however, because the Notes storefront is hosted by a service provider.

The Notes Inter-Enterprise Application

The Notes equivalent of a Web home page is the inter-enterprise application—digital storefronts fall into the category of inter-enterprise applications, which includes all applications that cross organizational boundaries. The bulk of Notes-based inter-enterprise applications fall into one of four categories, as follows:

➤ **Multi-enterprise collaboration.** Notes is the technology that helps you rapidly form teams consisting of people from multiple organizations. Notes is essentially the glue that holds these teams together.

➤ **Disseminate information to suppliers, distributors, and customers.** Notes is a good vehicle for circulating a variety of types of information, including product information, videos, and brochures.

➤ **Publishing news and magazines.** Notes' built-in search engines make it particularly useful for scanning, searching, and clipping news databases. More and more news organizations are now offering their information in a Notes format, typically selling it through several of the Notes services.

➤ **Electronic commerce.** Notes, with its digital signatures and verification technologies, is a good platform for electronic commerce. One drawback is that none of the encryption-based electronic payment systems covered in this book work with Notes. Each service provider must develop its own software to handle billing. Make sure your service provider can handle a variety of billing arrangements to provide you with the flexibility to experiment.

Most organizations that pursue a Notes storefront will be interested in publishing information. With its built-in search engine, application development tools, and agents (agents will be released with Notes v4), Notes can add value to information by enabling customers to easily organize, search, and clip information based on their own needs. The information provider no longer needs to anticipate all the needs of every customer, because the customer can customize the information themselves.

If you want to use Lotus Notes to distribute information, you should contact one of the service providers that can host the Notes servers for you. CompuServe, AT&T, Lotus, and others are hosting customer's Notes applications. In addition to hosting the servers, each of these providers is creating a Notes marketplace that spans the provider's network.

Throughout this chapter, it is assumed that you have some familiarity with Notes. Most organizations interested in publishing using a Notes format will already be using Notes internally, although there is no technical reason why a company that does not use Notes cannot publish information using one of the Notes services.

Introduction to Notes Lingo

Those of you interested in Notes as a possible publishing platform, but having no experience with Notes, will first have to learn some basic Notes terms before reading this chapter. The following is a quick primer on common Notes terms.

Rollout

Rollout is the process of planning, installing, and supporting a Notes network. A rollout can last anywhere from a few months to several years, depending on the number of licenses to be installed.

Replication

Replication refers to Notes' capability to automatically propagate changes to a database to copies of a database on other servers. Notes replication is *connection-oriented*, meaning that two servers must have a direct connection before they can replicate changes to common databases. The connection-oriented approach scales well to large numbers of servers and users.

Access Control List

Each Notes server and database has an *access control list* (ACL). The access control list is used to determine the rights a user has. Notes users can be given the following rights:

➤ Manager access—meant only for administrators

➤ Designer access—for application designers

➤ Editor access—can create and edit any documents not specially restricted

➤ Author access—can create and read, but cannot edit

➤ Reader access—can only read

➤ Depositor access—can create new documents, but cannot read

➤ No access

In addition, each Notes document can contain its own access control lists that limit the users who can read or edit the document. *Reader lists*—access control lists that govern who can read a document—are covered later in the chapter under Step 7, "Build Your Storefront." *Author lists*—access control lists that govern who can edit a document—work exactly the same as reader lists.

Domain

A Notes *domain* is a logical collection of Notes servers. Any group of Notes servers can form a domain. The servers can be on separate continents if desired. Each Notes server is assigned to a single domain when it is first installed. Although it is possible to change the domain of a Notes server after it is installed, this can entail considerable effort on the part of the administrator, and is therefore almost never done. Planning domain names before installing Notes servers is one area where a little planning can save considerable effort down the road.

Most companies have a single domain, not counting domains used only for testing. Some large organizations have more than one domain for historical reasons. Technically, there is no reason for a company to have more than one production domain, unless it is a company with more than 10,000 licenses—in which case it will have trouble using a single domain. The Notes directory of users and servers is incapable of handling more than 10,000 entries efficiently, which leads to terrible overall performance for the Notes network.

Hierarchical Naming

Any name that complies with the X.500 naming standard is called a *hierarchical name. X.500* is a global directory service that enables you to easily find contact information on registered individuals. One of the primary considerations used when creating the X.500 naming standard was elimination of duplicate entries. Notes can handle both the X.500 naming format and the older naming scheme known as flat names. Notes enables users and servers to use either flat names or hierarchical names. Each organization must choose one naming scheme for all users and servers. An example of a hierarchical name is as follows:

John Doe/Marketing/Acme/US

A flat name lacks all the special qualifiers, as follows:

John Doe

Name and Address Book

All users and servers are listed in the Name and Address Book, making the Name and Address Book the Notes address directory.

In addition to the corporate-wide Name and Address Book, each user can have a personal address book.

Certificates

A Notes certificate serves the same purpose as certificates on the Web. A *certificate* is used during the authentication process to guarantee the identity of a user. Notes servers store lists of the certificates they will accept—no server or user is allowed to access the server unless it can present a valid certificate.

Cross Certification

Cross certificates are used to allow servers from other domains to access your servers (you exchange certificates with the other server). In other words, you give the servers a certificate that provides access to your server, and they provide one that provides access to their server. This process is known as *cross certification.*

Designing and Deploying a Digital Storefront

If you have already rolled out Notes internally, you probably already have a methodology for developing Notes applications. This methodology may not be applicable to a Notes-based digital storefront. Many new issues arise when developing a digital storefront that are not part of an internal development effort. In this chapter, an eight-step plan is provided for designing and deploying a Notes-based digital storefront (or any other Notes inter-enterprise application). The steps are as follows:

➤ Form a project team

➤ Assess potential chapters

➤ Develop a business strategy

➤ Design your storefront

➤ Create a support organization

➤ Define your standard operating procedures

➤ Build your storefront

➤ Get the word out

Notice that most of these steps involve business, not technical, decisions. Most organizations use consultants to help build and roll out inter-enterprise applications, even if they have internal Notes skill, because the technical challenges are different when building an application that will be used by customers. If you compare this section with Chapter 9, "Planning Your Digital Storefront," you will notice that there is some overlap. Although there are similarities, a Notes storefront is technically more challenging due to the nature of Notes applications (integrated security, replication, search engines, agents, and so forth).

Step 1: Form Your Project Team

Several key issues arise when staffing for inter-enterprise applications. Customers using your applications will form impressions of your company based on these applications. Any application aimed at customers, therefore, should be considered part of the marketing message your company sends. All of your inter-enterprise applications should be consistent with the marketing message and materials that your company distributes through other channels.

You should consider whether or not you want your IS staff to develop your marketing materials. On the other hand, having your marketers develop software isn't necessarily a good solution either. Just as most firms hire an agency to handle their advertising, many companies now farm out the development of inter-enterprise applications. Most advertising firms have already added the capability to develop Web sites. Consulting companies specializing in inter-enterprise Notes applications are also popping up. Look for a firm that combines marketing and Notes experience when developing an application aimed at customers. For inter-business Notes applications aimed at distributors and suppliers, look for a company that combines business-to-business communication skills and Notes experience.

When staffing a project team for inter-enterprise applications, include members from your marketing and public relations staffs. The team for a inter-enterprise application will be considerably more interdisciplinary than for other Notes rollouts. Content and presentation become much more important.

Step 2: Assess Your Potential Customers

Before jumping into Notes-based electronic commerce, you should survey your potential clients. Make sure they are ready to take advantage of Notes. Potential clients can include the following:

➤ Your product distributors

➤ Your suppliers

➤ Your business partners

For each potential customer, you should find out if they already use Notes. If not, you should consider using the Web to reach these customers. Some companies are in the fortunate position of being able to convince their customers to install Notes just to access their storefront. If you are one of these companies, then you should consider helping your customers through a Notes installation.

Step 3: Develop a Business Strategy

The same business strategies that work for Web-based digital storefronts will work for Notes-based storefronts. The following strategies are particularly applicable to a Notes storefront:

➤ Use content, content, and more content

➤ Make your storefront interactive and easy to navigate

➤ Put your best face forward

➤ Make certain your storefront is error-free

➤ Know your competition

See Chapter 10, "Winning with Your Digital Storefront," for more details.

Step 4: Design Your Notes Storefront

If you plan to also publish information on the Web, you can create your documents using Notes, and then generate HTML documents from your Notes database. The Lotus InterNotes Web Publisher is the tool that translates Notes databases into HTML documents. For more information on InterNotes Web Publisher, see http://www.lotus.com/inotes/. You won't be able to use every bell and whistle on the Web, but you can create a decent-looking home page that can link directly to a Notes database. The primary advantage of this approach is the automatic management of links provided by Notes. Notes automatically tracks documents as they are changed, maintaining the correct links between documents. Lotus manages its home page using this method. Figure 8.1 shows the Lotus home page (http://www.lotus.com), which is created using Lotus Notes.

Figure 8.1
The Lotus home page is created using Lotus Notes.

When designing a Notes storefront, be careful in naming groups and roles in your access control list in your inter-enterprise applications. Names that you choose must not conflict with names in your customer's Name and Address Book, or your application may not work correctly. To accomplish this, you should prepend the name of your company or application to any name in the ACL. Avoid names that give away your internal organizational chart, because this information may fall into the hands of your competitors (you wouldn't want them hiring away your best Notes developers, would you?).

Step 5: Create a Notes Support Organization

The quality of support that you provide for your inter-enterprise application will affect your customers' impressions of your company. Even if you release a reliable, consistent application, you still have to provide excellent support for an inter-enterprise application. Even though all of your customers (presumably) have installed and are using Notes, you cannot assume that they have any Notes expertise. Your support requirements will go well beyond supporting your application. You should be ready to field general Notes support questions. Questions such as "It's not replicating—what's wrong?" are common. The problem may have nothing to do with your application; it may just be the first place the symptom appeared. Supporting Notes remotely can be an unexpected expense associated with inter-enterprise applications. Check with your service provider or consultant on the possibility of getting help with general Notes support. The author doesn't recommend building an elaborate support structure to rival the Lotus support structure—just make sure your support staff will handle these questions with grace and forward the question to the proper support channel.

Your inter-enterprise application should include a way to submit questions regarding usage and bugs. The author recommends having a general-purpose Help form, which customers can use to compose questions and comments. The form should be automatically routed to your support staff. You should also provide an immediate follow-up to all submitted questions. If you don't have an answer, give an expected time for getting back to the customer with an answer. Return a "thank you" for all comments.

In addition to requiring a higher level of support than may be needed in-house, there are additional challenges in administering an inter-enterprise application. Consider the case of

undeliverable mail. It may be that your Name and Address Book
has been corrupted, or that the customer's Name and Address
Book is wrong. It also may be that one of the intermediate servers
is not functioning properly. It's often quite difficult to resolve this
type of problem and requires cooperation over the phone between your administrator and your customer's administrator
(not easy for international clients). Because your customer's
administrators are at varying levels of skill and experience, the
administrator that you select to support your inter-enterprise
applications should be able to debug a Name and Address Book
problem over the phone. The administrator you choose to
support your inter-enterprise applications will have to be a good
"people person," having an infinite amount of patience and—if
applicable to your application—an ability to understand virtually
every spoken language in the world.

Because you'll be using hierarchical naming in your application,
you'll have to become familiar with cross-certifying servers. You'll
also want to provide a single external contact from your support
organization to support all of the inter-enterprise applications
that you deploy. You should require each of your end users to
provide a single point of contact for dealing with usage and
support problems.

Step 6: Define Your Standard Operating Procedures

Even if you do not enforce any restrictions on internal applications, you should develop and enforce standards for your
inter-enterprise applications—you need to ensure consistency
between your various inter-enterprise applications. *Consistency*
includes the look and feel, button naming, colors, fonts, and so
forth.

Document and enforce a change procedure for making design
updates to the application. You should clearly identify all sources
of information for the application.

Step 7: Build Your Storefront

Inter-enterprise applications differ technically from ordinary in-house applications, requiring greater security and reliability. Your application development methodology, testing procedures, application design, security precautions, and performance goals are all affected.

The issues that differentiate inter-enterprise applications from in-house applications include the following:

➤ Rapid application development methodologies may not apply.

➤ High reliability is required.

➤ Multiple domains are involved.

➤ Multiple client platforms must be supported.

➤ Your application must run small servers and clients.

➤ Users may be accessing your application with slow modems.

➤ You cannot rely on Notes' default security settings.

➤ You must protect customer information from unauthorized access.

➤ You may be forced into using hierarchical naming.

➤ Service providers may restrict the application tools you can use.

These factors affect the design of your Notes application, as well as the organization creating and supporting the application. Let's take a look at each of these issues in more detail.

Rapid Application Delivery Methodology May Not Apply

The overriding key issue that you must consider when developing, deploying, and supporting an inter-enterprise application is that your users are external to your application. Most Notes application development follows a rapid application development methodology where you work intensely with the targeted end users. This may not be possible for an inter-enterprise application. In this case, a marketing vision will replace user feedback. A phased delivery, where an application is delivered to customers one piece at a time, is not applicable for your inter-enterprise application. Releasing a constant stream of upgrades to the public may cause confusion among your end users. Less frequent, major upgrades are more manageable in this environment. The fact that your users are customers can have a dramatic impact on the methodology you use to develop your applications.

High Reliability Required

Inter-enterprise applications require extra testing resources. Your applications must be highly reliable. Releasing buggy applications on a service like AT&T Network Notes or CompuServe Enterprise Connect can have a detrimental effect on your company's image. This is true whether the audience is customers, suppliers, distributors, or joint venture partners.

Multiple Domains

The primary technical difference between an in-house application and an inter-enterprise application is the proliferation of domains. There are at least five domains in a typical inter-enterprise application, as follows:

1. Your internal domain

2. Your external domain

3. The service provider domain

4. The customer external domain

5. The customer internal domain

Figure 8.2 shows the domains involved with a typical inter-enterprise application.

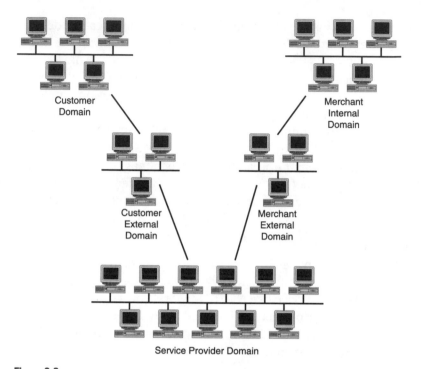

Figure 8.2

Typical domains in a Notes inter-enterprise application.

The service provider has a domain, the customer will have his external and internal domains, and you will have your internal and external domains—for a total of five domains. The number of domains affects the role of replication and mail routing, and requires a special test configuration. Create at least a three-domain test environment to do basic testing of your inter-enterprise applications. You can save yourself time by performing this testing even before placing an application on your service provider's host.

There are two strategies for tracking the full e-mail address of anyone submitting information to your database. You can have each user either fill out a form the first time he submits information, include this information in the submission, and replicate submissions, or have all submissions mailed to a central database. Because many users will not know the complete mail address, the author recommends mailing submissions to a central database. The Notes router will automatically maintain the full e-mail address as the submission is routed through the network.

Because there are five typical domains in any inter-enterprise application, replication will have to go through five hops to get from your input server to the customer server. This introduces a delay that may not be acceptable for your application. Even if you dial up your service host on a regular basis, you don't have any control over how often your end users dial in. Therefore, you need to plan on handling cases with a two-day turnaround from the time you put data out on your system to the time it actually reaches an end user. This situation can happen when a user who dials in once a day connects to the service provider just before your data reaches that host. His server won't get that data until the next day, when it dials in again. Then, at some point during that second day, the end user will check the data currently on his server. In a worst-case scenario, this can be a two-day turn-around.

If you have particularly urgent data, you'll have to use high-priority e-mail. This only works if your service provider will dial out to end users to deliver mail. In order to dial out, you have to have a phone number for each end-user domain. This will be problematic for publishing and electronic commerce applications, where you may not even know the identity of your customers. E-mail notifications work best for inter-enterprise collaborations. To avoid cluttering up personal mailboxes, provide each end-user domain with a mail-in database to receive e-mail notifications concerning your application.

The applications themselves must meet a higher standard of reliability than is typical for much in-house development. Customers will form an image of your company based upon their use of your inter-enterprise application. Therefore, you should rigorously test your applications.

Multiple Client Platforms

You cannot assume any restriction on the type of platforms that will be used to view your application. You must assume that every available Notes client will be used to view your application. Users will have a variety of monitors, resolutions, and colors when viewing your application. At a minimum, you should test your application in each of the standard resolutions (VGA, SVGA, and 1280×1024) to ensure that the screens are at the least intelligible. You'll have to stick to simple color schemes if you want them to look good across such a wide range of platforms—for example, don't use different shades of blue on a single screen. Some users will have difficulty differentiating the two colors.

Under-Powered Servers and Clients

Your application must perform acceptably on a minimally configured server and client. You should design your applications to have acceptable performance running on a 486DX server with 16 MB of memory. In most Notes networks, the server is the performance bottleneck. You cannot assume that every end-user domain will be using a high-powered server.

The primary performance benchmark to test when creating a Notes database is the length of time it takes to open a view. If views take several minutes to open, users will stop using your application. The design of your views and the size of your databases will have the greatest impact on application performance. When creating views, use no more than three sorted columns (if possible). In addition, avoid creating databases that have more than 100,000 documents.

Slow Connect Speeds

As of this writing, if you are deploying inter-enterprise applications, you can expect your end users to be using modems to access your service provider's host. Even at 28.8 Kbps with field level replication, you need to consider the amount of data that you change on a regular basis. You should also put in place special procedures to avoid massive updates to a database—

update fields instead of whole documents. Until Notes version 4 is released, you'll need to organize your application to use many small documents rather than one large one. This makes it easier to distribute changes to your data without having to replicate extremely large documents. Because of the slow connect speed, most users will access your data by replicating it to a server of their own rather than sitting online, running up access charges. Therefore, when building your applications, assume that users will be accessing replicated databases in a different domain. Notes v4 takes care of this problem by replicating only the changes to a document, not the whole document.

No Default Access Control List Entries

When designing your access control list, don't assume any default entries in the Name and Address Book. You need to set up the default access to enable end users to access all features of your application. At the same time, you must prevent information from accidentally replicating between customers.

The best way to prevent accidental replication of private information between your customers is to use reader lists (any field with the name ReaderNames is a reader list). As mentioned earlier, a *reader list* is a special field that controls access to a single document. If a document contains a field called "ReaderNames," Notes checks the field before enabling a person or server to read the document. The person or server's name must be listed in this field, or no access will be provided.

You should not overuse reader lists—they can cause headaches for an administrator, with people constantly calling to find out why a certain document isn't replicating (they aren't on the reader list for the document). Reader lists can make an application less flexible, because it is difficult to give new people access to a database that uses reader lists. It is sometimes necessary to modify the reader lists of every document when giving access to a new group. When dealing with inter-enterprise applications, modifying an entire database is usually an unacceptable solution, due to the replication overhead generated (which can result in erroneous billings if you are charging for replication time). When using reader lists, make sure you include the names of all people who may need access to a document when creating the reader list field.

Customers May Replicate with Each Other

When your database is replicated around the world to many organizations, you run the risk that two companies will replicate directly with each other. When two companies, both with replicas of your database, replicate with each other, confidential information can leak from one customer to another, and they may not be aware of this until it's too late. This will reflect badly on your company, and could result in liability if one of your customers suffers a loss as a result of using your application.

If each of the two companies creates a replica of your database, when their servers call up each other, your database will be updated. This may not be proper behavior for your database, however. In fact, if this results in the sharing of confidential information between potential competitors, you may be getting a phone call that you will definitely not enjoy! Your database ACL should explicitly list the domains that can replicate the database.

List your internal and external domains and the service provider domain. Your customers will want to replicate from their external domain to their internal domain. Because you cannot predict the names of these domains, you should provide details in the About and Using documents on adding entries to the ACL. Your default access must be set so that no information created at a customer site will replicate with any server other than your domains and the service provider domain.

You need to use reader's name and author's name fields to control access to documents. All documents composed and submitted should have a ReaderNames field. The ReaderNames field should include the person composing the document, the server name of the service provider's server, your external and internal servers, and your default inter-enterprise administrator group.

Must Use Hierarchical Naming

Your service provider will almost certainly require you to use hierarchical naming for all servers and administrators that will access a service provider host. This doesn't mean that you have to convert all of your internal users to hierarchical naming; it simply means you need to set up a hierarchically named external server for use with your service provider hosts. You may need to set up hierarchically named administrator accounts to directly access a service provider host.

To create hierarchical names for your servers and users, you must first create certificates, which will then be used to create the hierarchical names. For example, if you want to create the following hierarchical name:

> John Doe/Marketing/Acme

you must first create a certificate named Marketing/Acme. When you create an identification record (a Person Record in Notes lingo) for John Doe, a public/private key pair is automatically created for John Doe. You must certify John Doe's keys with the Marketing/Acme certificate. This causes John Doe to be known as John Doe/Marketing/Acme. The process is identical when naming servers.

You should consult the documentation that is shipped with Notes to determine the steps needed to create a certificate.

Restrictions on the Use of Agents

A service provider may impose some restrictions on your Notes applications. You may not be allowed to use all of the design features that Notes provides. For example, you may not be allowed to run agents, or doing so may be an additional charge. Your end users may not be allowed to create agents. All of these restrictions need to be described in the About document for your application.

Must Use Notes Interface Only

You should design your user interface using only the capabilities of the native Notes application builder. Building additional interfaces on top of your Notes database using Visual Basic, Power Builder, and so on, while possible, is an additional administrative burden that is not justified for most inter-enterprise applications. Some method of distributing and installing your application would need to be worked out. If you are going to develop an application using Visual Basic, Power Building, or C, and you want to reach as wide an audience as possible, you'll have to provide that application under Mac, Windows, OS/2, and Unix. Providing a consistent look and feel across all these platforms is difficult and expensive (and sometimes impossible). Providing a consistent look and feel is something that most corporate IS staffs are unfamiliar with and ill-equipped to handle. This means that your application developers developing your inter-enterprise applications will need to be more creative in their use of the Notes interface elements. You should strive to concentrate on the content, and to separate your applications from the rest of the pack, while still providing a consistent look and feel with your other marketing materials.

Step 8: Get the Word Out

You should advertise your Web storefront using the mechanisms provided by your service provider. You should consider developing and sending "getting started" kits to each potential customer. Due to the specialized nature of Notes storefronts, you probably need to use very focused marketing efforts, rather than the broad-based efforts recommended for Web-based storefronts. Advertising in a Usenet group, for example, would be nearly worthless. You will have to consider whether your Notes storefront justifies being mentioned in your other product literature.

Summary

The details involved with actually setting up a Notes network are too numerous to discuss here. There are many books available that will help you develop Notes applications. Your service provider will be able to help you locate a consultant capable of developing applications for deployment over their network.

Notes is well-suited to business-to-business information sales. Notes already integrates many of the technologies that are just now becoming standard on the Web. RSA security for encryption and authentication, agents, and a powerful search engine make Notes a powerful information distribution platform. Notes flexibility gives customers the power to quickly massage the data they receive. If your customers use Notes or could be talked into using Notes, and your information can take advantage of Notes features, then the author strongly suggests you consider publishing using Notes in addition to the Web.

Part III

Digital Storefronts

Chapter 9

Planning Your Digital Storefront

A well-done *digital storefront*—your own Web store—takes on a life of its own. Although it may start out small, a digital storefront can grow and become an important part of nearly any business. You wouldn't open a new retail store without laying out a plan, and a digital storefront is no different—planning is a critical part of any new business. This chapter covers the basic steps you should follow when building a digital storefront. Although you may not need to develop a full business plan, spend some time considering your goals before launching a digital storefront.

Eight Steps to Building a Digital Storefront

So you've decided to take the plunge. You want to set up a digital storefront and start to explore online retailing. Where do you start? What's the first step? In this chapter, you are provided with a step-by-step methodology for designing, developing, and maintaining a digital storefront. These steps are as follows:

1. Form a project team.

2. Set goals.

3. Register a domain name.

4. Select a service provider.

5. Develop a business strategy.

6. Design and build your digital storefront.

7. Promote your digital storefront.

8. Start over.

Step 1: Forming a Project Team

You should form a multidisciplinary team to plan and implement your digital storefront. Information systems (IS; also called MIS) departments tend to focus on the technical aspects of setting up a Web server, but this is actually the least important part of setting up a digital storefront. Far more important are your business strategies, products, prices, and advertising content. A good project team involves members from the following departments:

➤ Marketing

➤ Product development

➤ Public relations

➤ Information systems

➤ Graphics

The main role for your IS department is to design and build the links to your back end processing systems. These include your order fulfillment system and customer support. The authors strongly encourage you to consider outsourcing the hosting of your digital storefront. Most IS departments are not prepared to handle the security issues involved with hosting a digital store-front—a digital storefront involves many technologies new to most IS shops. Security, Unix or Windows NT, Web servers, and HTML skills are not present in most IS shops. In most cases, it is simply not possible to justify the expense of the hardware, software, and training required to build and host your own digital storefront.

Your team will almost certainly involve people outside your organization. Roles that are commonly outsourced include the following:

> ➤ Content providers
> ➤ Applications developers
> ➤ Internet service providers
> ➤ Advertising developers

Web content providers are usually referred to as *Webmasters*. Their role is to keep your digital storefront fresh to encourage repeat visits—thus, the ideal content provider should be a consultant, writer, artist, and business strategist. Make sure your content provider can help you identify workable Web strategies.

An applications developer is needed because a digital storefront goes well beyond simply publishing information. A digital storefront is closer to an interactive application than a simple magazine. An applications developer is needed to write the code that handles the processing of any forms. New Web technologies, such as Java, thus require the skills of an applications developer. If you want to use Java, for example, then an applications developer will be needed to write the Java code for your storefront.

Your Internet service provider may supply you with a link to the Internet or may actually supply the server that hosts your digital storefront. Internet service providers should be able to support a reliable, secure platform for your storefront. As is discussed in Chapter 4, "Internet Commerce Providers," there is no such thing as perfect security, and you should be suspicious of any provider that promises perfect security. A good provider should be able to support authentication, privacy, and digital signatures for your digital storefront.

Ad agencies are often involved in setting up Web home pages. There is a tradition in the United States of outsourcing the development of advertising. Web home pages, however, often fall under the advertising umbrella. Keep in mind that digital storefronts go well beyond simple advertising—they have the potential to shape and affect your entire organization over time. Check out Chapters 10 and 11 for details on digital storefront strategies and how they can affect your organization. At a minimum, a digital storefront will affect your customer support organization, because of the need to respond to online queries.

Each member of your team should be provided with a copy of the Netscape Web browser. Each member also should commit to spending some time simply surfing the Web to become familiar with other Web sites.

Step 2: Set Goals

For most existing organizations, your digital storefront is unlikely to be more than a sideshow in the near term. The experience of most storefront owners to date has been many visits and a few purchases (with exceptions!). As people's reluctance to purchase online falls and new secure software becomes commonplace, however, digital storefronts may become a viable part of your business plan. It is important when starting a project with the potential of a digital storefront to set some realistic goals up front. This will not only help you, but also any consultants or service providers that you involve to provide you with the appropriate advice and counsel. Although your eventual goal may be to have a digital storefront, you may want to start with a traditional home page and then move into a true digital storefront. Some of the options that you should consider when starting out are as follows:

➤ Distributing online brochures

➤ Publishing extensive product information

➤ Providing customer support

➤ Distributing financial information on your company

All of these options will give you experience in running a Web site, as well as move you toward a digital storefront—all of these elements are part of any good digital storefront. When you want to begin development of a true digital storefront, you will need to decide on products, strategies, and pricing.

Bring the team together for a few brainstorming sessions early on in the project. Use these sessions to discuss people's concerns and issues, as well as to generate ideas.

Step 3: Register a Domain Name

Internet domain names are hot items. *Domain names* are alpha-numeric names for your company, and are both the online address and online name of your company. If you want to use your company's name as your domain name, you have no time to lose. InterNIC, the company responsible for creating Internet domain names, services requests on a first come, first served basis. The very first decision your project team needs to make is the domain name you want to use. You can contact InterNIC at http:\\www.internic.net for more information. If you already have an Internet service provider, they should be able to help you register a domain name.

Step 4: Select a Service Provider

Although you do need to evaluate your ability to host your own digital storefront, most organizations will choose to outsource this function. Indeed, digital storefronts will bring back the outsourcing industry that existed in the '70s, which let people rent time on a computer so that they wouldn't have to buy one for themselves. The authors strongly recommend that you outsource your digital storefront host. (Disclaimer: the authors do not in any way stand to gain financially from this recommendation. They don't provide Internet hosting services.)

Reasons for Using a Service Provider

Most service providers charge less than what it would cost you to buy and install a *T1 line* (a high-bandwidth permanent connection). It simply makes economic sense, therefore, to use a time-share host for your digital storefront. Other reasons to consider using an Internet service provider to host your digital storefront are as follows:

➤ **Security.** Most IS shops, even in the largest organizations, are not capable of providing the level of security required to run a digital storefront. A single mistake can cost thousands (or millions) of dollars. Using a service provider can protect your internal network because the storefront is no longer running on your network, and because your storefront is protected from your own staff, the largest potential threat.

➤ **Cost.** Any serious digital storefront will require a T1 or fractional T1 line. If you decide to host your own Web server, the cost of this line alone will likely exceed the entire charge to have an Internet service provider host your digital storefront. The Internet service provider will also provide support (insist on 24-hour support) for your server, making the cost differential between using a service provider and hosting your own server even greater.

➤ **Technology is changing rapidly.** Your investment in technology and training is not a one-time investment. For the next several years, you will find yourself continually buying new hardware and software. In addition, your people will spend an inordinate amount of time keeping up to date on the latest Web application development tools. There simply isn't enough work involved with setting up a single storefront to justify the learning curve required to stay current.

➤ **Unix administrators are difficult to hire.** The preferred platform for Web servers is Unix (although Windows NT is growing in popularity). In many parts of the country, Unix administrators are hard to come by. If your organization is not currently using Unix, then obtaining a good administrator will be nearly impossible.

➤ **Internet service providers have a complete infrastructure in place**. There are a variety of other costs associated with running a Web storefront that a merchant would have to buy. A good service provider will have multiple high-speed connections to the Internet, making it more likely that customers will be able to contact your server. Service providers should also provide physical protection for our server (UPS, fire protection, electrical protection, and generators).

Just because you decide to use an Internet service provider does not mean that there is no role for your IS department. Your IS department, in conjunction with your storefront applications developer or Internet service provider, will be responsible for linking your digital storefront to your back-end systems. Your digital storefront must be linked to your order fulfillment, payment processing, and customer support systems.

Criteria for Selecting a Service Provider

You must be comfortable with your Internet service provider—it will function as a landlord and utility for your organization. The criteria you should use when selecting an Internet service provider are the following:

➤ **The technology the provider is capable of supporting.** As technology changes, different Internet service providers will adapt more or less quickly. Make sure your Internet service provider is technically capable. Your provider should be able to provide you with the latest release of HTML, as well as the capability to run CGI scripts, image maps, and three-dimensional storefronts (when the technology becomes available in early 1996). You may not want to use all of these features, but it's nice to have the option.

➤ **The bandwidth the provider can provide for your storefront.** Internet service providers vary in the amount of communications bandwidth they provide to the Internet. A service provider should be able to provide multiple connections to the Internet for your server. Make sure that any connections the service provider talks about can be used by your server, and that they are not reserved for some other usage. A service provider that is hosting multiple sites should have, as a minimum, multiple T1 connections to the Internet.

➤ **The financial stability of the company.** The age of the garage Internet service provider is already coming to a close. Competition has driven prices to a point where it is no longer economical for small shops to provide services to only one or two firms. Make sure that your service provider has a track record with other customers. At a minimum, your service provider should provide home pages to other companies. Ideally, the service provider you select would have some experience hosting digital storefronts.

➤ **24-hour support.** Your digital storefront will be open 24 hours a day, so you will need support 24 hours a day. Your digital storefront is truly an international store, and you should treat it as such. Support is expensive, and is often the first area to have problems when a provider is trying to cut prices or has more accounts than the staff can handle. Providers that have people on-site are better than providers that have people on call. If a provider only has people on call during the night, then you can count on having several 8–10 hour outages during the night over the course of a year. Companies with on-call support personnel also tend to provide lousy support on holidays.

➤ **Support quality**. Make sure the provider stocks spare parts for all hardware on-site to minimize the downtime associated with catastrophic hardware failures. Is the support center adequately staffed? Try calling the provider's support line 15–20 times in a week at all hours. Make sure you can get through to a human who can help answer questions and fix problems.

➤ **Value–added services.** Your Internet service provider should be able to provide you with some additional services beyond just hosting your digital storefront. You should be able to receive detailed reports on the activity for your storefront, including the number of individuals accessing your server, the pages they access, and popular links. Ask to

see examples of reports that you can expect to receive on
your digital storefront.

Step 5: Develop a Business Strategy

A digital storefront, like any business, needs to have a strategy
that motivates the decisions made regarding the storefront. The
business strategy for a digital storefront should be based on the
strategy used by the rest of the company, but does not have to be
identical. For some real-world examples, review Chapter 2,
"Commerce on the Web," for examples of storefronts and the
strategies they use. Some key points to remember when developing your business strategy are the following:

➤ Integrate your digital storefront with the rest of your business—your storefront cannot exist in a vacuum. The rest of
your company, including marketing, shipping, accounting,
and so on, should be involved with the storefront.

➤ The materials you publish through your digital storefront
should be consistent with other marketing materials in both
content and look. You don't want to confuse customers by
providing mixed messages—one through traditional media
and one online. A consistent look can also help customers
remember your online store.

Some key decisions you will need to make are as follows:

➤ Will you offer special products?

➤ Will you offer discounts?

➤ Should you build partnerships with other companies?

➤ What information should you offer?

➤ What forms of payment should you accept?

Make sure your storefront offers something that is unique so that
customers have a reason to patronize your store. Business
strategies are discussed in detail in Chapter 10, "Winning with
Your Digital Storefront."

Step 6: Design and Build Your Digital Storefront

There are three steps in building a digital storefront, as follows:

➤ Decide what content to offer.

➤ Design the individual pages.

➤ Program each page.

Decide on Content

The content that you offer will be dictated in large part by your business strategy. Involve the firm that will be developing your content when deciding what content to offer. Internal sources for content include existing product literature and advertising. You should also identify external sources (mainly other Web pages) to which you may want to build links.

Design Individual Pages

The first step in designing the individual pages of your storefront is to take a step back. You first need to think about the total system that will surround your digital storefront—you need to design both the human and computer processes involved with managing your storefront. You should think of your digital storefront as more than simply a collection of Web pages. Your storefront includes the following:

➤ The internal processes needed to support your digital storefront, including content development, order fulfillment, and customer support. Make sure you have a process in place to correct any content mistakes within one business day.

➤ The integration with your current systems.

➤ The flow of money from your digital storefront into the bank.

➤ The security requirements for both your digital storefront and your internal network.

After you have designed the overall system, identify the individual pages of your storefront. Next, decide how to link the pages together. Each page should have a link back to your main page. A good reference for developing quality home pages is http://www.mcp.com/3362026762376/general/workshop/.

When designing your digital storefront, keep in mind your overall business strategy. Don't get caught up in fancy graphics just to have fancy graphics. Make sure each graphic adds value to the page. Except for your company logo, each graphic should either present information or provide a link to another Web page.

Your digital storefront will be viewed by potentially millions of people—any mistake will be quickly noticed. People will form an opinion of your company based upon your digital storefront. Everybody on your project team must be sensitive to the fact that thousands (or millions) of people external to your company will be using your digital storefront. Most IS departments are experienced at developing applications for internal use, but have little or no experience developing applications for external use. The reliability and look-and-feel requirements of an external application far exceed those produced by most IS organizations. When building your digital storefront, *always* keep in mind the end user.

Program Each Page

When building your pages, use a prototyping methodology. The basic approach you should use is to make a series of small changes to your storefront, rather than a few large changes. This reduces the amount of time it takes develop the storefront by minimizing the amount of work that is discarded. When building a storefront, you should go through several cycles of designing, building, and reviewing. Make sure to have your content provider and applications developer build several different prototypes for your digital storefront. Having multiple prototypes will help generate additional ideas. You should continue to refine your storefront even after going public.

After you have designed the individual pages for your digital storefront, you need to analyze each exchange that your server will have with your customers. Each time you send information to the customer or the customer sends information to you, analyze the security requirements for that exchange. Don't provide more security than is required—if your introductory screen does not require privacy, don't specify it when creating your screen. For each exchange, decide whether you need to provide privacy, authentication, and/or a digital signature. Chapter 4 provides background on privacy, authentication, and digital signatures. After deciding the security requirements for each message exchanged between the browser and server, design and build any necessary connections to your back-end systems.

Make sure each page on your digital storefront contains some method of contacting a human being. You should indicate what kind of response customers can expect. Include the hours that your support staff will respond to queries and the amount of time that might pass before a customer receives a response. Setting a proper level of expectation for your customers is a key part of your digital storefront.

Before rolling out your digital storefront, test it. Make sure that several different people, not just the applications developer, have tested your digital storefront.

Step 7: Promote Your Digital Storefront

There are a variety of ways to promote your digital storefront. You can participate in relevant Internet Usenet groups and provide the address of your storefront, or have other home pages provide links to your storefront. A total promotion package should include offline advertising as well. You should include the address of your digital storefront in any advertisement. You should also consider including the address of your digital storefront on business cards and correspondence. As a minimum, you should include the address of your digital storefront on e-mail that you send to external clients and contacts.

Step 8: Start Over

After a few months of experience with a home page, people's creativity really kicks in. You shouldn't treat your first attempt at a digital storefront as the Holy Grail. After a few months of experience, pull the team together, review successes and failures, and decide how to proceed. This second phase of your digital storefront is when most companies begin to plan out specialized products for the digital storefront. You should also consider developing a customized marketing ability at this point.

Summary

In this chapter, a step-by-step methodology for designing, building, and running your digital storefront has been provided. Although many organizations have had their IS department develop their first home page, the authors recommend outsourcing your digital storefront. The cost of the hardware and software, not to mention the learning curve involved, justify outsourcing your digital storefront. Don't outsource control of your business strategy or the design of your products, however. These key items should always be kept in-house, although you may still want to consult with outsiders to get some ideas.

A multidisciplinary team is required when developing a digital storefront. A member of your marketing or product development staff should take the lead on developing your digital storefront. The key role for your IS organization is to build the links from your digital storefront into your current systems.

Your digital storefront should be consistent with and integrated into your other marketing efforts. Your storefront does have some special requirements not found in typical advertising—it is less like a printed ad and more like an infomercial or newsletter. Your storefront will also undergo constant change. The content, product software, payment systems accepted, and look and feel will all change over time. You may need to repeat the steps outlined in this chapter several times before you are truly happy with your digital storefront.

The next chapter, "Winning with Your Digital Storefront," will review business strategies used by real Web merchants, and will also help you generate ideas to make your own storefront unique and compelling.

Chapter 10

Winning with Your Digital Storefront

You can sell products, services, advertising, and information on the World Wide Web if you are smart about it, and at the very least, you can promote your existing business. A repeat customer base is important to success in both the online and offline worlds. Repeat business depends on knowing your customers. Identifying customers and developing profiles is something that is just beginning to be explored on the Web.

Ultimately, consumer attitudes toward the Web will drive the success of digital storefronts. Anticipating the needs and wants of your likely clientele is the first step in shaping customer attitudes. This chapter explores the following strategies that you can use to position your digital storefront in cyberspace:

➤ Generate a plan

➤ Use content, content, and more content

➤ Have a clear, concise, and direct message

➤ Put your best face forward

➤ Make your storefront interactive and easy to navigate

➤ Entertain

➤ Offer giveaways as incentives

➤ Offer discounts

➤ Update your storefront frequently

➤ Integrate humor into your storefront

➤ Project a "bigger than you are" professional image

➤ Seriously consider your clientele's interests and needs

➤ Make purchasing easy

➤ Monitor your Web activity

➤ Know your competition

➤ Make certain your storefront is error-free

➤ Draw a crowd

➤ Maximize your visibility

➤ Advertise

Use all the strategies or only the ones that match-up well with the nature of your business to take advantage of the Web's size, demographics, and potential growth, and enjoy success with your digital storefront.

Generate a Plan

Before starting a business, most people put together some sort of business plan. Approach taking your business to the Web in the same thoughtful manner. If you already have a business and are establishing your first Web site, or if you are launching a new, purely Web-based business, you need to spend some time developing a plan. Begin formulating your plan by asking yourself these important questions:

➤ Why should I put my business online?

➤ What should I sell?

➤ Who am I selling to?

➤ How will I market my digital storefront?

➤ Who will manage technical issues and keep the server running?

➤ Who is responsible for keeping the site graphically fresh and updated with new content?

➤ Who will monitor the competition?

Use your answers to these questions to generate a list of priorities and establish a focus before you begin development of your digital storefront. Also, use your list of priorities to help you establish some short-term and long-term goals, and then keep them in perspective as you continue to develop your online business.

Have Content! Content! and More Content!

The Web is an information medium. If you don't have any worthwhile information to offer, you are totally exposed, and no one will take you seriously. Make certain that only good, solid, accurate information gets the widespread exposure the Web offers.

Make your best information easy to locate. A customer should be able to get the core information about your products and services with three clicks or less. Customers can easily compare the depth and breadth of your product information to that of your direct competitors if they so choose, and you can count on them comparing prices. Because customers are in control of how they view information, they can visit your site and your competitor's site in a matter of a few seconds. Consequently, quality and price are issues you cannot afford to ignore.

Help-Net, shown in figures 10.1–10.3, is an example of a digital storefront driven entirely by content. Help-Net is a group of qualified psychologists who will answer your questions quickly, professionally, and privately for $20 per inquiry. The content is interesting, entertaining, and informative. Model questions and answers are provided so that you can determine the quality and professionalism of the responses. Qualifications and bios of all the participating psychologists are also readily available.

Welcome to Help-Net

This site is growing every day - visit us in a few days and see what else is new!

Accomplished psychologists and psychiatrists from many specialties, on-line to answer your questions.

Have a problem or concern? A question about yourself or someone else? We will answer your questions quickly, professionally, and privately.

Figure 10.1

For $20, customers can get answers to their questions by qualified psychologists.

Topic: Prescription Drugs

Question: I have joint and muscle pain and my doctor has recommended an anti-depressant. I don't think I'm depressed. Does this mean that depression is causing my problems?

Answer. No, it does not necessarily mean your doctor thinks you are depressed or that depression is causing your problems. Pain is a complex interaction of neurobiochemical, physiologic, and psychological systems. Recently, physicians have discovered that some of the antidepressants have been helpful to people suffering from chronic pain and headaches. In addition, people with pain such as you describe often have other symptoms such as sleep disturbance (perhaps from the pain), appetite changes, and altered libido that antidepressants have been found to be helpful for. The antidepressant can make other pain medications more effective, and can act as an analgesic (pain killer) itself. The antidepressant, even in low doses,

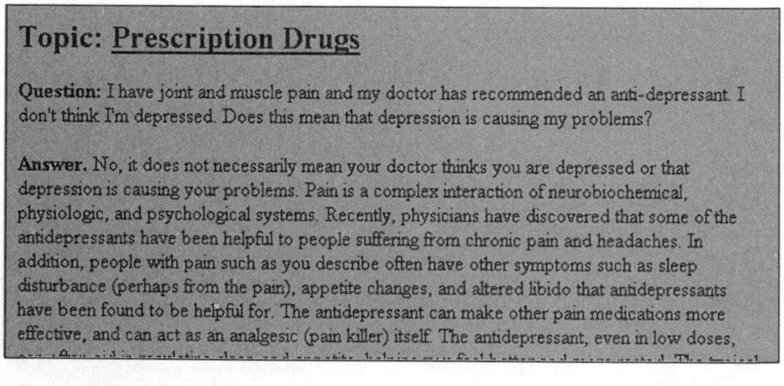

Figure 10.2

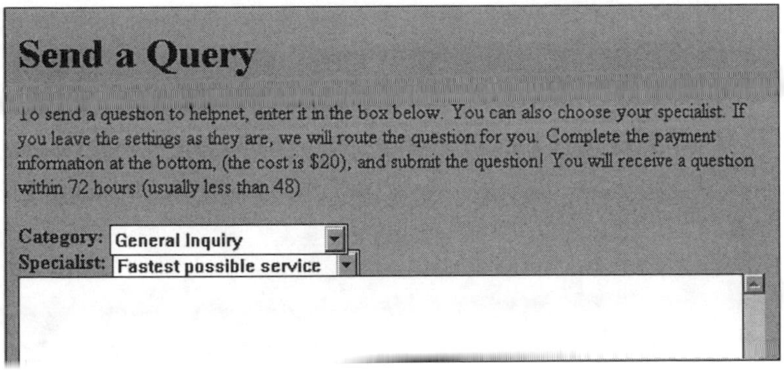

Send a Query

To send a question to helpnet, enter it in the box below. You can also choose your specialist. If you leave the settings as they are, we will route the question for you. Complete the payment information at the bottom, (the cost is $20), and submit the question! You will receive a question within 72 hours (usually less than 48)

Category: General Inquiry

Specialist: Fastest possible service

Figure 10.3

There is no need to panic about having enough content for your digital storefront. Look around your business for work already done. You can draw your content from a variety of existing sources: customer brochures, press releases, newsletters, annual reports, and company databases.

Finally, every storefront should have the following information on the storefront: a header that clearly identifies who you are and what you sell, an e-mail address, copyright information as it applies to online content, contact information, a mailing address, a fax number, and a phone number.

Have a Clear, Concise, and Direct Message

Although the importance of providing meaningful content was just stressed, understand that quality does not mean quantity. Textually dense sites are tiresome, and they get in the way of doing business.

Concentrate on capturing the essence of your business without overdoing the message. Avoid information overload, and get to the point. As shown in figures 10.4–10.6, Hot Hot Hot is a premiere online hot sauce source with over 100 varieties—it is an effective and efficient site that targets a specific audience and interjects some entertaining subtle humor with its graphics and product descriptions. Within four clicks, you can select a product, read about it, make a purchase, and be entertained in the process.

Figure 10.4

Hot Hot Hot is a fun, effective, and direct storefront.

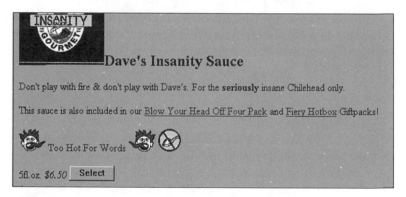

Figure 10.5

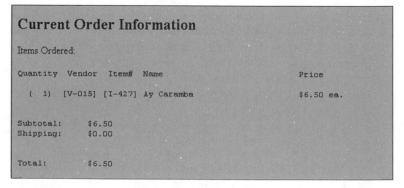

Figure 10.6

Move more in-depth information to other pages, because visitors will not be willing to wade through too much extraneous text to get at the "heart and soul" of your message, they will quickly become frustrated and leave. Use your storefront to set the tone for your online business by letting your customers know what is available and showing them the fastest way to get where they want to go.

Put Your Boct Faoo Forward

First impressions do make a difference. Invest the time, resources, and energy to make an attractive site. Word will get around, and on the Internet word travels fast. An attractive site does not necessarily mean complex, expensive graphics. Often clean, crisp lines work just as well.

Organize your storefront so that all of your core options are in view without the customer having to scroll to see more. If you have a number of links, present them in a organized manner, grouping similar links together. This approach gives your page a clean rather than a cluttered look. Storefronts like software.net, a software product distributor, offer a large volume of information, but they still manage to present it all in one screen. Adding prices to the storefront is consistent with the marketing message of guaranteed low prices, and saves consumers time searching the product catalogs. Notice how similar types of information are grouped together graphically, making the software.net storefront easy to read and manage (see fig. 10.7).

Value-added features like the ones on software.net's digital storefront (software catalog, magazines and news, support and service, and cool deals and free stuff) make a good first impression when they are organized and presented well on your storefront.

Carrying a unified theme throughout your site presents a consistent and professional image. Most people coordinate their letterhead, envelopes, note cards, and business cards. Think of your Web pages in a similar light, as just another part of your professional image package.

Figure 10.7

The software.net storefront.

Coordinating your Web site with other promotional materials is an effective, cost-conscious approach. Matching your letterhead, envelopes, business cards, brochures, and so on presents a unified, professional image, and can also help you save on design costs.

Make Your Storefront Interactive and Easy to Navigate

You want your digital store to be easy to use, fun to use, and fast. Set up purposeful and meaningful links. Don't send customers on wild goose chases through your site unnecessarily. Make certain that your links accurately represent the information the customer will find. Utilize the interactive nature of the Web to your advantage. Remember that people browsing on the Web are learners, not just passive receivers of information. Your storefront must have more to offer than just pictures and text. Give your customers something to do. Make it as interactive as possible.

Add search features if you offer large amounts of information at your Web site. Customers will appreciate being able to easily get what they are looking for. software.net offers a search feature for its software catalogs (see fig. 10.8).

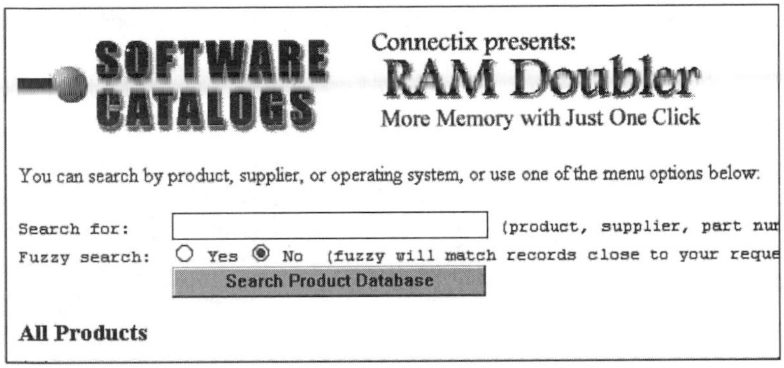

Figure 10.8
Search the software.net catalogs by product, supplier, or part number.

software.net also does a good job of anticipating customer needs by including product reviews on its product data pages, making the site easy to navigate (see fig. 10.9). The customer doesn't have to remember the product as he goes to look up the reviews on a separate page.

CLARIS

CLARIS ORGANIZER V1.0 SINGLE

Supplier: CLARIS
Product: CLARIS ORGANIZER V1.0 SINGLE

Figure 10.9
A customer can conveniently read a review before making a purchase.

Your Web site has to have action or challenges to match the consumer's skills; otherwise, they will become bored or frustrated. The richness of the site also helps to keep them at your site, but don't make your graphics so complex that they take too long to load. The current maximum size for graphics is 50–60 KB. Larger graphics take too long to download using a 14.4 modem.

If you would rather not design with a 9600 modem in mind, consider offering a text version of your site as a friendly alternative for slower modem speeds.

Take a conservative approach to images in terms of picture size and color in the near term until all those 14.4 Kbps modems are almost a thing of the past. The Web is slow enough as it is without having to wait on complex images.

Also, correct server problems immediately. Have a system in place that lets you know immediately if your customers are having access problems.

Entertain

People like to be entertained—they actively pursue a good time. If your online store is fun, customers will visit. Be careful, however, that the entertaining qualities of your Web site do not over-shadow your message. Entertainment does not necessarily mean lots of "bells and whistles." It could be as simple as posting a daily or weekly comic, asking trivia questions, starting discussion groups, and so forth.

Ragú has developed a very entertaining storefront, with humor sprinkled like parmesan cheese throughout the Web site—even their Web address is whimsical (http://www.eat.com). The pages are built entirely around an Italian theme and a character called Mama Cucina. You can enter a family reunion contest, get a couple of recipes, learn about the products, make a few purchases, and listen to phrases like "That spicy red pepper sauce is as hot as the Sicilian sun" spoken in Italian.

Finding a balance between entertainment, content, and a great product or service targeted at specific groups is the foundation of a successful Web site. The kind of site you are developing should drive the kind of entertainment you offer. Always keep your target audience in mind when creating fun and entertaining dimensions to your Web site.

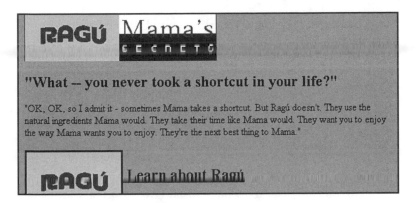

Figure 10.10
Ragú is a fun site guaranteed to entertain.

Offer Giveaways as Incentives

Frequent contests and giveaways draw crowds. Online coupons and store discounts can increase retail store traffic. TDK is not currently selling online, but the company is running a $1,000,000 contest to stimulate retail store traffic (see fig. 10.11).

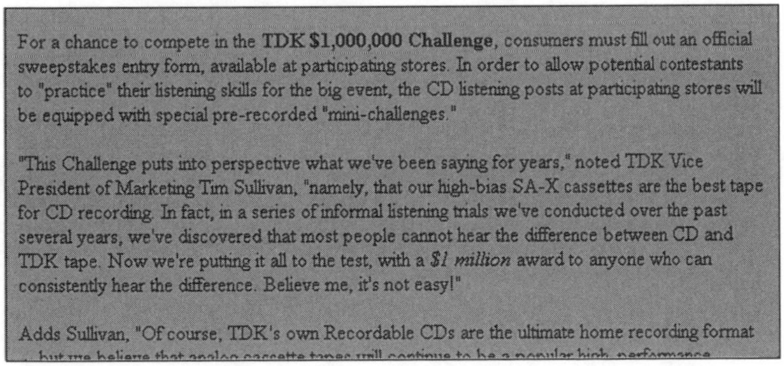

For a chance to compete in the **TDK $1,000,000 Challenge**, consumers must fill out an official sweepstakes entry form, available at participating stores. In order to allow potential contestants to "practice" their listening skills for the big event, the CD listening posts at participating stores will be equipped with special pre-recorded "mini-challenges."

"This Challenge puts into perspective what we've been saying for years," noted TDK Vice President of Marketing Tim Sullivan, "namely, that our high-bias SA-X cassettes are the best tape for CD recording. In fact, in a series of informal listening trials we've conducted over the past several years, we've discovered that most people cannot hear the difference between CD and TDK tape. Now we're putting it all to the test, with a *$1 million* award to anyone who can consistently hear the difference. Believe me, it's not easy!"

Adds Sullivan, "Of course, TDK's own Recordable CDs are the ultimate home recording format but we believe that analog cassette tapes will continue to be a popular high-performance

Figure 10.11
TDK uses an online contest to stimulate sales at retail outlets.

The computer industry has set the precedent for giving away free products online. For many companies, it has proved to be a brilliant marketing strategy. Free samples, demonstration software, or trial subscriptions are increasingly being used to attract customers. Demos, simulations, and modeling can have the effect of a giveaway, while enabling you to hold on to your core product. In figure 10.12, software.net (http://software.net/specials.htm/SK:NONE) is offering a free one-month trial version of Interprint for Macintosh by Intercon, so customers can access the power to networked Unix PostScript printers.

...and Free Stuff

Here's some of the free stuff available through *software.net*:

For Macintosh:

Interprint by Intercon:
> One month trial version. Macintosh users can now access the vast power of networked UNIX PostScript printers through InterPrint, the industry's first commercial LPR client for the Mac.

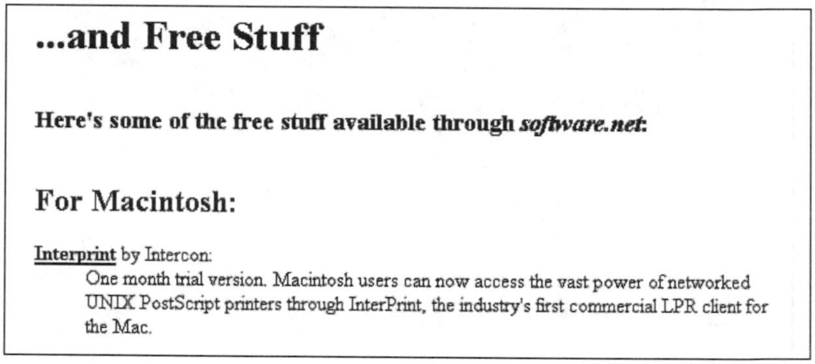

Figure 10.12

Free trials are effective giveaways.

Other sites leverage information to increase traffic through newsletters and FAQs. Developing a reputation for quality industry information can increase traffic in your store, but also goes a long way toward quality name recognition. For example, Astra Network—(http://www.man.net), an Internet service provider in Winnipeg—has put together a brief but very informative and helpful FAQ about how to choose a good Internet service provider. Giving quality expert advice about your business helps to build customer confidence.

Information sites can also give away condensed versions of articles and books in order to encourage the customer to buy the entire publication.

Don't be afraid, however, to charge for what customers are willing to pay for. Businesses, for example, are accustomed to paying for information. Most businesses have corporate subscriptions to a variety of publications for their employees.

Offer Discounts

Selling at a discount will be a must for most businesses venturing onto the Web, at least in the early days. You are going to have to be willing to sell at a discount, because you are asking customers to do something different and unfamiliar—make a purchase online. As a rule, customers are resistant to any kind of change, and you will have to give them a reason to buy online—price is always a great motivator.

Update Your Storefront Frequently

Change your display as much as money and time will allow; fortunately, many changes that can be made on a Web site do not necessarily have to cost you anything extra. Traditional retailers change their store windows on a regular basis to keep the store looking up-to-date. Digital storefronts need to change their displays as well. Keep the following in mind:

➤ Keep it fresh.

➤ Set a schedule for updating your site and stick to it—reliability is appreciated and noticed. If you have the luxury of updating everyday, do it.

➤ Offer promos like What's Coming! and promise something special for a future date to encourage repeat visits.

➤ Refresh your graphics.

➤ Use "new" banners to mark pages that have been changed, so your regulars know where to find updates, changes, and new features.

➤ Be creative.

➤ Pay attention to customer feedback and immediately make the changes that you can. Responsiveness encourages buy-in and trust with your customers.

Integrate Humor into Your Web Site

Humor is an effective tool, but difficult to do well. Humor interjects a more relaxed tone and takes the edge off a hard sell image; however, sarcasm is a dangerous area, especially when you are dealing mostly with text and graphics. Harmless sarcasm in text form is often misinterpreted. This is not a hard and fast rule, however. If you know your targeted audience, it can work to your advantage. Coca-Cola is clearly aiming at a young audience and uses sarcasm effectively, as shown in figure 10.13. This humorous storefront will undoubtedly entertain its targeted audience, but may leave the older generation of Coca-Cola drinkers unimpressed.

Figure 10.13

Coca-Cola uses humor specifically directed at a young audience.

Above all else, make certain that if you use humor, match it to the profile of the customer base you are trying to attract.

Project a "Bigger Than You Are" Professional Image

No one who meets you for the first time online needs to know how big your company actually is, so consider putting effort into looking bigger than you really are. You can accomplish this by projecting an expert image. Provide content that is well thought-out and professionally presented. A few professional-looking graphics go a long way to boosting your image. Also, a well-designed home page that flows well, and a good product backed by good service, are also keys to creating an image of a well-established and profitable business. Use Web links to round out your image: discussion area, customer service, What's New, A Message from the President, and so on.

Consider Your Clientele's Interest and Needs

You really need to understand the user community of your Web site. If you own an offline business, carefully rethink your relationship with customers before you go online. Get to know them through discussion groups, e-mail, and customer service. Watch what they buy, and customize your site accordingly.

Give your customers a vehicle to contact you and respond immediately to any e-mail you receive. Don't list a contact number unless you are ready to respond promptly. Letting unanswered e-mail stack up, especially after you have solicited customer feedback, is bad form. Not only that, you will have wasted an opportunity to build a goodwill relationship with a potential customer.

In addition, carefully evaluate new technologies as they become available for the Web. The technology trap is a seductive one, which can cause you to lose the most important focus—your customers.

Here's an example of a business getting enamored with a new process and losing touch with what their customers really want. A grocery store nearby put in automatic checkout lanes—you scan and bag your own groceries. They marketed the process as "fun for the family." "No more waiting!" Well, mothers with young children were furious after just one shopping experience, because trying to keep track of the children and scan their groceries proved too much for a mere mortal; consequently, the store put off the customers they most wanted to please, because they got too enamored with the technology.

Provide a reliable storefront, so that customers can count on your site to be up and running any time of the day or night without long delays or downtimes.

Beyond having a reliable site, you must offer a consistent high-quality product, have good customer service, quick order processing, and reliable shipping if you are going to sell hard goods. If it's information or services you are selling, make certain that you can deliver what you promise. Regardless of what it is you are selling online, provide an easy way for customers to get in touch with you.

Make Purchasing Easy

The easier you make the process of buying, the more likely it is that you will generate revenue. Remember that you want them to buy—make the process as quick and painless as possible by following these guidelines:

➤ Do not bother customers with lengthy surveys and unnecessary forms. Make surveys voluntary, in any case.

➤ Don't make them wade through too many instructions.

➤ Don't make them scroll unnecessarily.

➤ Develop flexible pricing plans.

➤ When appropriate, offer pricing options, especially if you are running an information site. For example, offer a subscription price, monthly price, and an individual search price.

Even if you offer secure credit card transactions or some other secure electronic payment system, be sensitive to customers' uneasiness with the unfamiliar. Keep in mind that they have been bombarded with Internet security horror stories from the press. Until perceptions change, offer your customers at least one offline payment alternative, such as the telephone, fax, or traditional mail.

Monitor Your Web Activity

Programs are becoming available to track user activity at Web sites. These programs identify organizations with multiple host and domain addresses, and chart Web site activity to determine what is popular and what is not. Server companies are also building marketing analysis tools into their machines to help drive sales. One drawback of this approach is that it can only measure the number of users who contact the server where the monitor software is running. With all the large Internet service providers *caching* Web pages (storing merchant Web pages on the ISP servers for a short period of time), this method will always underestimate the true activity level of a Web server. There will always be some customers accessing the temporary copy of the merchant Web page from the ISP cache, and these accesses cannot be recorded by the tracking software.

For now, online coupons and store discounts are tangible ways to track Web customers. Remember, customers are still figuring out what they want and expect from the Web. This process could be a long one.

Know Your Competition

Bill Gates made his fortune watching, learning, and doing what's already been done—better. Keep a close eye on businesses marketing similar products and services. The Web makes the monitoring of your competition easier, so take advantage of it. Who has the good ideas? Who is failing? Who is taking risks? What's the next trend?

Make Certain Your Storefront is Error-Free

Mistakes are inevitable. Prevent as many as you can by having more than one person review your Web site. Test and retest before you go to market. The fact is there are many error-riddled, poorly written Web pages, even on very high profile sites. Yours will stand out if you take the extra time to create clean, professional Web pages.

Online mistakes are not difficult to remedy, but many people may see your error before you catch it. Remember, the online world can be an unforgiving place, and word travels very quickly.

Draw a Crowd

Virtually nothing is known about how to effectively develop storefronts to maximize business. For example, how does a firm maintain consumer attention, move consumers to the purchase decision, and secure repeat visits?

It is known that most of the people currently on the Web are visiting a series of Web sites out of curiosity and to browse content. Some are searching for information. Others are looking for advertising and product information, and a few are beginning to buy online. While the data to address these issues is becoming available, no established framework exists to guide the analysis. In reality, everyone is operating from their gut.

The other wild card is the extent of customer control in the Web environment. Consumers, for now, do have greater control, because the Web is more accessible, flexible, and responsive, but it remains to be seen how consumers will react to this control in cyberspace.

Maximize Your Visibility

Many businesses are taking a multiple strategy approach to get people to their storefronts, because they know that visibility helps to build credibility. As the Internet continues to grow, it will become easier and easier to get lost in the sea of information. Here are a few suggestions:

➤ **Make yourself easy to find by establishing as many links as possible from other sites to your own.** Concentrate first on the Web sites that match your own in interest and similar customer base. The higher your Web visibility, the more visitors you'll have. Many links can be established at no cost, but seriously consider paying for links that are likely to generate the right kind of traffic for your site.

➤ **Exploit the traditional media: television, radio, newspaper, magazines, and direct mail.** Always include your digital storefront URL in your traditional publicity, and make a special effort to draw attention to it. For example, many companies are including the URL of their home page in their print and television advertising. Don't underestimate these traditional media vehicles for boosting Web sales.

➤ **Register with directory services like Yahoo.** Directory services are often perused by editors of publications about the online world, who are looking for interesting web sites to include in their publications. Many businesses have gained a surge in online traffic as a result of being included in "hot spot" on the Web lists.

Consider linking your site to New Riders' Online World Wide Web Yellow Pages (http://www.mcp.com/newriders/wwwyp). The site is averaging nearly 500 new links per day, and at last count had over 25,000 sites!

➤ **Tap into both the consumer and the business markets.** Tailor your product information separately to your business markets and consumer markets. For example, if you are doing business with government agencies, create a path specifically for them and direct consumers down another, more appropriate path.

➤ **Personalize your site to meet different customer needs.** Different users of the Web have different priorities. Some may want to close a deal; others may just be looking for the latest interesting sites. For example, CDNOW has made it possible for customers to bookmark their favorite page on the site using their browser, so that they can just go to that page without having to log on to the site and cycle through pages in which they have no interest. They made this adjustment after a request was made by one of their regular customers. They made it possible for customers to personalize the site themselves.

➤ **Extend your reach to the global market if your product or services would be of interest in other countries.** Translate your home page into other languages if it makes economic sense. CCF, a financial and banking institution, offers both an English and a French version of their site, as shown in figures 10.14–10.16.

Advertise

Everyone is accustomed to advertising ploys and gimmicks designed for the masses, particularly the masses with economic clout. The World Wide Web is standing the advertising industry on its ear, and there will be casualties. Companies like Toyota are beginning to demand an advertising campaign that includes an interactive approach—specifically, a Web presence. On the whole, advertisers are not accustomed to presenting interactive approaches, and no effective tools exist for measuring its effectiveness. Advertisers are beginning to partner up with Web providers or starting their own internal shops. They are also beginning to realize that advertising on the Web requires smart target marketing that takes advantage of the Web's unique ability to get immediate customer feedback.

There are no passive, captive consumers on the Web. At least for now, you cannot be a couch potato and surf the Web. The medium requires continuous decisions about where to go next. Unlike traditional advertising, the customer can choose whether or not to click on your advertising banner and go directly to your site for a more extensive message

Figure 10.14

When tapping into global markets, be sensitive to language and cultural barriers.

> *CCF's International Private Banking arm provides custom services geared to the precise needs of its clients.*
>
> From Switzerland, the pivot and origin of its private banking business for the past twenty-five years, CCF has built up a global specialized network. It has extended and reinforced this network since the beginning of the current decade. Through its fifteen units, including three representative offices, CCF offers high net worth customers a first-class wealth management service to protect their assets and provide multinational legal advice.
>
> CCF International Private Banking registered satisfactory results in 1994. This was especially true in Switzerland, which accounts for 70% of its total trust and custody operations, as well as in Luxembourg and Monaco. The latter has doubled its trust and custody activity in the space of two years. They failed to meet the forecasts made at the end of 1993, at the end of a bull year in the markets. However, bearing in mind the prevailing market gloom in 1994, revenues held up

Figure 10.15

> *La Banque Privée Internationale du CCF offre des prestations sur mesure à ses clients.*
>
> A partir de la Suisse, pivot de ses activités de banque privée depuis vingt-cinq-ans, le CCF dispose d'un véritable réseau mondial spécialisé de banque privée qu'il a étendu et renforcé depuis le debut de la décennie.
>
> Ses quinze implantations, dont trois bureaux de représentation, lui permettent d'offrir un service de grande qualité à une clientèle internationale de haut niveau.
>
> Son approche, fondée sur des prestations sur mesure, couvre la gestion et la protection des avoirs de sa clientèle, ainsi que des conseils patrimoniaux combinant plusieurs législations nationales.

Figure 10.16

MC² Cyberspace, Ltd. (http://www.mc2-csr.com) is one of the top 40 Internet marketing and communications firms in the United States whose clients include CheckFree, Frigidaire, Ashland Inc., and Consolidated Stores (see fig. 10.17). MC² has a loose business relationship by invitation with SBC Advertising, a firm with a capitalized volume of over $42,000,000. Initially, the relationship between the two companies was based on the fact that SBC saw the advertising industry rapidly changing, and decided that it was easier to form strategic relationships rather than ramp up internally. MC², an expanding company in its own right, saw SBC's commitment to the online medium and saw access to their existing clients as a powerful advantage to the company's continued growth. They co-market services, but both SBC and MC² operate as independent companies. This relationship is an effective one for both companies, but particularly for MC², which builds Web sites and houses them in addition to focusing on careful marketing efforts to provide the best Internet positioning possible for their clients.

Brock Polling, one of the principals at MC², regularly explains to customers that getting your first site up and running on the Web is only the beginning. Putting together a media packet that gets your site noticed by the public, media, and, ultimately, the customers is an important step. Frequent updates and modifications will be necessary as your site evolves, and you learn more and more about your customer base. By watching the daily stats on your Web activity, you can make some assumptions, although not foolproof by any means, about the kind of traffic your site is generating. Polling helps customers design approaches based on those assumptions for increasing their Web site traffic.

Figure 10.17

MC² offers a Web presence and a Web marketing plan.

Advertising on the Web should, therefore, attract the online user, involve some kind of fun, and provide opportunities for interaction. Offer something free or something cool to get users to click on your banner. Advertise on successful sites and when you buy ads, request that your banner be positioned next to exciting articles and features to increase your visibility. Avoid buying ads at the bottom of pages (see fig. 10.18)—everyone sees the top of the page, but not everyone scrolls to the bottom before they link to another page or another site.

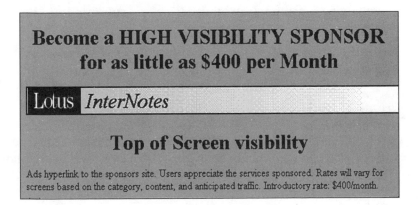

Figure 10.18

If you purchase ads on other Web sites, try to get good visibility.

The "What's New?" directory's on digital storefronts is a desirable advertising location as well, because it's often the first link chosen by surfers.

You can also make money from advertising if you have a successful site. Advertising rates fluctuate widely, because no real way exists to measure an ad's effectiveness. The number of hits is no barometer. Some businesses sell advertising based on guaranteed impressions—the number of times an advertiser's logo is guaranteed to be seen by viewers. But until some hard data becomes available, it's anyone's guess. Some sites get around what to charge for advertising by auctioning off ads. Some Web navigators charge $15,000 a month; others, such as Netscape, charge between $25,000–$60,000 monthly. CDNOW charge $3,000 per month for a full banner. Other, even more popular, sites charge as much as $12,000 a month for an ad, but there are also those who only charge $100 per week.

Sites that sell content build their revenues literally a nickel and a dime at a time. You have to sell a lot of articles, newsletters, newspapers, and so forth to amass any kind of substantial revenue. Some industry experts believe that advertising will be an important revenue generator for these sites, especially as they make the transition from providing information for free to charging for snippets of information and subscriptions. Because many people currently on the Web regularly frequent information sites, it's a good trend for the advertisers, as well as a good trend for the information service provider.

A Pet Peeve

Avoid putting up a Web site before it is completed. Construction site signs on the Web are annoying and a complete waste of time for the surfer. If you drive by a construction site in your car and happen to see a sign announcing that a business is coming, it does not get in the way of where you are going, but landing on a construction site on the Web is frustrating. You get there, you can't do anything, and then you have to get out. It's like visiting empty cages at a zoo. There are supposed to be pandas here. Where are the pandas??

Summary

Everyone one is in the midst of a tremendous learning curve when it comes to doing business on the Web. Success stories are beginning to crop up and tools are being introduced to monitor customer activity. The initial success stories may not be good indicators of the trends that are likely to emerge, as more and more businesses put up their own digital storefronts, and the monitoring tools may take a long time to tell the real story. Watch and learn, but don't expect clear answers to your questions. Also, pay attention to the failures—there will be failures, but they will not be so widely publicized. Learn as much as you can from both the successes and the failure. For your own online shop, make the best decisions that you can, taking into the account the potential and limitations of the technology and how well they match up with the essence and direction of your business. Don't do things just because you can—do them because they make sense for your business.

In the next chapter, "Digital Storefronts," you will have an opportunity to read about specific digital storefronts that are successfully implementing some of the strategies discussed in this chapter.

Digital Storefronts

This chapter is an extension of some of the basic principles put forth throughout this book. In this chapter, additional digital storefronts doing business online are included. Some are using encryption to make secure credit card transactions, and others are making the transition from "telling" to "selling" online. Included are a range of businesses that illustrate different approaches to doing business on the Web. Some of the sites have done an excellent job of creating customer-friendly features that work and mesh well with the types of products and services they offer. Each of the sites is examined in detail, so that you can see what the overall strategy of the site is. Hopefully, you will get some good ideas for your own digital storefront.

L.L. Bean

http://www.llbean.com

Some businesses do a wonderful job of capturing the essence of their business online. L.L. Bean is just such a site. The look and feel of their digital storefront is exactly what you have come to expect from this giant catalog company, retailer of casual wear, outdoor wear, and accessories for men and women. The park-like signpost helps to establish the outdoorsy theme and is useful in its role of directing customers to the site's links. Considerable effort is made to provide free information that would be of interest to their customers.

Figure 11.1
Visitors to L.L. Bean begin here in the great outdoors.

In their fall catalog, L.L. Bean takes advantage of the time of year by focusing on the fall products available in its online store using both graphics and text. Figure 11.2 displays the L.L. Bean fall product offerings.

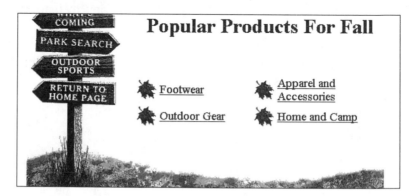

Figure 11.2
L.L. Bean's fall product offerings.

L.L. Bean informs its customers that it is considering online transactions, but is not rushing into anything. This is a goodwill builder for customers nervous about sending their credit card numbers over the Internet. They provide three traditional ways to make a transaction: order by telephone, download an order form, or either fax or mail it to L.L. Bean. Figure 11.3 shows the screen customers can use to order from L.L. Bean.

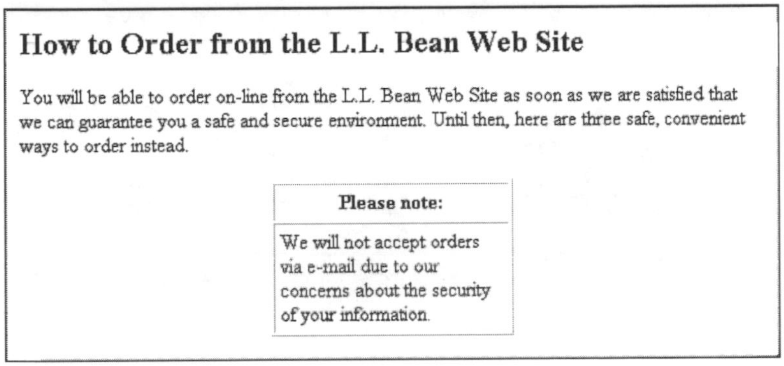

How to Order from the L.L. Bean Web Site

You will be able to order on-line from the L.L. Bean Web Site as soon as we are satisfied that we can guarantee you a safe and secure environment. Until then, here are three safe, convenient ways to order instead.

Please note:

We will not accept orders via e-mail due to our concerns about the security of your information.

Figure 11.3
L.L. Bean is taking a conservative approach to online transactions.

The What's Coming link is designed to give customers incentive to return to the site by updating them on new products and services; however, the link could probably be a little more compelling. On this page, What's New and What's Coming is all jumbled together on one page. This site could benefit from separate What's New and What's Coming links. Also, sprinkling "New" banners throughout your site is always a good idea, making finding the latest information easier for your customers. In addition, more emphasis should be placed on What's Coming to encourage repeat visits. Figure 11.4 shows the L.L. Bean What's Coming Link.

Continuing with the park theme established on the home page, L.L. Bean offers a Park Search where customers can browse nearly 900 parks, forests, and other outdoor locations. These are not make-believe parks with more marketing material—this is information about real parks that L.L. Bean customers might find useful (see fig. 11.5). You can search by park name, activity, and site, and read fact-filled summaries that will help you plan trips and vacations. After you've planned an outdoor weekend, you may need to go back to L.L. Bean's product page and pick up a few things.

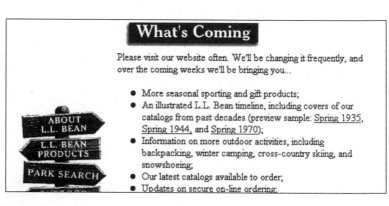

Figure 11.4

The L.L. Bean What's Coming Link.

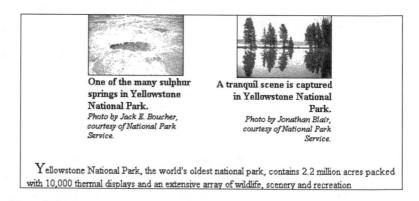

Figure 11.5

Use the park search to plan a weekend camping trip.

Visit the Outdoor Sports links to find out more about L.L. Bean's discovery program, a year-round series of workshops, classes, and symposia held in Freeport, Maine, on a wide range of outdoor activities (see fig. 11.6). Check out the Guide to the Outdoors for tips on hiking, camping, and first aid, as well as special links to cross-country skiing information and winter camping.

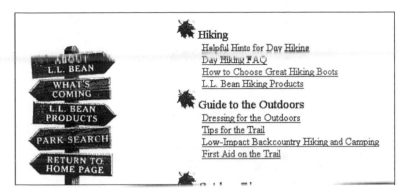

Figure 11.6

The Outdoor Sports link offers content of interest to L.L. Bean customers.

The L.L. Bean digital storefront has a clear, concise, and direct message—"our company is all about being outdoors." Their graphics, products, and value-added information all revolve around that specific message. L.L. Bean has seriously considered their clientele's interests and needs, and has thus built upon them.

Holiday Inn

http://www.holiday-inn.com

Holiday Inn is the first commercial hotel chain to accept online reservations. The hotel is using its Web digital storefront to make finding a Holiday Inn and getting a reservation as easy as possible. You can search for a Holiday Inn by city, highway proximity, and by attractions in your destination city, and receive a detailed list about the best Holiday Inn location that meets all your criteria. Holiday Inn's digital storefront creatively uses images of the usual hotel room items to transport you to your information destination (see fig. 11.7).

You can select U.S., Canadian, or foreign travel, and then highlight your city of choice, highway access, and attraction preference in order to find the Holiday Inn best suited to your travel plans (see fig. 11.8). By including a highway access search, Holiday Inn anticipates information that is likely to be very important to the customer.

Figure 11.7

Click on a familiar hotel room item to travel to another page of information.

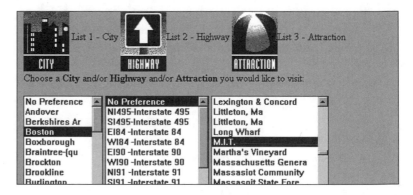

Figure 11.8

Holiday Inn offers online reservations.

After you have made your preference selections, a list appears about the Holiday Inns and their amenities, which details each of the hotels' features, including distances to local attractions (see fig. 11.9). This kind of information goes a long way in sending a message to customers that you always have their needs in mind.

When selecting a room, the usual options are available—bed size, single or double occupancy, dates, and so on, as shown in figure 11.10. The Holiday Inn system offers customers as many options as they would have when dealing with a live reservation agent.

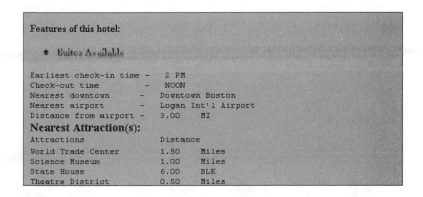

```
Features of this hotel:

    • Suites Available

Earliest check-in time  -   2 PM
Check-out time          -   NOON
Nearest downtown        -   Downtown Boston
Nearest airport         -   Logan Int'l Airport
Distance from airport   -   3.00    MI
Nearest Attraction(s):
Attractions                 Distance
World Trade Center          1.50    Miles
Science Museum              1.00    Miles
State House                 6.00    BLK
Theatre District            0.50    Miles
```

Figure 11.9

A list of choices is presented.

```
Rate is quoted for 1 person(s) in Dollar (United States) per room no tax included.

*Rate Codes: E=Weekend Rate; D=Weekday; S=Special Events; N=Seasonal
Rate Codes*:        D           D           D
                    04/01       04/02       04/03
                    Mon         Tue         Wed


Available Room Types:
 O    Kng 1 King Bed  179.00      179.00      179.00
 O    Kng Executive   199.00      199.00      199.00
 O    Parlor King Bd  189.00      189.00      189.00
 O    2 Dbl Beds      179.00      179.00      179.00
```

Figure 11.10

Select the kind of room you desire.

Holiday Inn is the first hotel to offer direct booking, not through e-mail or through an Internet provider, but live on the Internet. Guests can make their own reservations right from their personal computers, and secure those reservation with a credit card.

Holiday Inn accepts the usual range of credit cards over the Internet on its Netscape/RSA dynamic encryption-enabled site (see fig. 11.11). This mode of security offers some protection, but it is certainly not absolute; however, neither is giving your credit card number out over the telephone to an unknown clerk. If you are using a Netscape Web browser 1.1 or above, software encryption can be optionally invoked on all of Holiday Inn's pages, including pages where you provide your credit card number, name, address, telephone number, and so forth.

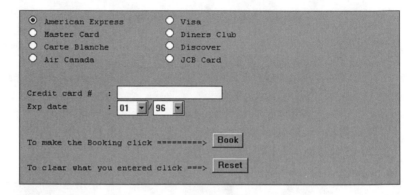

Figure 11.11
Secure the room with a credit card.

This is an error-free, attractive Web site with well-done graphics. It was obviously designed with a clear goal in mind—making reservations at Holiday Inn easier and more convenient. This is accomplished by making it possible for people to secure reservations from their personal computers. The effort to connect customers with the Holiday Inn best suited to their needs demonstrates an effort on the company's part to seriously consider their clientele's needs.

Amazon.com Books

http://www.amazon.com

Amazon.com Books offers a wide selection of books for online purchase at discounted prices—the home page boasts of a million-title catalog (see fig. 11.12). The digital store's special feature is its personal notification service, which searches the inventory for books you might enjoy based on your online search history at the digital store. It also notifies you of new book arrivals that you might enjoy.

amazon.com
Welcome to Amazon.com
Books!
One million titles,
consistently low prices.

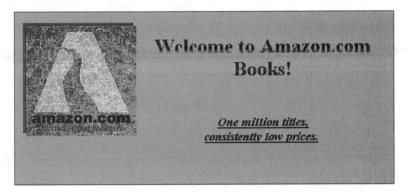

Figure 11.12
Amazon.com's digital storefront boasts a million-title catalog.

The free personal notification service, called Eyes (an electronic search agent), lets you know when new books are available by your favorite author, or when a particular title you want comes out in paperback (see fig. 11.13). Departmental editors let you know about books that might interest you based on your favorite subjects and genres. Eyes can even let you know when new books are published in any Library of Congress subject category.

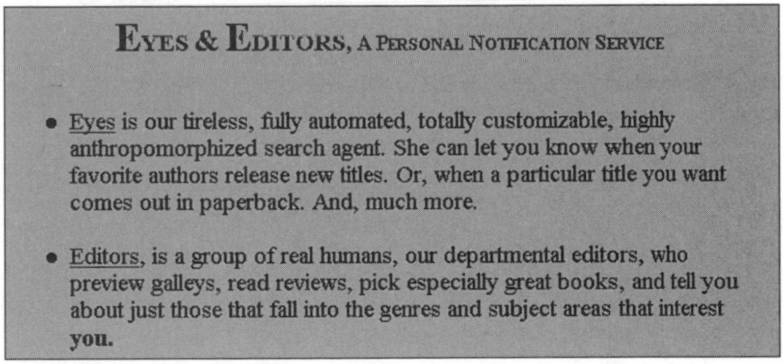

EYES & EDITORS, A PERSONAL NOTIFICATION SERVICE
• Eyes is our tireless, fully automated, totally customizable, highly anthropomorphized search agent. She can let you know when your favorite authors release new titles. Or, when a particular title you want comes out in paperback. And, much more.
• Editors, is a group of real humans, our departmental editors, who preview galleys, read reviews, pick especially great books, and tell you about just those that fall into the genres and subject areas that interest you.

Figure 11.13
Use Eyes to keep you updated on the latest available books.

Eyes can help you look for any existing books that are similar to the ones you would like to hear about in the future. For instance, you might search for a specific author or subject, as shown in figure 11.14. Once you get the results, you are offered the chance to sign up for the notification service. Select the link Personal Notification and Amazon asks you for your e-mail address to send information to when your title becomes available. Also, to keep their customers coming back, Amazon.com updates their Spotlight link every day with staff and customer favorites (see fig. 11.15).

- **Search Amazon.com's One Million Title Catalog**
  - ☐ By Keyword
  - ☐ By Author, Title, and Subject
  - ☐ Using our Full-featured Search Form
  - ☐ Using our Search Language

- **Award Winners**

- **Bestsellers**

- **Customer Reviews**

Figure 11.14

You can search for books in a variety of ways

Figure 11.15

Amazon.com's Spotlight link.

This digital storefront leverages information to keep you interested and coming back on a regular basis. Amazon adds a personal touch to their storefront with the use of Eyes. They also give you a reason to return often by spotlighting a different book and author daily. In addition, if you give them the opportunity, they can send e-mail directly to your account on a regular basis.

Kaleidospace

http://kspace.com

The Kaleidospace houses a collection of independent artists (writers, musicians, sculptors, painters, and so on) who sell their wares on the Internet (see fig. 11.16). Various entertaining activities are available on the site, designed to entertain and market the artists, and selling is also a very serious part of the equation. All the artists have links to their own home pages, where they display their products for online purchase.

Figure 11.16
Kaleidospace is an interactive space with plenty to offer in terms of art and activity.

Select one of the following areas to explore from the Kspace (Kaleidospace) wheel: Art Studio, Center Stage, Cyberfaire, Interactive Area, Music Kiosk, Newsstand, Reading Room, Screening Room, Spotlight, and Tool Shop (see fig. 11.17). For example, you may want to start with the Music Kiosk to see a listing of all the artists listed by music genre, select an artist, download a demo of the music, and maybe place an online order for a CD. Next, you might want to explore the comedy and performance videos at Center Stage before you move on to the Art Studio, where you can view lithographs, oils, sculptures, and so on available for purchase by various artists.

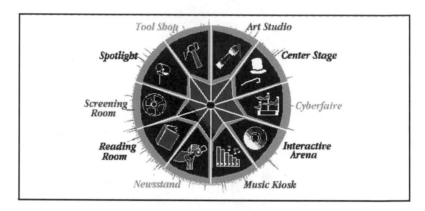

Figure 11.17

Select a destination on the Kaleidospace wheel.

At the time this book was written, Clive Barker was the Artist-In-Residence (see fig. 11.18). The Artist-In-Residence link is an entertaining value-added feature used to draw a people to Kspace and its compilation of independent Internet artists. You could view some of his artwork, read a few selections of his writing, and try your hand at contributing to one of his unfinished works. Kspace is building a relationship with its customers by letting them use their creativity, rather than just filling out biographical information on boring forms.

Interactive ordering helps you find out if an artist's work is right for you—by taking a quiz prepared by the artist, as shown in figure 11.19. After the quiz, you will end up on the artist's home page, where he or she will tell you if you would like their art based on your quiz performance. At the writing of this book, interactive ordering was available for five of the artists housed in Kspace: Bartz, Emote, Robin Frederick, Forrest Rew Mathis, and Newmatic Slam.

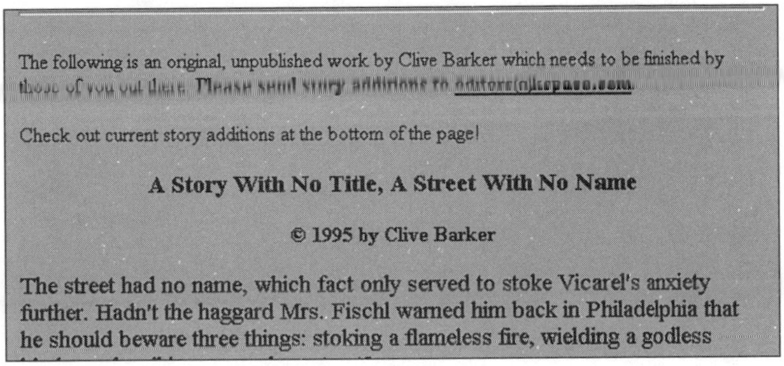

The following is an original, unpublished work by Clive Barker which needs to be finished by those of you out there. Please send story additions to editors@kspace.com.

Check out current story additions at the bottom of the page!

A Story With No Title, A Street With No Name

© 1995 by Clive Barker

The street had no name, which fact only served to stoke Vicarel's anxiety further. Hadn't the haggard Mrs. Fischl warned him back in Philadelphia that he should beware three things: stoking a flameless fire, wielding a godless

Figure 11.18

Visit one of the artists in residence.

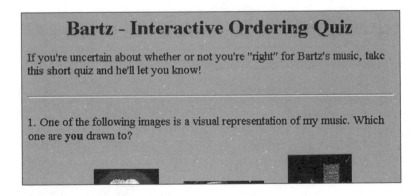

Figure 11.19

Participate in interactive ordering to determine if the artist's work is for you.

The questions are whimsical, and the artist's feedback is immediate. Even if you get all the answers wrong, you can still continue on and view, read, or listen to the artist's work. Online ordering (encrypted credit card numbers) is available to users of the Netscape Web browser (see fig. 11.20).

Kspace is all about fun and entertainment, and plenty of it; however, all the activity does not get in the way of the real purpose of Kspace—purchasing independent artists' works. With all the participating artists' home pages linked in and easy to access, a purchase is waiting to be made regardless of where you start on the wheel.

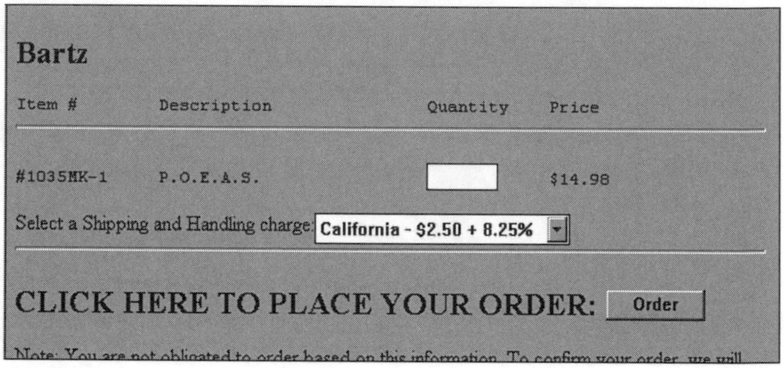

Figure 11.20
Visit the artist's home page and make an online purchase.

Cars@Cost

http://www.webcom.com/~carscost/

Cars@Cost is selling "car buying convenience" online (see fig. 11.21). They provide a service that takes care of all the negotiations with the dealer. The digital storefront is designed to make the car-buying process easier if you know what kind of car you want. You simply complete a form and e-mail it to Cars@Cost. They send you a vehicle spec sheet and factory pricing information, as shown in figure 11.22. If you decide you want the car, Cars@Cost confirms the price and sends you to a convenient dealership where you can pick up your car. The service guarantees the car at factory invoice without haggling over price with the dealership. Cars@Cost charges a small fee, $199 for factory orders, and $399 for stock orders, compared to the dealership's usual percentage—anywhere from 3–8%, depending on the price of the car. You pay Cars@Cost once your order has been established. Cars@Cost requests a $75 deposit, with the balance due only after you have visited your local dealership and purchased your car.

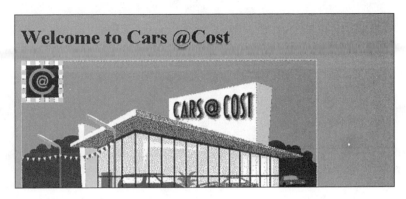

Figure 11.21
Cars@Cost negotiates car deals for you below the sticker price.

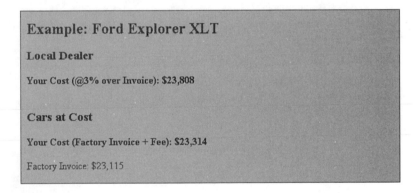

Figure 11.22
Cars@Cost sends you vehicle spec sheets with factory pricing information.

Customers fill out a stock request form to place an order (see fig. 11.23). You must provide your name, address, telephone number, e-mail address, vehicle make and model, trim level, model year, and vehicle options (color, two- or four-door, automatic or manual transmission, and so forth), as shown in figure 11.24.

Stock Request Form

If you are currently in the market or planning to purchase a new car in the next 30 days, please fill in the Stock Request form below. **Cars at Cost** will provide you with a Vehicle Spec Sheet & Factory Pricing Information by email, fax or telephone (please allow up to two business days). There is no charge until you decide to use the service and place an order for the vehicle you want at Factory Invoice!

When you have entered all the information, click on the "Submit Query" button at the bottom. To register additional purchasers, click on "Reset", then enter them and click Register again.

(Note: Availability of certain 1995 models may be subject to local availability during the Summer transition between the 1995 and 1996 model years. Normal availability will return in September with introduction of 1996 models.)

Figure 11.23
Fill out the stock request form and e-mail it back to Cars@Cost.

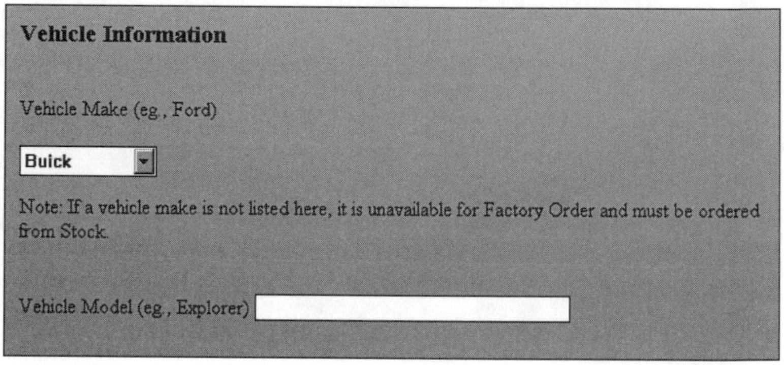

Vehicle Information

Vehicle Make (eg., Ford)

[Buick ▼]

Note: If a vehicle make is not listed here, it is unavailable for Factory Order and must be ordered from Stock.

Vehicle Model (eg., Explorer) [_____]

Figure 11.24
Enter your vehicle of choice information.

InfoSeek

http://www.InfoSeek.com

InfoSeek is a popular search service on the Internet that offers a flexible pricing structure based on usage. It was rated the #1 search engine out of the top 14 search engines by *PC Computing* and *Internet Magazine*. This site demonstrates effective ways to get customer buy-in, so that customers are likely to continue the service. You can see a demo of the service and use a trial subscription before deciding whether or not to sign up. Click on the

"Rated # 1 link..." on InfoSeek's home page to read a review (see fig. 11.25).

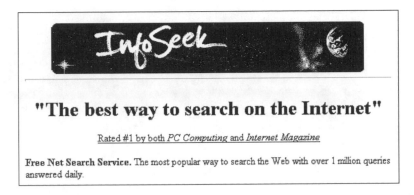

Figure 11.25

You can link to reviews of the service right from the digital storefront.

InfoSeek lets customers conduct a sample search of their own or try out the sample demonstration query, so they can try out the service before deciding whether or not to sign up as a paying member (see fig. 11.26).

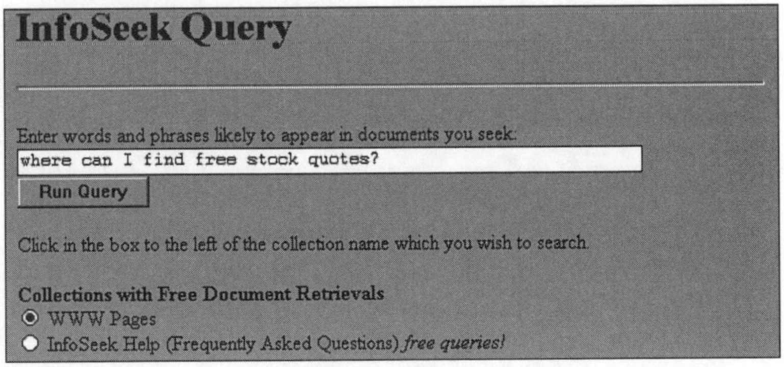

Figure 11.26

InfoSeek's sample demonstration query.

After you sign up for a trial account, you receive a $14.95 credit to use the service, and you do not need to cancel to avoid being charged (see fig. 11.27). InfoSeek will ask you for payment information to continue the service.

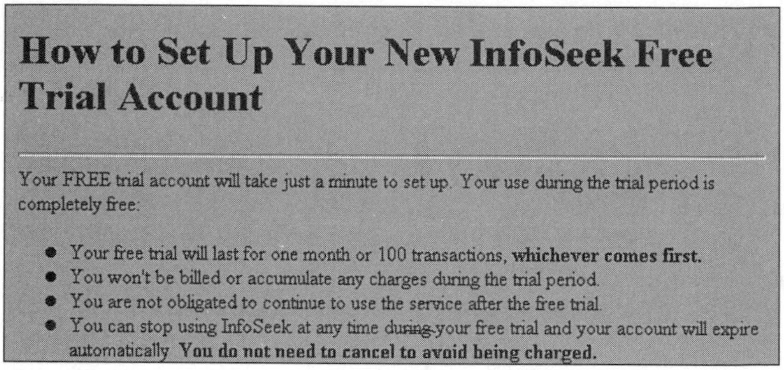

**How to Set Up Your New InfoSeek Free
Trial Account**

Your FREE trial account will take just a minute to set up. Your use during the trial period is
completely free:

- Your free trial will last for one month or 100 transactions, **whichever comes first.**
- You won't be billed or accumulate any charges during the trial period.
- You are not obligated to continue to use the service after the free trial.
- You can stop using InfoSeek at any time during your free trial and your account will expire
  automatically. **You do not need to cancel to avoid being charged.**

Figure 11.27
Set up a trial account and receive a $14.95 credit.

You can choose among the standard membership plans and the
premium service for the option that best meets your needs (see
fig. 11.28). A standard membership is $9.95 per month and
includes 100 free queries per month, with a 10-cent charge per
query thereafter.

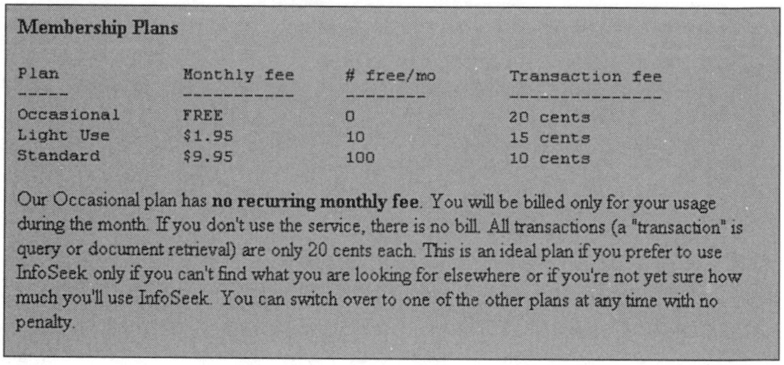

Membership Plans

Plan	Monthly fee	# free/mo	Transaction fee
Occasional	FREE	0	20 cents
Light Use	$1.95	10	15 cents
Standard	$9.95	100	10 cents

Our Occasional plan has **no recurring monthly fee.** You will be billed only for your usage
during the month. If you don't use the service, there is no bill. All transactions (a "transaction" is
query or document retrieval) are only 20 cents each. This is an ideal plan if you prefer to use
InfoSeek only if you can't find what you are looking for elsewhere or if you're not yet sure how
much you'll use InfoSeek. You can switch over to one of the other plans at any time with no
penalty.

Figure 11.28
The membership plans offered by InfoSeek.

InfoSeek recognizes that different people will use InfoSeek to find
information in different categories, ranging from the latest in
financial news to the latest in fun and entertainment on the Web.
InfoSeek offers more than one pricing structure because they
realize that one size does not fit all; consequently, they appear

flexible and adaptable to customer needs. "Trying before buying" is another effective strategy that gets customer buy-in before you ask for a commitment.

Summary

All the sites included in this chapter represent some of the different types of businesses going to market on the Web, and they employ many of the strategies that have been discussed throughout this book. The L.L. Bean digital storefront is an example of a business with name recognition and name-brand products that has successfully taken the image and feel of the company to the Web. Another company with name recognition is Holiday Inn, but this company is an example of a business attempting to do something that has never been done before—taking hotel reservations over the Internet.

In addition, intelligent agents, discussed at greater length in the next chapter, are being used by Amazon.com to keep customers coming back to the digital storefront. A more unusual site, Kaleidoscope, houses individual artists' home pages and puts energy into updating their site and keeping it fresh with their Artist-In-Residence feature, as well as with their artist spotlight and chat room features. And then there is Cars@Cost—a site breaking down all barriers about what can and cannot be done online. Who would have thought that you could shop for a car from your living room? Finally, InfoSeek uses demonstrations, free trials, and flexible pricing to draw customers in and eventually sign them up.

Hopefully, you have gotten a few ideas for your own digital storefront. Remember, a strategy employed by one business site may not necessarily fit well with your particular business. Spend a considerable amount of time surfing the Web, browsing, and learning. Examine the competition closely and continue to do so after you go to market.

Part IV

Looking into the Future

Chapter 12

Agents in Commerce

Imagine not having to spend hours bargain hunting. No more driving from store to store looking for the best deal. No more feeling guilty that you paid too much for an item. No more pesky salespeople looking over your shoulder. In the future, you will let your agents do the walking. Eventually, intelligent software agents will be the primary way customers interact with digital storefronts. Agents—acting as digital clerks—will respond to customer agent requests. For example, a customer looking for new shoes will have his agent send out requests to different shoe stores. The shoe store agents evaluate requests from the customer agent and send in a bid. The customer agent sifts through the bids and can recommend a purchase to the customer. All of this activity can take place after traditional business hours while the customer is sleeping. He doesn't even need to leave his computer on, because agents can run independently on service providers' computers at any time—day or night.

What is an Agent?

A *software agent* is simply a computer program owned by an individual, group, or institution that automates data acquisition by traveling around cyberspace performing specific tasks. All the tasks an agent performs involve some kind of information transfer—whether it is exchanging data with other agents or people, or handling business and personal transactions. A learning agent, an advanced type of agent, watches what a user does, recognizes repetitive patterns, and carries out appropriate tasks after getting the permission of the user.

Today's agents can take care of mundane repetitive tasks such as automatic back-up, mail management, database queries, desktop management, and so forth. Merchants can use these agents to send reminders to customers and manage their digital storefronts. Agents can also help route mail inquiries to the proper person by searching for keywords in the body of the inquiry as triggers. For example, inquiries that mention a product name could automatically be routed to the group that supports that product. Basically, agents are at their best when the application domain is small and the amount of knowledge needed to function accurately is limited.

Tomorrow's Agents

Tomorrow's agents will be even more sophisticated than the current ones. A commonly used metaphor to describe intelligent software agents is that of a personal assistant, because soon agents will be able to handle the following tasks:

➤ Answer the telephone

➤ Recognize and forward important calls

➤ Automatically schedule appointments while being respectful of your personal habits and idiosyncrasies

➤ Manage your e-mail by sifting through all incoming mail, recognizing which messages you are interested in and discarding those you do not want to read

➤ Shop and buy presents for business associates, family, and friends

➤ Monitor your stock portfolio's performance and notify you when it is time to buy and sell

➤ Retrieve information of interest to you that was recently posted on the Net

Tomorrow's agents will be sophisticated information handlers that are highly tailored to the desires of the user who owns them. The ideas mentioned in the preceding list barely scratch the surface of the possibilities. Each user, however, will probably own several specialized agents, with each dedicated to a specific task.

Types of Agents

In order for a software program to be considered an intelligent information agent, it must be able to perform at least one of the following tasks:

1. Draw conclusions from an existing database.

2. Add facts to a database to help it make better decisions in the future.

3. Recognize patterns and match them with the correct actions. The more patterns the agent sees, the better it can recognize what actions the user wants to take.

Intelligent agents have dramatically varying degrees of sophistication. Generally speaking, there are three types of intelligent agents: low-end, mid-range, and high-end. *Low-end agents* perform repetitive tasks triggered by external events. They execute the same steps every time they are run, without getting smarter. An agent that backs up your e-mail system is an example of a low-end agent that does not adapt to changing conditions.

Using an existing database, *mid-range agents* apply reasoning to monitored events. They usually have a limited responsiveness to changing conditions and typically do not get smarter with time. A shopping agent that places orders only when the bank account balance will cover the cost is an example of a mid-range agent.

High-end agents can both learn and reason. By building an increasingly sophisticated model of a user's actions, these agents become smarter over time and can adapt to changing conditions.

Uses for Agents

The online world is becoming increasingly more complex. As the online world continues to grow at an alarming (exciting, mind-boggling) rate, search engines will begin to return too much extraneous material. Help at managing information will become critical to having a competitive business edge. The type of help needed becomes more sophisticated as the amount of information increases.

Agents as Database Monitors

When the Web was young, individuals could browse manually. When the amount of information increased, keyword search engines were developed to help users find relevant material. Keyword searches work best when run against a database dedicated to a particular topic. The Web, however, is most certainly not a specialized database. Currently, keyword searches are used in conjunction with specialized hotlists.

Hotlists can be thought of as the specialized databases of the Web. A hotlist containing quality links on a particular topic can be used by Web surfers to quickly find relevant information. Even hand-crafted hot lists cease to be useful when it is no longer possible for a human to monitor the entire Web for quality information. At this point, agents must be used to automatically and continuously search for relevant information, because they are capable of handling enormous amounts of information (which will soon be available on the Web). So much new information and software will become available that agents will become necessary for monitoring databases and parts of networks. Agents must be highly personalized in order to perform the task. Users must personalize their agents over time, by correcting mistakes and providing additional instructions.

Further Uses for Agents

Anyone who has spent any time on the Internet will tell you that it is problematic when it comes to efficient and effective information retrieval. With agents, people will spend less time gathering information and more time analyzing it. Because intelligent agents can consider a much wider base of focused data, they will enable customers to carefully consider purchases using their PC.

Business will also benefit. Agents are being touted as a time and cost saver for businesses online and offline, because they can automate repetitive tasks like gathering competitive information, waiting for sales, taking phone orders, and checking on order status. Managers can make better decisions as well, because agents can both search and filter a large volume of information, making more informed decisions possible.

In the next few years, agents are likely to have the greatest impact on information sales. Newspapers, magazines, and research reports are all examples of information products that will be affected by agents. Agents promise to be significant time-savers for customers by helping to automate the synthesis of information. Customers can selectively access news and information and will no longer necessarily need editors to filter and package the information for them; consequently, the product actually sold by an information provider will change. In addition to providing small packages of filtered news, such as a newspaper or magazine, information providers will be creating databases that can be easily scanned and searched. Agents will be able to scan an entire AP news wire for weather reports, weather forecasts worldwide, sports scores, and so on. You will no longer need someone else to pre-package daily news for you. Agents probably won't replace today's press as we know it, but they will give consumers more options for getting information.

Agents in Action

An ideal agent essentially observes a user's, keeping track of these events over days, weeks, or months. An agent receives user feedback through the acceptance or rejection of the agents' recommendations. By remembering these acceptance/rejection actions, the agent can, over time, build up a history that it can use to guide future decisions. This feedback is critical in training an agent.

Ideal agents will not only make recommendations, but act on behalf of users. For each action, the agent will calculate a *confidence level*, the statistical probability that the action under consideration is correct. The confidence level represents the agent's level of belief that its user actually wants it to take an action. Each agent will have its own method of calculating a confidence level; the mathematics involved are beyond the scope of this book, but a user does not need to understand the mathematics before being able to use an agent. A user can build up confidence that an agent will take the correct action based on past experience with the agent. Users decide whether the agent is allowed to act on their behalf, and how confident the agent has to be before it is allowed to do so.

Users can also instruct agents, giving them rules for special situations. You can tell the agent whether the rule is soft or hard—*soft* being accepted as a default that can be overridden as the agent learns, and *hard* meaning it cannot be overridden by the agent.

Because an agent needs to be highly personalized before it can be effective, the issue of privacy arises. Running an agent on a service provider's computer enables that service provider to learn some very interesting things about you—some people may not even realize the amount of information about themselves that they are broadcasting to the world. One way to avoid this problem is to create two classes of agents, one that contains non-personal information that lives on the Net, and another that lives by your side (on your PC). A service provider could still watch the behavior of your personal agents (if they were so inclined), but they wouldn't have access to the rules the agent is using to gather information. The rules that an agent uses convey the most sensitive information about the user. In addition, if the agent running on your PC is encrypting all messages it sends out, then the service provider will not even be able to monitor your agent's behavior. The personal agent and non-personal agent are two distinct agents. The difference is in the type of information the user programs into the agent. The user doesn't store any highly personal information in the non-personal agent running on the service provider's computers.

Agent Learning

Agent learning is based on research in the field of *artificial intelligence* (the study of human learning and computer simulation of human decision making), using the following strategies:

➤ Directly query the user to obtain information, as needed

➤ Dialog-based learning methods that identify common procedures by watching the user perform tasks manually

➤ Memory-based learning, where the agent finds the closest match against a memorized set of situation-action pairs

➤ Hybrid neural network and knowledge base system architectures, where the neural networks perform knowledge acquisition and use knowledge-based techniques to perform inference and knowledge maintenance

Agents can "talk" to each other, and through collaboration, can share knowledge they have learned from their respective users. This process is helpful to people who work in groups and share habits or interests. Agents observe user behavior, detect regularities, watch for correlations among users, and exploit those correlations. This is one area where standards will help the development of agents. A standard way of saying "I want a red pair of shoes, size 11" is needed before agents can realize their full potential.

Qualities of Effective Agents

Agents will have different abilities—some will be more capable than others. There are some basic qualities, however, that any agent must have for it to be effective. These qualities are as follows:

➤ Mobile, independent, and know when to take action.

➤ Able to learn and remember user actions over time to better reflect the wants and desires of the user.

➤ Provide a mechanism for two-way feedback so that the user can direct the agent and the agent can ask questions of the user; therefore, maximize confidence and minimize risk.

➤ Predictable. The user must be able to reasonably predict what agents are likely to get wrong.

Risks with Agents

Agents have tremendous potential, but their very nature gives them an element of unpredictability. Communication mismatches between the user and the agent can occur without either one recognizing that a problem exists. For example, if you reject an agent recommendation to purchase a pair of shoes from a specific company, and the agent recognizes that you have rejected this shoe company in the past, the agent may decide that you don't like this particular shoe company—when in fact you didn't like the colors available. It is important that user expectations match the reality of what an agent can accomplish. With every action delegated to an agent, an element of risk and trust exists. If you give agents the power to make purchases, then you take the risk that your agent will purchase an item you really don't want.

Agents will never be 100-percent accurate. Whenever you delegate work (whether it is to another person or an agent), you get errors. Managers must balance the risk of delegating tasks to the benefit gained on a daily basis. Even for non-managers, delegation is a fact of life. You need to be especially careful when delegating tasks to agents. Choose tasks that are easy to carry out and that will not cause much loss if performed incorrectly.

If you are using agents to help run a digital storefront, then you need to carefully consider the risk that using an agent involves. Setting up an agent that accepts bids, but forwards them to humans rather than automatically responding, is a *low-risk strategy*—the agent cannot make a mistake that costs the company money. Letting an agent respond to bids, accept payment, and ship goods, on the other hand, would be a *high-risk strategy*. This strategy may be appropriate for information providers, but not for clothing stores.

Available Agents

The technology for intelligent agents is rapidly advancing. Businesses and universities are working at a fever pitch to bring software agents to market. Some of the agents available now or currently under development include the following:

➤ AT&T's PersonaLink (http://www.genmagic.com/att.html) enables customers to place software agents in a huge data network with instructions to search for products offered at the cheapest prices. Figure 12.1 shows the PersonaLink home page.

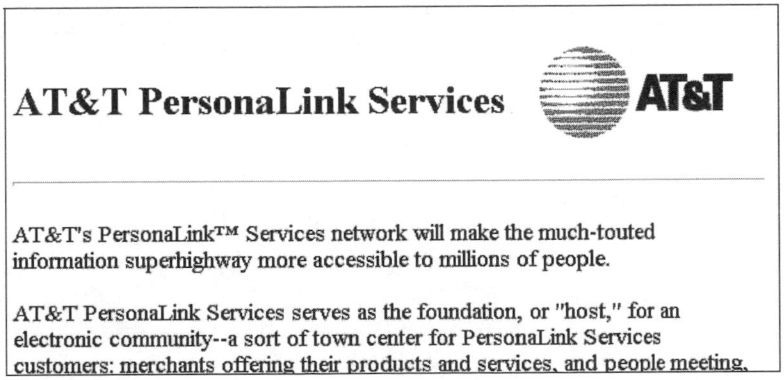

AT&T PersonaLink Services  **AT&T**

AT&T's PersonaLink™ Services network will make the much-touted information superhighway more accessible to millions of people.

AT&T PersonaLink Services serves as the foundation, or "host," for an electronic community--a sort of town center for PersonaLink Services customers: merchants offering their products and services, and people meeting,

Figure 12.1
AT&T PersonaLink enables customers to use agents to shop for products.

➤ British Telecom is creating corporate and personal agents for its customers. Once developed, a customer can make a phone call, perhaps requesting special services (a video connection or a scrambled line) and their personal agent will confer with the corporate agents to agree on the best mix of services at the best price.

➤ Open Sesame from Charles River Analytics (http://www.cra.com) is an intelligent agent that streamlines everything you do on you desktop and improves productivity. Open Sesame observes your activities, learns which tasks you repeat again and again, and then performs those repetitive tasks automatically. Figure 12.2 shows the Charles River Analytics home page.

Figure 12.2

Charles River Analytics offers Open Sesame, a simple agent.

➤ Telescript is a product from General Magic that really shows promise. A software language for creating applications on a network, Telescript includes intelligent agents. The product eventually will handle online shopping by placing software agents in a huge data network with instructions to search for products offered at the lowest price, but initially it will do simpler chores such as routing e-mail messages.

➤ Fishwrap, a personalized news service for freshman, is being developed at MIT. Fishwrap is covered later in this chapter.

Examples of Real Agents

You can tell a computer agent what you want and when you want it by drawing on the collective reasoning of the past, present, and future (memory, user commands, and inference). Agents will then travel the digital marketplace knowing what you are looking for, and thus find the best deal for the best price. Eventually, software will be embedded into consumer goods, gathering information about your usage, making suggestions, and automatically reordering when needed. For merchants, the opportunity to learn from user behavior will lead to the ability to provide highly customized service and products. More and better shopping agents will likely emerge as value-added tools.

BargainFinder

Andersen Consulting, one of the largest computer consulting companies (they do accounting also), is conducting an experimental intelligent agent research project on the Internet. The name of the agent they are developing is BargainFinder. The goal is to explore issues lying ahead for retailers engaged in electronic commerce. Figure 12.3 shows Andersen Consulting's home page.

Figure 12.3

Andersen Consulting experiments with shopping agents and records customer's reactions.

Using BargainFinder, an intelligent agent, users can compare prices among stores selling compact discs online. Compact discs were selected because of the volume of product available and the well-known nature of the commodity. Users can shop high-class stores offering electronic reviews, ratings, and background information, and then use BargainFinder to find the store where they can buy the CD for the cheapest price. A questionnaire linked to BargainFinder is designed to record user's reactions to intelligent agents, and then compile data and determine implications for virtual retailers. Issues to be investigated are as follows:

➤ Key attributes online shoppers value other than price and availability, such as customer service, cost of delivery, product information, and so on

➤ The ways shopper would be willing to compensate Internet merchants in exchange for service offered by an intelligent agent, other than paying a higher price

➤ Other products or services Internet users see as being ideal for an intelligent agent

BargainFinder is being used as part of the Smart Store project. Visit Smart Store® Virtual (http://smartstore.ac.com/smartstore) to test-drive BargainFinder. The objective of Smart Store Virtual is to research and report on issues affecting electronic commerce.

BargainFinder is an experimental prototype of a potential commercial service that will begin to explore what customers are looking for in the world of electronic commerce and how they will react to the use of an intelligent agent.

Fishwrap—Agents as Editors

Fishwrap (http://fishwrap-docs.www.media.mit.edu/docs/dev/CNGlue/cnglue.html) is an experimental electronic newspaper system available at MIT. This system uses agents to create personalized newspapers for incoming freshmen. Figure 12.4 shows the front page of a typical Fishwrap newspaper. Fishwrap provides its readers with an egocentric window into world affairs, enabling them to receive news from their home town, as well as stories of personal interest. In addition to personally selected

stories, Fishwrap provides a continuous update of selected
general news items and features, thus connecting readers both to
the MIT community and the world.

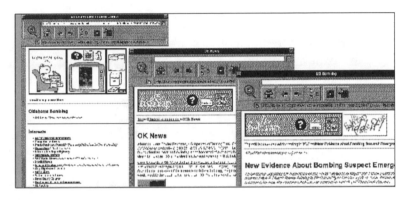

Figure 12.4
Fishwrap is a personalized newspaper generated by agents.

Each edition of Fishwrap is more personalized than the one
before. Fishwrap records how users navigate the paper in order to
adapt future presentations to their reading habits. A user can
change his agent's news filter by selecting from a list of existing
news topics.

Users can view news categories for each article their agent selects.
This enables readers to quickly find similar articles or add new
news topics to their profile. Handling this meta information
(information about information) will be a critical part of agent
behavior. Meta information enables users to understand the
behavior of their agent and to build on the work the agent has
already done.

As the Fishwrap experiment progresses, it will be interesting to
see how "coarse" the information filter is, or how much "fine-
ness" is needed or desired by various individuals. A *coarse filter*,
one that returns lots of general information, would imply that
people don't consider it worth the time it takes to create a highly
personalized newspaper. On the other hand, if most people

develop a highly personalized agent, this would imply that there might be a huge demand for custom newspapers.

Summary

Agents are clearly not a technology that merchants need to incorporate into their digital storefronts right now. There are some experiments underway, such as BargainFinder, in which interested merchants can participate. Important questions remain to be answered, as follows:

➤ Who will develop the best application?

➤ Will standards emerge?

➤ How much of the Net can be searched by a single agent?

➤ What are the implications of the information on your server being indexed by someone else's agent?

If agent creators succeed, agents will perform such jobs as re-searching databases, managing investments, buying and selling products, and keeping an eye on almost any specified area of interest. In the future, agents will simply be placed in cyberspace and report back when something you care about (a sale, a new product introduction, a shift in the stock market, and so forth) happens.

Agents eventually could change the face of conducting business online, but not in the next year. Keep an eye out for them, though, because they're coming.

The next chapter, "Electronic Banking," reviews the state of online banking, an area that should be of interest to all Web merchants. Banks will probably be involved with all online financial transactions, and the direction they take could impact the type of payment systems customers are willing to accept. Banks, through the trust that customers have in them, can have an important role in setting customer expectations.

Chapter 13

Electronic Banking

Why was the U.S. government all up in arms about the potential deal between Intuit, the makers of Quicken (a leading financial package for PCs), and Microsoft? The deal is dead for now, but what could it have meant for commercial banks?

Here was the plan: Bill Gates wanted Intuit, Inc. because he saw the potential of Intuit's software and his online service, the Microsoft Network, working together to be the banking and shopping choice of millions. Customers could use Microsoft's online service to pay bills, get financial advice, and shop. The potential that frightened the Justice Department was that Bill Gates and Microsoft could become not only the largest worldwide software distributor, but the largest and most powerful banking and financial service provider as well. Fears of a powerful monopoly moved Justice officials to block the deal. Some feared that successful banks would be out of the market before they even realized what happened.

This example is just one threat that banks will face from online banking. All of the electronic payment systems (EPS) covered in Chapter 4, "Internet Commerce Providers," represent both a threat and an opportunity for banks. They are a threat because new EPSs represent an opportunity for competitors to steal customers from banks. They are also an opportunity for banks to regain customers lost to mutual fund companies and other competitors in recent years. As a merchant, you need to recognize the pressures facing banks so that you can make intelligent decisions about where to keep your money, decide which EPSs to support with your digital storefront, and minimize the risk to your company of possible bank closures. This chapter will therefore:

➤ Provide an overview of the banking industry

➤ Discuss the state of online banking today

➤ Look at some banks that are pioneering online banking

➤ Show how online banking will affect digital storefronts

➤ Outline some strategies banks might use to keep market share

➤ Examine some of the competition banks are likely to face

Banking Trends

Banks compete on price and services. The Web exposes price differentials and broadens the potential services banks can offer their customers. Thus, the Web has the potential to intensify competition among banks. Banks on the Internet are not limited to the customer base within their geographic region. The result is that smaller, regional banks, which are already under the gun, will find it difficult to retain their customers.

Many banks are already trying to economize by shutting down some branch offices. The percentage of transactions being handled electronically is already increasing quickly, and banking on the Web has barely started. Web banking will lead to further layoffs within branches.

The large customer base that the WWW can reach will result in lower banking costs (and perhaps lower banking prices). The primary costs involved with online banking are the support personnel needed and the cost of the equipment involved. Both of these cost factors favor large banks over small banks. A bank that has 100,000 customers will need to charge less per customer than a bank that has only 10,000 customers. Online banking is expected to be a highly competitive market, so even small price differences can separate winners from losers. Web banking economies of scale will also favor large banks over small banks.

The net result of the Web and other regulatory factors (interstate banking regulations, which mandated the creation of regional banks, are being scaled back or eliminated) will be fewer, larger banks and significantly fewer bankers. According to *Business Week* magazine, as many as 500,000 bankers (mostly branch personnel) could lose their jobs in the next five years. The WWW will help globalize the banking industry, because many of the logistical and cost constraints are removed.

This is all good news for merchants, who can expect lower prices and better service. Internet merchants will need to work with banks that can support transactions on a global scale, because Internet merchants are reaching a global audience. Merchants currently relying on regional banks will want to closely monitor the price and service level offered by competitive banks, so that their worldwide customers can get the best service possible.

The changes in the banking industry will have an effect on merchants (both online and offline). As a merchant, you need to keep on top of online banking trends. You don't want to have your money frozen for days or weeks during a bank failure. If you need local personal service, choose your bank carefully. Bank mergers and branch closings are going to be a weekly occurrence over the next few years.

Consumer Banking on the Web

Home banking is becoming a reality—no more banking hours or long lines at the drive-thru. Banks are beginning to offer customers the ability to manage their accounts over the Web. This is a significant development that will enable banks to offer easier access and more features than are available using other technologies, such as a touch-tone phone. Making the transition to home banking via the Web, however, will take some time. Consumers are going to need good reasons to jump online, and are also going to expect a much wider range of value-added products and services than is available to offline customers.

What can consumers expect? Online banking will enable 24-hour graphical access to your personal accounts from your PC. The graphical interface will be easy to use, and record keeping will be done for you. Like the old "bank book," the checkbook will soon find its way out to pasture. Customers will be able to quickly check their balances and then compare the checks they have written (at least the checks written using online software) against the checks that have cleared.

Other conveniences online banking will bring for customers involve managing their personal accounts, as follows:

➤ The ability to shop around for the best interest rates for checking accounts, CDs, money market funds, and brokerage accounts

➤ Downloading customized bank statements with digital images of each cleared check

➤ The convenience of being able to electronically write and send checks

➤ The ability to apply for credit cards

Banks will also need to figure out a way to handle small money transfers as information purchasing on the Internet continues to grow. Online banking customers will demand a system that can support the needs of online merchants. For example, information providers will need a secure, inexpensive system that can process $.25 transactions. This represents a challenge for banks that want to take a small cut of every transaction. Cumbersome verification processes substantially cut into profits as much as 50 percent for small value transactions. Chapter 4 discusses several possible solutions, including the creation of *electronic cash*—electronic tokens that can be traded over the Internet and exchanged for real currency.

Security First Network Bank

In case you doubted the predictions mentioned in the previous section (online consumer banking will offer consumers many new features), this may make you a believer. Security First Network Bank (http://info.sfnb.com) is the first operational, government-approved online bank on the Internet. The online bank offers a direct link between the bank and its customers, who can open accounts, pay bills, and reconcile accounts 24 hours a day, seven days a week. Multilayered secure software created by SecureWare, Inc. puts layers of security around each individual account. Deposits at Security First are insured by the Federal Deposit Insurance Corporation (FDIC).

Security First Network Bank is actually the creation of several other banks. Wachovia Corp., Huntington Bancshares, and Area Bancshares Corp. are among the investors in Security First. Wachovia and Huntington, which plan their own Web storefronts, have also purchased the software, Virtual Bank Manager, used by Security First. Figure 13.1 shows the Security First home page.

As shown in figure 13.1, the Security First storefront offers a comprehensive demo of the new customer banking services. You can regularly check your accounts, and also review your electronic payments, deposits, and ATM transactions (see fig. 13.2).

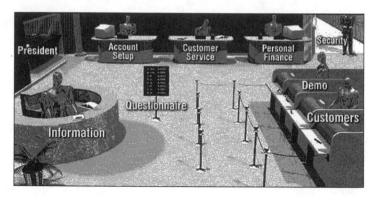

Figure 13.1

The Security First home page.

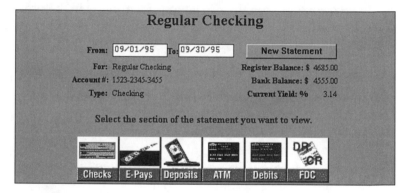

Figure 13.2

Review your balances and percent yield.

Security First uses a simulation of a regular check for its online checking interface in order to make electronic check writing comfortable for customers. You can enter your regular check destinations and add them to a scroll list to cut down on retyping the same information. The customer fills out the check with the usual information. The only difference is that the check is digitally signed, rather than signed by hand. Figure 13.3 is an example of an online check.

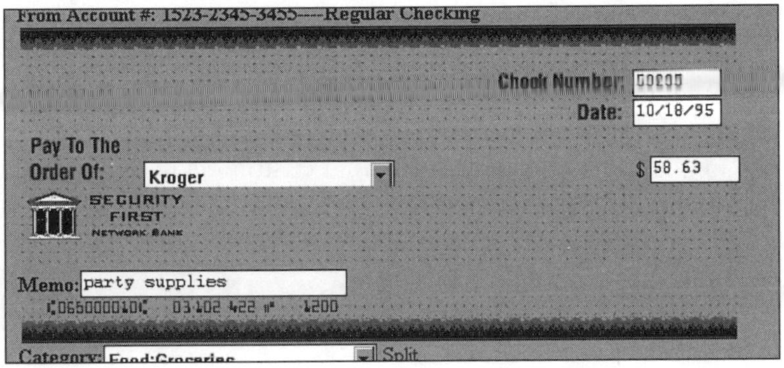

Figure 13.3

An online check.

Security First provides a worksheet to help customers with their record keeping. Customers can change anything they want on a check, except the date the check cleared, for their own record-keeping purposes. For example, a customer may want to break the amount paid into more than one category. Changing fields in the check after is has cleared has no effect on the actual transfer of funds—it is useful for record keeping only. Figure 13.4 shows the worksheet used by the customers.

Figure 13.4

Customers can use a worksheet to help with their record keeping.

You can set up your account to make automatic payments. You simply enter all of your regular monthly fixed payments and the dates they should be paid. Security First then removes the money from your account on the date entered under Transmit Date. Figure 13.5 shows the screen that customers need to fill out when creating an automatic payment.

Pending Payments List

Payee	Bank Account	Category	Transmit Date	Payment Date	Amount
⦿ Forest Green Apartments	Regular Checking	Rent	10/01/95	10/05/95	600.00
○ Georgia Power	Regular Checking	Utilities:Electric	10/01/95	10/05/95	70.00
○ Midland Bank Visa	Regular Checking	Credit Card	10/01/95	10/05/95	200.00
○ Southern Bell	Regular Checking	Telephone	10/01/95	10/05/95	135.00

Figure 13.5

Setting up regular payments using Security First.

The New Transaction window enables you to select the type of transaction and payee, and then store the information so you only need to enter it once. The images at the top of the screen enable you to jump immediately to the next transaction. Figure 13.6 shows the window used to create new transactions.

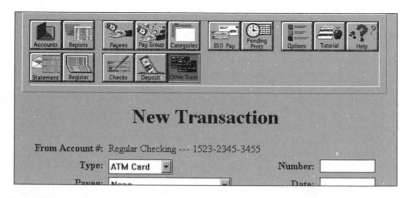

Figure 13.6

The Security First New Transaction window.

Security First also provides you with regular checks that you can use like you do your current checkbook. The bank then returns a scanned image of the check after it clears. This enables customers to do all of their checking with Security First.

Digital Storefronts and Banking

A Yahoo search (http://www.yahoo.com), a searchable index of categorized Web sites, turned up over 100 banks with Web sites on the Internet. For the most part, these banks are not very customer-friendly. Most banks are still in the learning process, establishing an information site for now with plans to expand later. Some are just publishing their brochure information on Web pages without much thought, while others have nothing but "Under Construction" signs posted. The same rules apply to banking storefronts that apply to other digital storefronts. They must be interactive, easy to navigate, and be consistent with the bank's offline image. Banks need to create an interactive environment that displays useful information on their products and prices.

As the level of competition increases, banks will start to respond faster to the opportunities and challenges presented by online banking. History shows that when banks are unable (due to regulations) or unwilling (due to banks' natural conservative behavior) to respond to competition, people will move their money to other institutions. Banks cannot ignore the following statistics, reported by *The Wall Street Journal* on August 1, 1995. Since 1990:

➤ Direct deposits have nearly doubled.

➤ Automated clearinghouse payments have increased by 63 percent.

➤ The dollar volume of ATM transactions has risen 50 percent.

➤ Sales of personal computers has risen 85 percent.

Many of these changes are being encouraged by the banks, because of the need to lower costs. Banks are raising charges associated with non-automated transactions, including teller-assisted transactions and bounced checks. As more transactions become automated, banks will have to work hard to avoid becoming faceless computer centers.

Wall Street Online

Investment firms are beating the commercial banks in the race to the World Wide Web by offering extensive online support for their customers. Over 100 banks have a presence on the Web, but they are mostly information sites that are not doing much in terms of actual transactions. Some investment firms, such as Charles Schwab and Fidelity, are already offering interactive financial planning, real-time stock quotes, electronic prospectuses, regulatory filings, and company research.

The Portfolio Accounting World Wide Web (PAWWS) Financial Network is one of the comprehensive financial services emerging on the Internet. PAWWS was the first to have real-time trading on the Internet. You can enter your existing investment portfolio online and get graphs that reflect value changes in real-time. The service enables you to conduct research, track stocks, and monitor emerging trends in other markets. Figure 13.7, 13.8, and 13.9 show some examples of the type of information available through PAWWS. PAWWS offers a free trial period for the service.

Figure 13.7
The PAWWS home page.

Figure 13.8

A variety of services are available, including non-paying ones like this newsletter.

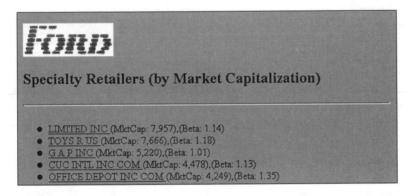

Figure 13.9

An example of a retail tracking system.

According to industry experts, the use of the Internet for financial investing is booming. This should not come as a surprise—the WWW is a tremendous information tool, and the financial market is entirely information-driven.

America Online, CompuServe, and Prodigy also offer substantial services for hefty fees, but they boast more secure systems. For example, CompuServe members can track the stock market and place bids. Because CompuServe maintains its own network, the transactions are more secure than those that pass over the Internet.

The increasing availability of consumer choice in financial services is working against banks. One example most people will be familiar with is the growth of nonbank-issued credit cards. The continuous flow of credit card applications in your mailbox is there for a good reason. Non-bank credit cards are very successful and now hold 25 percent of the credit card market. Banks are trying to lure you back, while other nonbank credit card issuers are continuing to try to increase their market shares. As the number and variety of financial institutions grows, some people are beginning to ask, "Are banks even necessary?" Customers need someone to help them manage and secure their money, but this no longer needs to be a bank. Banks will thus need to offer a wider array of products directly to customers to retain their current market position.

Intuit Corp. recently announced that some of the largest financial firms in the U.S. are working with it, so that their customers can conduct banking transactions online using Quicken, Intuit's personal finance software. *Quicken* is a popular personal financial management package that can track bills and help families analyze expenditures. Using Quicken, customers will be able to do their regular banking, financial planning, and use brokerage services all at one site.

Smart Strategies

If they want to succeed online, banks must develop Web-based online banking services. The competition to provide this interface is fierce, however, and the stakes are high. Microsoft's recent failed attempt by Intuit is only one indication of the stakes at play. Merchants will be affected by the outcome of this battle, although there isn't much they can do to determine the outcome.

Banks cannot wait for others (Microsoft, Intuit) to develop the home banking interface for the following reasons. If a bank relies on a third party to provide the interface, there is no way for the bank to differentiate itself from another bank. To the user, all banks would look alike because they all use the same software package. There would, moreover, be no way to offer services not available through the third-party interface. If banks are relegated to being nothing more than electronic vaults, then there won't be a need for banks at all—it wouldn't take others long to provide an even better, cheaper electronic vault.

Prime examples of third-party interfaces that may be a threat to banks are Quicken and Microsoft Money. These programs (and a few others) already control the market for desktop money management. If banks cooperate in moving these programs to the Web, then they will cut off their own ability to compete.

Banks that have worked to develop their staffs' expertise of the online world are well-positioned to react quickly to the competition of other commercial banks and the financial services industry. Banks must develop their own digital storefronts. This expertise can be rented (consultants), but long-term success will only come when people inside the organization have a good sense of how to use the technology.

If they haven't already, banks will soon come to these same conclusions. The number of banks constructing their own Web sites is one indication of this. Banking on the Web will not be done through popular programs such as Quicken, but rather directly through the Web browser. Quicken and other financial packages will play a lesser role. Of course, the final decision rests with bank customers—if customers refuse to use Web browsers to manage their money, then the banks will be forced to build gateways to personal financial management packages. Because online customers will be familiar with the Web, however, and most other applications are taking a Web-centric view of the Internet (most Internet applications are being marketed as browser add-ons rather than the other way around), customers will be accustomed to using their Web browsers to browse the Internet and purchase items. Thus, there is good reason to believe that customers will accept a Web interface for online banking.

The software that banks use to handle online banking is important to other merchants on the Web. First, everyone should learn the same lesson about controlling the interface to your organization. Second, merchants will also be helped by the fact that banks will put up Web-based banking services. Customers will become acclimated to passing money online quicker when banks are directly participating on the Web. Banks can help legitimize online commerce by having an active online presence.

Summary

Banks are losing capital to non-banks already. They need to make bold moves to reverse this trend by improving the convenience of their services. If banks don't manage to win a major role in running these new payment systems, the rise of the Internet and the new electronic payment systems may cause banks to lose even more customers.

Banks currently have one enormous advantage over Microsoft, CyberCash, and others, however—trust. People will only store their money in institutions they trust. Microsoft, CyberCash, and other companies that want to handle online transactions will have to build trust over time. How long will banks enjoy this advantage? Five years? Ten years? There is no way to know, but it is clear that once people trust an organization, huge sums of money can shift very rapidly from the banking sector into the organization.

Banks need to use the Web to build customer relations and continue to play the trust card before Wall Street closes them out. Will banks be more than large computers processing transactions? Merchants need to know the answer to this question.

For now, merchants should evaluate every organization offering electronic commerce services. You may find that banks provide you with the highest level of security and convenience. In many cases, this will not be true. Most merchants will be better off going with another provider of payment services that takes care of the link back to the bank. These may grow and take over more banking functions over time, eventually turning banks into highly specialized institutions. The legal monopoly on the ability to create money by participating in the fractional banking system may be the banks' saving grace. (The fractional banking system allows banks to lend out more than they have in assets.)

Chapter 14, "The Future of Internet Commerce," examines the impact that online commerce will have on industries and individual businesses. The chapter also presents some guidelines to help you evaluate the impact new communications technology will have on your life and business. In addition, the advertising and retail industries are examined in depth, because they will feel the greatest impact over the next few years.

Chapter 14

The Future of Internet Commerce

Now it's time to gaze into our crystal ball. We do this with some trepidation, because we are going where many people have failed before us. But instead of simply making random predictions about Internet commerce, we want to also provide you with a format for understanding how technology can shape future communications, specifically through the medium of the Internet.

Claims made about the Internet are grandiose indeed:

➤ The Internet will enable people to live and work wherever they please.

➤ The Internet will create new communities of people who never need to meet each other.

➤ The Internet will improve the lot of poor people or alternatively, depending upon which way you lean, the Internet will divide society into the information "haves" and the information "have nots" (see the section entitled, "The Haves versus the Have Nots," later in this chapter).

Some believe, of course, that all of this will happen only if government either keeps its hands off or takes total control, depending upon which side of the fence you are on. Another viewpoint is that if the government doesn't regulate the environment, the Internet will become the playground of international criminals.

Before examining more claims about the Internet, it may be instructive to go back in history and look at predictions that were made about another revolutionary communications device. These predictions about this other technology will sound familiar to anyone who has done even a little reading about electronic cash. The communications technology? Why it's the telephone, of course. All of the predictions for the Internet have an extremely familiar ring—so to speak—if you just take yourself back 120 years to 1876, the year of the telephone's invention.

How soon we forget predictions that don't come true! The telephone was going to bring peace on earth. It would eliminate accents. It would revolutionize medical surgery, stamp out heathenism by spreading the word of God, and make rural areas more livable and less lonely. The moral tone of society and its entertainment was going to be vastly improved, because only the best material could survive with such broad public scrutiny. Presidential speeches and three-dimensional plays were going to be made possible because of the invention of the telephone.

Fast forward now 100 years to any of your favorite Internet conferences, and you hear very similar claims. The Internet will bring peace by making it impossible for governments to control information. The Internet will result in English becoming the universal language. The Internet will enable people to move back to the countryside. We'll all soon have over 500 channels of entertainment. The Internet is an ideal vehicle for distributing porn and children's minds will become polluted. These are predictions being made today about the Internet.

Predictions—Then and Now	
Telephone	**Internet**
Will let people live and work wherever they please.	Will let people live and work wherever they please.
Will eliminate accents.	Will make English the universal language.
Smut will be eliminated.	Smut will prosper.

What is the point of this comparison? The point is that predictions have a way of not coming true. The telephone was supposed to stop the dramatic population shift to the cities by making it possible for you to communicate over long distances, but we know that the opposite is true.

Cities continued to grow as people learned how to use the telephone. Peace did not reign, and people pretty much were still people. It turns out that even though the telephone can connect you to anyone around the world, over 90 percent of phone calls, even today, are local. We learned that just because you can call someone around the world, doesn't mean you want to or even know of someone on the other side of the globe. Then, as now, the factors that will decide the ultimate shape of new technology do not rest with the technology alone, but rather are influenced by what society does with the new technology. This is where Internet commerce and its future comes into the picture.

History has a way of repeating itself. Just as the technically savvy at the turn of the century laughed at people's inability to understand how to use a phone, Internet nerds today scoff at the newbies who barely know how to turn on their modem.

This chapter examines Internet commerce's impact on society. Specifically, you will read about the following:

➤ The future of specific industries

➤ The future of Web technology

➤ The impact on society

➤ Guidelines for evaluating communications technology

Evaluating Communications Technologies

As a merchant thinking about using a new communications technology, it is important that you be able to anticipate the best uses of a technology. You can get ahead of the competition if you have the ability to focus on the most likely uses of technology and can anticipate the ways customers will use it. The criteria you should use to evaluate technology are the following:

➤ Cost

➤ Bandwidth

➤ Interactivity

➤ Types of information

➤ Privacy

➤ Geographic and time restrictions

In this section, we provide an overview of how to think about new communications technologies, and discuss the likely ways they will be used. The key question that you should always ask yourself when evaluating a new communications technology is, "What type of conversations between people does this technology encourage?" Examine closely all the different aspects of the technology to answer this question. Once you know what types of conversations are likely, you can start to imagine the different possible applications and ultimately, the effect these might have on society. Remember, technology doesn't directly lead to change. Technology affects economics, which is the true driving force in our society.

Cost

An important question to ask is what are the costs? If a technology is too expensive to become widely used, then no more analysis is necessary.

No technology will have a major impact on society until it is cheap enough to become widespread. For communication technologies, this means that individual exchanges need to be very cheap. Different communities will be able to justify the expense sooner than others.

Bandwidth

Bandwidth, as it is used in this section, refers to more than the connection speed to the Internet. *Bandwidth* is the amount of information that is typically transmitted using a particular communications technology. Even if it is theoretically possible to send huge amounts of information using a particular medium, you need to understand the typical usage so that you can anticipate the ways your customers will expect to use the technology. The questions you need to answer are the following:

➤ How much information is typically transmitted in a single exchange?

➤ What are the bottlenecks?

Bandwidth is affected by the number of people that can participate in a single conversation. The more people that can participate, the greater the bandwidth. Not all communication technologies are the same. Some technologies, like TV, enable one person to broadcast a message to an unlimited number of people. Other technologies, like the telephone, can connect a small number of people at a single time—generally two people at a time, but it can be more. Conference calls can carry a number of people, but very few calls ever include more than a half dozen people. Huge conference calls are just not a natural way to distribute information, but there is one exception. Companies often have more than one hundred brokers on a single call when announcing major plans. These calls actually resemble a TV broadcast without the picture. Very few of the people on a large conference call ever get to talk, because there just isn't enough bandwidth for everyone to get their two cents in. Supplementing the amount of information that can get transmitted via the telephone is not practical.

E-mail differs from the phone and face-to-face communication in a way that was probably not clear to the early adopters of e-mail. The bandwidth bottleneck of e-mail isn't the computer or the modem, but people's willingness (or ability) to type. Even though networks have enormous bandwidth, e-mail messages tend to be very short. The limitation is mainly on people's ability to quickly type in long answers. They are not the same as other forms of written communication. E-mail encourages an exchange of short snappy messages. While each individual message in an e-mail conversation is short, the technology supporting e-mail does have the capability to transmit large amounts of information. One way this capability is put to use is when people add their comments to a message without deleting the previous comments. In this way, an e-mail message can become a complete record of a conversation.

Bandwidth is also affected by the number of senses people can use at one time. If a person can use both his eyes and ears to receive a message, more information can be understood in the same amount of time. When talking in person, you can send information with not only the words that you speak, but your tone of voice, your posture, gestures, and facial expressions. When giving a lecture, you can supplement your words with overheads or slide shows. Over the telephone, you have your words and your facial expressions, and if you are sending e-mail, you have only your words. TV, print media, and the Web use integrated graphics. Each communications technology varies in its capability of handling voice, graphics, text, and other types of information.

Interactivity

There are several questions that determine the level of interactivity supported by a communications technology, as follows:

➤ Is the communication interactive or one-way?

➤ How many people can talk? How many can listen?

➤ Does the interaction happen instantly, or is there a delay?

As a merchant, you should take every opportunity to interact with your customers, to help build relationships, and to better serve your customer base. A Web storefront will probably include at least two different communications technologies—the Web and e-mail—so you need to understand when to use each when setting up a storefront.

When you are talking to someone face to face, it's easy to ask questions and get quick answers. The same applies when you are talking on the phone. E-mail is different. A conversation takes considerably longer when carried out using e-mail. Therefore, e-mail is not commonly used when giving long explanations. The ability of the parties to interact is another important aspect of communications technology.

Make sure that your digital storefront follows people's expectations based on the current technology capabilities. It may be wonderful, for instance, to incorporate sound, but if the technology can't support it well, then customers will be turned off by the experience.

Types of Information

Each technology handles different types of information. Voice, text, still images, and movies are all different types of information that may be supported. The key question to ask is:

➤ What type of information is appropriate for this medium? Voice? Text? Graphics?

The types of information supported by a technology changes over time. In general, there is a trend toward more graphics and sound with nearly every communications technology.

Privacy

Communication technologies also differ in their capability to protect the identity of one, both, or all parties involved. Some communications mediums enable you to hide some information, but not all. For example, people who work at home and communicate over the telephone can work wearing sweats if it pleases them—the telephone enables them to hide their appearance. The information that is not typically revealed using a particular communications technology is an important part of customer expectations that merchants should anticipate and honor. If a merchant tries to collect information that is not typically revealed, customers may resist and/or stop patronizing that merchant. The important questions to ask are:

➤   Who knows who?

➤   What information is revealed?

With television, the viewer is completely anonymous, while the television station is clearly identified. With e-mail, both the sender and recipient are clearly identified (usually). Over the telephone, in most cases, both people are identified, and in virtually all cases, the person receiving the call is known, while the person placing the call may remain anonymous. The Internet supports both anonymous interaction and non-anonymous interactions. Despite great publicity about privacy concerns, however, people today seem comfortable using credit cards, even though a credit card transaction empowers a company to easily track the what, when, and where of your purchasing habits.

Geographic and Time Restrictions

It is no longer unusual for people to work on the same team, complete a project, and never meet in person. Technology has freed us from the need to be in the same room at the same time. Of course, each technology accomplishes this to a different degree. The key questions are:

➤   Do people need to coordinate their schedules?

➤   Do people need to be in the same location?

E-mail's big advantage over other forms of communication is that people do not need to coordinate their schedules. The capability to avoid personal contact is also an important aspect of e-mail. The lack of personal interaction can increase the efficiency of communications. The lack of personal interaction can also lead to some big misunderstandings, but that's not unique to e-mail. The telephone is good for communicating at a distance with one other person. The ability to communicate without coordinating schedules is the last important aspect of a communications technology.

Technology's Influence on Communication

You can see how the preceding factors have influenced the way we use different forms of communication. We use face-to-face communication when interpersonal relationships are important—where a high level of trust is required, nothing beats looking someone in the eye. The telephone is good for exchanging small amounts of information at a distance or for idle chitchat. It is also useful for transmitting instructions to subordinates, as well as keeping in touch with family and friends. Phone calls in a business setting are used to exchange information and tend to be quite short and to the point, revolving around a specific question or task. E-mail encourages a similar form of interaction, with the actual messages being even shorter than telephone messages. Cost restrictions have limited e-mail to business uses, although this is beginning to change.

How do these factors (cost, interactivity, bandwidth, privacy, time and place restrictions) apply to the Web and Internet commerce? The World Wide Web is both a publishing medium and an interactive communications technology—it is appropriate for transmitting nearly every form of written communication. Internet advertising on the surface can feel much like TV and magazine advertising, but there are several key differences. You can transmit much more information using the Web than you can in a magazine advertisement, and gather customer information more readily. A Web page can have an interactive form available that you can fill out instantly, send, and get an immediate response, whereas a magazine is limited to business reply cards that customers have to fill out, mail, and then wait for a response. We will return to these issues throughout the chapter.

The Future of Web Technology

The future of the World Wide Web will be shaped more by the back-end systems used by merchants than the front-end glitz (graphics, sound, and animation) that gets all the press. *Back-end systems* are the order processing, accounting, financial, and other systems used to run a business. The connections to back-end systems will enable the processing of secure transactions.

Because present Web servers are little more than fancy file servers, Web browsers give the Web its personality. We are only just now beginning to see the roll out of software that provides secure connections all the way to a merchant's back-end processing systems. The Web servers will be able to receive and validate transactions, but they will need to hand the transactions off to the correct automated processing system in order to fulfill the customer's order. We predict that Web servers will begin to integrate true database functionality, enabling them to do some of the processing involved with online transactions. Secure Web servers might be able to fulfill simple orders for information-based products.

Although Web servers will start to integrate database functionality, the real powerhouses will continue to be the database vendors. They are simply too far ahead of Web browser companies such as Netscape and Spry in the database field to be caught. Servers running Oracle, Sybase, and DB2, therefore, are likely to be the workhorses fulfilling online transactions.

While Web browser technology is important in giving your home page personality, you as a merchant need to seriously evaluate a Web server's capability to connect to your back-end processing systems. The technology in the trenches is every bit as important as the glitz that gets the press.

As Web technology continues to advance, merchants must evaluate potential uses in their digital storefront. Not all technologies will be worth the cost, however, so carefully evaluate each one. The advancements that will find their way into more

Web pages soon will include 3D Web pages, animation, and sound. Merchants that understand the costs and capabilities of each of these technologies will be able to create unique Web sites at a reasonable cost.

3D Worlds and Animation

Sun Microsystems and other companies have written programs that make it possible to display animated logos. These animated logos can display on the same page as static text and graphics. The logo can be set to play automatically or at the click of a button.

We have to add our voice to that of the skeptics on the value of three-dimensional Web pages. Certainly Web pages that incorporate 3D will generate quite a bit of press. Whether the cost of a 3D page can be justified by increased sales remains to be seen. The development of affordable tools to support the development of 3D pages could make a big difference in the cost benefit analysis. For now, the performance of three-dimensional Web pages leaves something to be desired. 3D is a technology that, while currently available, will take some time to come into general use.

3D worlds and animation certainly sound like fun, but avoid being recklessly enamored with all the bells and whistles and expensive play toys. The cost of developing a high-quality Web site already can run into the tens of thousands of dollars before you even get to all the glitz. This would include high-quality graphics and well-linked information that is kept up to date on a regular basis. Adding the additional cost of 3D and animation won't be justifiable for many merchants. Sound, on the other hand, may very well become an integrated part of nearly every Web home page.

Sound

Sound is inexpensive and a value-added extra. In the past, sound files have taken up to five times longer to download than they take to play. Progressive Networks, Inc., based in Seattle, is selling a package that can play files while they are being downloaded. Sound is already being incorporated into several leading edge Web servers, including the Hot Wired server.

Web Page Trends

Over the last two years, the primary method of developing Web pages was to create HTML files by hand using ordinary text editors. This method is being quickly supplanted by popular word processors and desktop publishing tools adding HTML format capability to their products. We expect that even these new products, in turn, will be supplanted by complete application development environments targeted at developing complex Web applications. Web development tools will span the range from Word with HTML extensions to PowerBuilder or Visual Basic type tools capable of generating Java code. The good news is that merchants will have a number of cost/benefit entry points for generating their Web pages.

Merchants who are outsourcing the housing and development of their Web page will need to evaluate the technical capability of their service provider. Advertising firms can add the ability to generate static Web pages without too much difficulty; however, adding a real development capability may be trickier for most advertising firms. Make sure, as a merchant, that you carefully evaluate the HTML version number you are using and your provider's ability to support it, as well as their capability to support full application development environments.

Web pages will, in the near future, have more variety. Currently, Web pages are a mixture of slick magazine type pages and fill-in-the blank forms. Soon, more active Web pages involving animation and continuously updated information will become common. A full variety of interface development tools will be applied to home pages, creating a nearly infinite variety of functionality. Designing an easy-to-use home page could involve a full user development interface effort.

Successful Web pages will need to have well-designed user interfaces. Before creating your own, examine other home pages that incorporate custom interfaces for their ease of use. Consumers visiting a home page are not willing to read a manual in order to access the information, products, or services that you are offering.

Unfortunately, good user interface developers are rare today—a decade after the introduction of the first graphical interfaces. Well-done home pages will incorporate custom application development and can help you gain a competitive advantage in the world of digital storefronts. Poorly done Web pages probably would have been better off sticking with straight HTML.

The Future of Electronic Cash

We are not ducking the issue, but we feel it is too soon to know the impact Internet commerce will have on the non-Internet based commerce. Electronic cash raises many questions that we cannot answer at this time. Will there be regulations regarding who can issue electronic cash? If so, how would they be enforced in the international forum of the Internet? How will taxes be applied? How will police monitor money laundering and counterfeiting? Regulations will certainly vary between countries and states. Complying with the various regulations may well prove impossible. On the other hand, enforcing the regulations may also prove to be impossible. The outcome is far from clear on these issues.

Will Electronic Cash Replace Other Currencies?

In today's society, it is hard to predict which technologies will be successful and which will fail. Consider the future of electronic cash in terms of the stoplight analogy, in which the green light represents favorable attributes of electronic cash forms that could lead to their proliferation. The following list describes these green light attributes:

➤ Electronic cash will expand the types of transactions for which cash will be used. During the Wymar Republic in Germany, people needed wheelbarrows of money to buy their weekly bread. Anyone trying to buy a car with cash today is in much the same position. There are certain transactions for which cash is inconvenient. It's just as easy to carry a million dollars of electronic cash as it is to carry five dollars of electronic cash. This will bring back the era of paying cash for large purchases.

➤ Electronic cash is more flexible than traditional currency—it is appropriate for lending a few bucks to friend. Electronic cash can be earmarked for specific purposes, and can also support thousands of small payments.

➤ Processing electronic cash transactions will be considerably less expensive than processing checks and credit card transactions. The economics of electronic cash may very well transform the banking industry, reducing the number of staff required.

➤ Some forms of electronic cash will afford more privacy to consumers than credit card transactions. Chapter 4, "Internet Commerce Providers," details various payment systems and the amount of privacy they offer.

➤ Electronic cash enables anonymous transactions at a distance. Currently, the only way to buy goods anonymously is with cash, but cash requires you to meet in person to exchange money. Electronic cash will enable cash-like transactions at a distance. Not all electronic cash transactions will be anonymous, however—merchants still need to have a name and address to ship goods. When purchasing soft goods (i.e., software and information), electronic cash will enable a new era of anonymous transactions.

There are, of course, certain factors that can be considered detrimental to the eventual widespread use of electronic cash forms. These red light factors include the following:

➤ Electronic cash may undermine the current bank- and government controlled monetary systems. The use of branded electronic cash may result in a less efficient economy, despite the fact that individual electronic cash transactions are efficient. The inefficiency arises from the need to track the value and reliability of individual brands of electronic cash.

➤ Electronic cash can be lost or stolen. Yes, money can also be lost or stolen, but people are familiar with the steps they need to take to protect money—it is essentially common sense. You just don't leave money lying around. The same cannot be said of electronic cash. Not all people are familiar or comfortable with computers and other electronic gadgets. They are thus unlikely to understand what it takes to protect their money in this format. The result may be a less secure form of money.

If the use of electronic cash forms becomes widespread, the following problems will have to be overcome. Some of these yellow light factors are highlighted here:

➤ Electronic cash may enable a new level of money laundering and tax evasion. Branded electronic cash, not tied to any state or nation, may prove untraceable. An international underground economy could develop. Although an underground economy is most attractive to criminals, don't think for a moment that many citizens would not dabble in a little bit of tax evasion given the chance.

➤ Electronic cash is only as secure as the systems used to generate it. If a company issuing electronic cash were to have a break-in, counterfeiters could quickly print more money than the entire net worth of the company. The result would be an instant collapse of the value of that particular brand of electronic cash.

➤ Software-based electronic cash creates an environment where hackers could steal vast sums of money. Once a hacker breaks into a system holding electronic cash, there is very little you can do to protect yourself. If a robber were to break into your house, the amount that he could steal in the few minutes that he may have is quite limited. This is certainly not the case with electronic cash.

Branded Cash

Branded cash is cash that is issued by a corporation and is not denominated in any monetary unit. Branded cash derives its value from the assets of the company that issues the cash. The best example of branded cash so far is DigiCash's Ecash. Merchants accepting Ecash trust in DigiCash's capability to convert Ecash into hard assets or government-backed denominations. The claim has already been made that branded cash will become preferable to government-issued cash. Let's examine this claim.

The prediction has a certain allure to it. Compare branded cash backed by hard assets to government cash backed by full faith and credit of the issuing government. There have been several incidents over the last few years when a currency quickly lost more than a third of its value. Government-backed currencies are subject to speculation and policy changes. Because branded cash derives its value from the assets of the company issuing it, the value of branded cash is only as vulnerable as the company's assets.

We expect that rating companies will begin to rate the credit worthiness of electronic cash companies just as rating companies today rate banks and insurance companies. Because the value of branded cash relies on the assets of the company, it should better hold its value through inflationary times. To minimize your exposure to the failure of any particular electronic cash company, however, merchants will have to monitor the amount of any particular branded cash that they are currently holding.

Most international corporations today already protect themselves against currency swings. Branded cash simply extends this problem to any merchant doing business on the Internet. While

electronic cash in general is likely to be more stable than government backed currency, a particular electronic cash is subject to
wild swings in value should that company's investments fail or
should the company fall prey to embezzlers or hackers.

It won't take many widely publicized failures of electronic cash
companies to spook off most consumers. Overall, we don't expect
electronic cash to be preferable to government-backed currency
in developed countries. People doing business in developing
countries, where currency fluctuations can be dramatic, will
probably prefer electronic cash. Furthermore, just as bond
markets have disciplined several governments, the existence of
electronic cash may cause governments to adopt a stable currency policy.

Branded cash will certainly have its place, particularly in conjunction with the smart card. We expect that smart card technology
will be very popular once the infrastructure to read these cards is
in place. It took about a decade for ATM's to become widespread
and commonly used. Because of the foundation laid by the ATM
technology, the spread of smart cards should take considerably
less time, perhaps as little as five years. Branded cash seems quite
appropriate for international transactions—this type of cash
avoids the expense of converting currencies, while making
anonymous purchases at a distance possible.

One big disadvantage often associated with electronic cash is the
possibility of money laundering. Merchants need to be aware of
this issue and to track any legislation that may be introduced to
try to deal with any potential problems.

Electronic Cash and Money Laundering

We haven't seen an article yet on the future of money that hasn't
mentioned the prospect of large-scale money laundering. *Money
laundering* is the process of legitimizing money earned from illicit
activities. The primary concern is drug dealers taking the cash
that they have earned through drug deals and turning that into
legitimate income.

In the United States, merchants and banks are required to report transactions in excess of $10,000 to the IRS. This prevents criminals from spending large amounts of cash. This, in essence, makes their cash worthless. In theory, drug dealers can't spend the money that they have earned. The reality has been something quite different. Even today, with hard currency, money laundering is a common activity. Money laundering doesn't apply only to drug dealers though—it applies to nearly any criminal activity.

The fear is that electronic cash, because it is international and anonymous, will enable criminals to spend their cash easily. Whereas it is inconvenient to carry and spend large amounts of cash, it is extremely convenient to carry and spend large amounts of electronic cash. The difference between carrying one dollar and a million dollars is nothing more than a few extra zeros typed at a keyboard. Of course, criminals would still need to convert cash into electronic cash in order to distribute their gains. Businesses that engage in money laundering would have a much easier time of it.

The anonymous nature of electronic cash would make it difficult for any government to collect taxes on unreported income. Just as the IRS in the United States has an extremely difficult time tapping in to the cash society that already exists, nations across the globe would find it extremely difficult to collect taxes on electronic cash. That, in essence, is the argument that says that electronic cash will result in an explosion of international money laundering. We feel that it is far too early to tell whether electronic cash will result in an explosion of illicit financial transactions. We certainly acknowledge that there are legitimate concerns. International terrorism depends on the ability to move and spend large amounts of cash, for example. Rogue nations across the globe routinely print hundreds of millions of dollars of fake U.S. currency to support their particular economies.

In order for these predictions to come true, anonymous branded electronic cash would have to come into widespread use worldwide. Electronic cash tied to a banking system won't work for criminals. Only cash that can be used completely outside our

current financial systems would enable criminals to collect and
launder large sums of money.

Gaps in our regulation currently enable money laundering. For
example, there are no laws that limit the amount of currency that
can be loaded into a single smart card. The ability to transport
large amounts of cash in your wallet is a major opportunity for
money launderers.

Other gaps in regulation include determining whose tax laws apply
in cyberspace. When a merchant based in the United States sells
goods to a customer in Germany, whose tax laws apply? Does that
make the merchant in the United States an international firm
subject to the tax laws of Germany? Even domestically, a firm in one
state selling to a customer in another state is currently not subject
to any sales tax. Does this law extend to sales made over the
Internet? Some states are attempting to charge sales tax on interstate sales. How will this carry over on the Internet? Currently, in the
United States, a company is not subject to sales tax in a state unless
it has a physical presence in a state.

In a never-ending quest for more tax revenue, states are closely
looking at ways to expand the definition of physical presence.
One idea is to expand the idea of physical presence to be a
customer's PC screen. Simply transmitting your home page to a
PC in another state, under this regulation, would count as having
a physical presence in that state. These regulations clearly would
favor large organizations who already have in place the necessary
accounting structures to deal with filing and tracking sales tax in
50 different states. Small companies, ma-and-pa shops, and one-
person shops are simply not capable at the current time of
tracking and filing accurate tax reforms for all 50 states, much less
international tax forms.

One thing is for certain—there is no going back. Pandora's box has
been opened and, like it or not, we are going to have to find a way to
live with the consequences. If electronic cash systems enable
widespread money laundering, then we will simply have to find a
way to combat it. The Internet doesn't have an off switch.

The Future of Publishing

Magazines and newspapers are rushing to publish information on the Internet. It is not clear at this point, however, if any of them are making money. Internet publishing may, in fact, be siphoning off customers from traditional publications and hurting the value of traditional publishing outlets. If this turns out to be the case, advertising revenue for traditional publications will certainly fall. Whether this lost income will be made up through money made online is not yet known.

Postponing the Paperless Office

While we see a definite future for publishing on the Internet, we don't agree that traditional books, magazines, and newspapers will disappear. It has been nearly twenty years since the first predictions of the paperless office were made. As we look around our offices, we see that there is quite a way to go before that prediction comes true. In fact, the use of paper in offices has grown even as more information is stored online. How can this be?

While computers are extremely useful tools for developing and transmitting information, they are fairly lousy presentation mediums. People can scan a paper book far faster than they can scan or search a computer publication. Paper is also portable, foldable, and lightweight. Computer screen technology is not likely to ever advance to the point where it erases these advantages. Paper is still the presentation medium of choice, and we feel it will remain so for the foreseeable future.

Micropublishing on the Internet

What the Internet and World Wide Web will enable is micropublishing. In the past, publishing a book or magazine required a large up-front investment. The types of information available through traditional outlets are limited by the need to recoup this investment. To justify the expense of publishing, information must appeal to a wide audience. Mass distribution is required in order to recoup the up-front investment required to develop and distribute publications. Micropublishers on the Internet, on the other hand, may be profitable with as few as 300 subscribers. Because you only need 300 people drawing on an Internet audience of over 30 million (and growing every day), we feel that the number of micropublications may become truly astounding.

The saying goes that ideas want to be free. While publishing information over the Internet is extremely inexpensive, all information will continue to have a price tag. Information has value and anything that has value costs money. As you peruse the Web today, you will find vast amounts of free information and software. When you look at the quality of the information though, you will understand why it is free. You won't find in-depth, reliable information for free very many places, and the places where you do find this info are normally heavily subsidized. Information sales on the Internet will grow. Publishers may need to protect themselves against an onslaught of micropublishers, but the publishing industry overall will continue to exist.

The Future of Retailing on the Internet

The Internet and electronic cash represent a highly efficient way for companies to reach customers. The Internet is far more efficient and cost effective than any retail outlet or mall. Over time, goods sold over the Internet and paid for with electronic cash will have a price advantage over those sold in traditional retail outlets.

Malls won't disappear. Catalog sales, while growing, certainly haven't resulted in the closure of any malls. Retailing is affected by far more important factors than catalog sales and electronic commerce. Rather than replacing retail or catalog sales, the Internet and electronic cash will supplement these venues. Brand identities established in retail malls will carry over to the Internet. New brands will emerge online, but we don't feel that is any different from the development of new brands on a regular basis in traditional retail outlets.

The real impact of direct marketing over the Internet will be in the types of products that are offered. Customization is frequently not an option in many of today's retail outlets, because there simply isn't enough shelf space in malls today to offer highly customized products. Distributing and advertising costs would be prohibitive to anyone attempting to sell highly specialized goods through normal retail outlets today (yes, there are exceptions, but that's all they are—exceptions). Direct marketing over the Internet eliminates these production and distribution costs. By dealing direct with the customer, many companies will be able to ship completely customized products direct, completely bypassing retail outlets.

Internet commerce will bring the era of mass customization manufacturing to a new level. The contact that merchants will have with their customers will enable them to develop highly specialized products. Products developed specifically for an individual are certainly within the realm of possibility. There is no shelf space to compete for and there is no advertising costs involved. The true impact of electronic commerce and direct marketing over the Internet will be in the alteration of people's expectations in terms of quality and value. If you can get a product manufactured to your personal specifications, why would you purchase an ordinary off-the-shelf product at a retail mall? Women's jeans are already being made-to-order online. Other markets, which are traditionally underserved, will be the first to feel the impact of direct marketing over the Internet.

Selling Soft Goods on the Internet

Software, insurance, and information all fall under the general category of *soft goods*—goods that can be delivered online. Businesses that sell goods that can be distributed completely online will be affected to a far greater degree than more typical businesses.

The Future of Software Sales

Already many software companies are selling their goods online, and this trend will grow. The distribution channel is there, and it's cheap, so this is inevitable. Anyone buying software presumably has a computer. Because you cannot buy a computer without getting some kind of modem, software customers will universally have access to the Internet. Selling software online is, therefore, a natural progression for this marketplace.

Insurance Agents Beware

Software is not the only product that can be sold completely online. Because insurance will be sold online in the future, the need for human insurance agents will be eliminated. The use of agents, the salesmen of the insurance force, constitute one of the major costs for any insurance company. With some forms of insurance, such as life insurance, the payment to an agent exceeds the total premiums paid over the course of the first year. The insurance company does not make a return on its investment until the second or third year at a minimum. The combination of the Internet and electronic cash has, therefore, the potential to drastically change the insurance industry.

The primary customers for insurance companies are the upper middle class. They are the ones who have things that need protecting with insurance. These customers are also the ones most likely to have access to computers and the Internet. Just as with software, insurance customers will be online. By selling directly to customers, insurance companies can drastically lower their costs. It is only a matter of time until insurance contracts are predominantly made online. The result of this will be a drastic reduction in the number of insurance agents nationwide. We are not predicting the demise of the insurance agent by any means. Some demand will always exist for face-to-face contact in insurance sales, particularly business insurance.

Middlemen in general will be the ones most affected by the advent of the Internet, electronic cash, and electronic commerce. Companies will have an inexpensive way to sell direct to the customer. It is only a matter of time until anyone with the word "agent" in their job title starts to feel the pressure.

The Future of Advertising

No discussion about the future of the Web is complete without some comments on the world of advertising. The Internet will certainly have as big an impact on advertising as the television did. Historically, the ability to advertise on TV affected both the style and content of ads, as well as the structure of both the television and advertising industries. TV advertising was instrumental in the rise of national name brands. The Web will, in time, have a similar impact.

At first, people will try to anticipate the nature of Web advertising by drawing parallels to advertising today. Some common analogies are the commercial and infomercial (a very long commercial). The true winners on the Web, though, will be those that can anticipate the new applications of the technology. The first new application that will clearly affect Web advertising is the ability to create individualized ads on a mass scale. Web strategies based on these new applications will be the most effective. The good news for many companies is that you don't need to have a large budget to take advantage of many of these strategies. The Web enables small companies to put forth a professional appearance. Because of security and cost concerns, most companies, big and small alike, will use Web page hosting services.

Web advertising will be affected by and affect the Internet culture. Many people think that it is impossible for the current *netiquette*, the unwritten code of conduct that has grown up on the Internet, to survive the rapid introduction of so many new people. This issue is dealt with later in this chapter.

Commercial or Infomercial?

The Internet has already changed advertising—you won't find a major advertising house that isn't capable of developing online advertising. Advertising over the Internet is still a sideshow in most advertising houses. A few firms are popping up that specialize in Internet advertising. These firms will expand into other areas and become full-fledged advertising agencies. We don't feel that direct marketing over the Internet by itself will drastically alter the face of the advertising industry. Direct marketing will have more impact on the companies advertising their products than on the companies generating ads. The largest impact will be on the structure and content of advertising, and on the types of organizational structures needed to produce highly customized products.

A jingle and a pretty face may work well in a 30-second TV commercial, but will prove to be highly inadequate over the Internet. Information-based advertising is likely to dominate. The force driving this is the fact that the Internet can transfer more information than can possibly be packed into a 30-second commercial. The Web gives customers the ability to research a product in-depth before making a purchase. Impulse buys will continue, though, and glitz will continue to sell. To build a steady clientele, however, a merchant's home page will have to offer much more than a slogan. Advertising over the Internet will more closely resemble an infomercial than a commercial.

Advertisers are going to have to make a shift in attitude. In order to bring people back on a regular basis, constantly refreshing your Web site is a must. Writing a single infomercial is not enough to keep people coming back—continual updates and changes will be key to a successful Web site. For example, an oatmeal company wanting to be viewed as a health food company could publish government reports on cholesterol on a regular basis. Other merchants will, in effect, be publishing newsletters online to draw in customers. In the age of interactive advertising, content providers will become more important than ever. Companies that can reliably generate interesting material will be essential in drawing repeat visits.

Mass-Customized Advertising

Advertising on the Web is a sideshow for most of the companies involved. This situation applies to both the advertising agencies and the companies generating advertising with those agencies. Companies that want to take full advantage of their digital storefronts will need to think hard about their advertising strategies.

The industrial world has been shaped by the technology of mass production. *Mass production* is the process of building one standard item in great quantities and distributing this item to the masses. The success of firms using mass production depends on their ability to anticipate market demand. Manufacturing firms have needed to anticipate demand years in advance. With the advent of computerization in the early '80s, mass production has given way to a technique called mass customization.

Mass customization is the process of manufacturing a wide number of items using a single production line. The ultimate mass customization is custom made to order goods that are manufactured using a production line. The technology of mass production and later mass customization totally dominate the entire structure of an organization. The internal structure of a company, its distribution channels, support strategies, and advertising are all affected by the basic production technology. Mass customization implies that an organization is closer to its customers than with mass production.

For years, advertisers have been practicing mass production. They produce a standard commercial and distribute it to the masses, be it TV, magazine, or newspaper. This will change, however. The ability to converse with individual customers will force the change.

Web technology enables a new form of advertising, one different from what is available through any other medium. We call this new form of advertising *mass-customized advertising*. This enables Web advertisers to do the following:

➤ Track the exact information accessed by any particular visitor to their site

➤ Develop a profile for each of their regular visitors

➤ Present information that may be of special interest to a particular visitor

➤ Alert customers to special savings or remind them of past purchases

When a Web server senses that a repeat customer is accessing the server, special links can be inserted into a home page, enabling that customer to quickly navigate to information of interest to him. You may be able to track the links that have been accessed by a customer and give some visual indication as to whether that information has been updated. This can save your customers considerable time accessing information repeatedly, only to find out that it hasn't changed. Other mass customization techniques will surely be applied to Web advertising. Web advertising at its best will be an interactive, two-way exchange between a merchant and a potential customer.

Another form of advertising mass customization will be simple notices sent out to individual customers, reminding them of products that they have purchased in the past. For example, a flower shop that knows that you have ordered flowers for your anniversary eleven months ago may send out a reminder of exactly what it was you purchased previously and a recommendation for this year's anniversary, along with an order button. Mass-customized advertising doesn't need to be passive, waiting for repeat visits from customers. This type of advertising can be aggressively distributed to consumers. Mass-customized advertising using the Web is a natural progression of targeted marketing efforts that are common today.

Future Marketing Strategies

Web technology will drive the mass production paradigm, which is already showing considerable signs of strain, to the graveyard. The new marketing paradigm will be driven by direct contact between a customer and merchant and depends on several things, as follows:

➤ A dialog between customers and merchants

➤ A marketing process based on a share of customer concepts (vs. share of market)

➤ An organization strategy targeted to support this share of customer strategy

Whereas mass media advertising focuses on selling one message to as many customers as possible, a share of customer strategy focuses on getting as much of a particular customer's business as possible. The focus changes from demographics to an individual. Corporations that sell a variety of goods will only be able to exploit this new arrangement if they break down internal barriers between different product groups.

The introduction of mass customization has caused a proliferation of products chasing very limited shelf space. The prime competition for many consumer product companies is for shelf space in grocery stores. Prime grocery store shelf space is perhaps the most valuable asset to national name brand companies.

The essential characteristics of Web technology that will force a change in the mass paradigm is that the Web and the Internet provide a means for merchant and customer to participate in a dialog. The fact that it's just as cheap for a ma-and-pa shop to engage in a dialog as it is for Pizza Hut means that many organizations are going to be empowered. Niche marketers will be able to more fully exploit opportunities, forcing corporations to change or die.

Is Big Beautiful?

You can hardly pick up a newspaper and not read about the third wave or the information economy. One of the predictions for the information-based economy is that the ability to react quickly will determine success. This is supposed to favor smaller, nimble firms over large corporations. The reasoning goes that because the cost of doing business on the Internet is so low and you can reach such a wide audience, major corporations no longer have an advantage over small ma-and-pa shops.

We feel that there are too many variables to make a sweeping generalization. Each industry is different. A good product idea can make up for many mistakes, so it is far from clear that the race always goes to the best informed or the fastest. Sometimes the race goes to the one with the best distribution channel or the best product, or the one with a history of solid products.

Large corporations have one advantage over niche marketers on the Internet. The ability to track the spending habits of a particular household is most useful when applied across different product categories. By focusing on a share of customer strategy, large organizations can fight back against smaller competitors, offering something that they can't. By combining information garnered through the sale of multiple products, a large corporation should be able to put together a more complete picture of an individual customer's habits than would be possible for a small organization selling a single product. So while a small niche competitor will be able to more fully exploit a niche than ever before, large organizations will be able to offer a higher level of service to any single customer than a smaller competitor can through their ability to co-market multiple products. In our minds, it is not clear which force will win out. Whether this will result in a concentration of power in large corporations or whether this will result in an explosion of small niche competitors is yet to be seen.

We believe that corporations will have to reorganize themselves around the concept of customer relations, rather than the concept of product lines. Managers will become responsible for managing relationships with a particular demographic group rather than responsible for managing the production and distribution of a single product to all demographic groups. This change will ripple through the entire organization.

The Return of Outsourcing

Many companies will be using the Web for advertising and nothing else. These companies are prime candidates to outsource their Web site. Just as most major companies today outsource their advertising to an agency, Web advertisers will outsource the housing and maintenance of the Web server. For the cost of the communications line to your own business, most Web server providers can house your digital storefront. The age of outsourcing will return, however. There is simply no reason for most companies to spend the time that it would take to become experts in running their own Web server. Although running a simple Web server is no challenge whatsoever, security remains a major concern. Isolating an in-house Web server from the rest of your internal network requires a fair amount of expertise and baby-sitting.

The Rise of Pay-Per-View

Traditional mass media involves an implicit agreement between customer and merchant that if the customer will only watch a particular show, then the merchant will help pay for that show. This arrangement is threatened by the arrival of Web advertising, in which a fundamentally different relationship between merchant and customer exists. With Web advertising, the merchant is no longer in control of what a customer sees. The customer is no longer a passive viewer, but is actively seeking information. This puts the customer in greater control of the information that he sees.

Web advertising is only one technology driving this change. The proliferation of channels and the remote control play an equally important role. Every household now has a remote and people aren't watching the commercials anymore. There are now so many channels that there aren't enough advertisers to support them all. The rise of pay-per-view and commercial subscription channels is a supplement to the traditional advertising-supported mass media.

Partnering on a Home Page

Many of the most compelling digital storefronts will be those that combine multiple products that will be attractive to a particular customer group. A Web page that combines the products of synergistic, but noncompetitive, companies will offer more value and convenience than one dedicated to a particular niche company. By forming these partnerships and sharing demographic information garnered through these pages, niche companies will also be able to get a complete picture of a particular customer's buying habits. Making this vision a reality, though, will require a high level of trust between the smaller companies participating in a partnership on a home page.

We believe that Web pages are a natural medium for connecting synergistic companies. It allows a natural entry point for companies to co-market. The problems with co-marketing aren't technical, but have more to do with ego and control. We believe that the companies that can overcome these problems and work together effectively will be far more successful than companies that attempt to go it alone.

By partnering with other companies, merchants can afford a much higher quality Web page than can be justified individually. By spreading the cost of providing content over several companies, a merchant enables a higher and deeper level of information to be developed for a home page. A more active Web page offering a variety of synergistic products will be far more attractive to Web surfers than static single product pages. We believe that the Web will result in the formation of many business partnerings that would otherwise not happen.

The Haves versus the Have Nots

Merchants aren't the only ones closely watching the rise of the Internet. Many people are very anxious about the impact the Internet will have on society in general. Legitimate concerns and unfounded fears alike are driving many people to lobby for increased government regulation.

One of the primary arguments advanced to justify government regulation of the Internet is universal access. Just as the government stepped in around the turn of the century giving AT&T a monopoly in return for providing universal access, regulators today are considering ways to provide universal access to the Internet. *Universal access* in this case implies free or reduced cost access. The argument is that, without universal access, the Internet will split society into a class of information "haves and have nots."

Our view is a little different. We don't view the division of society into information "haves and have nots" as a result of the Internet.

Our society always has and, as far as we can tell, always will be divided into information "haves and have nots." In an age with declining educational standards and rising illiteracy, talk of universal access to the Internet seems somewhat myopic. Government regulations based on the concept of providing universal access would do nothing to advance egalitarian causes, but would do tremendous harm to the advancement of Internet technology.

Information is power. Information has value. Those who understand how to apply information have always had an advantage and will always have an advantage. The information available over the Internet isn't the kind likely to lead to a leveling of society in any place. Information increases in value as the number of people with access to that information decreases. Information that is widely distributed is worth very little. Information widely dispersed over the Internet is of relatively little financial value. The information that is most valuable is information that is completely secret. For example, a stock tip distributed over the Internet quickly becomes worthless as the share price adjusts to a proper value. A stock tip known to only one person, however, becomes extraordinarily valuable, enabling that person to buy vast quantities of the stock at a reduced price. The same concept applies to virtually any bit of information.

We don't expect highly valuable information, the kind that can be used as a weapon, to be freely available over the Internet. Universal access to the Internet would do no more to break down divisions between classes than universal access to a phone, even though phone access at least plays an important role in emergencies. Universal access to the Internet won't even have that role to play. On balance, we simply do not buy the argument that the Internet will create or even exacerbate a division between information haves and have nots. Of far more importance is the basic education received by individuals. We will make one prediction and that is that universal access to the Internet will have no measurable impact whatsoever on the distribution of opportunity in our society.

The Future of Journalism

A.J. Liebling once said that the freedom of the press is guaranteed only to those who own one. If true, then the Internet represents a journalist's ultimate dream. Anyone with a computer and a modem can now be a reporter. In fact, one of the main ways the Internet has been used is to distribute information without using traditional media outlets. This has become particularly important on some historic occasions, such as the changing of the guard in Russia and Tiennamen Square in China. As self-styled reporters multiply, it will become increasingly difficult to sift fact from fiction.

Self-styled reporters also need to keep in mind that the libel laws don't cease to apply simply because reporting is being done online. People have been successfully sued for articles they have written that were published only on the Internet.

Traditional journalism is a top-down affair. An editor decides which stories to cover and reporters go out and gather facts and pictures; the news is then put together into a coherent package and distributed. This process applies to both the newspaper and television media. Journalism on the Internet, by contrast, follows a decidedly different process. There is no editor to determine which stories to cover—each reporter covers whatever his particular interests are. While this may lead to reporting that is incorrect, we don't feel that this will be anything new or unique to the Internet. Errors in traditional publications are extremely common. In fact, by enabling experts to publish their reports directly without being filtered through the eyes of a non-expert journalist, the Internet will bring a new level of in-depth and reliable reporting to the masses. The Internet will enable people to get closer to the true source of information. Scientists, politicians, and advertisers no longer need to encapsulate their messages into 30-second sound bites or to get their message sent through traditional media outlets. They now have the ability to reach out directly to people with huge amounts of information.

The Rise of the Virtual Corporation

Communication is at the heart of any business organization. From the pony express through the fax machine, businesses are shaped by the communications medium of the time. The World Wide Web will have an equally important impact on the shape of corporations. We predict that the Internet and World Wide Web will lead to an ever-increasing number of virtual corporations.

Virtual corporations are corporations that have no geographic presence and are made up of diverse geographically dispersed or mobile employees. Virtual corporations may have short lives, being formed quickly to exploit a market opportunity and then dissolving as the market opportunity closes.

The Internet and particularly the World Wide Web offer two important enabling technologies, as follows:

➤ The ability to transmit vast amounts of information in real time

➤ The ability to communicate without regard to limitations of time and space

At first, we'll see the rise of the officeless salesman. Roaming the countryside connected to their corporation only through their laptop and a phone, these salesmen can give real-time demonstrations, take orders, check on the status of orders, and process and follow leads all without ever coming into the office.

Sales force automation software is currently an extremely hot area in the software development arena. We predict that the Internet and World Wide Web will spread this to other parts of the corporation. Product development, product marketing, sales, and accounting may soon all reside in different geographic locations, indeed, even in different nations. Airlines already send most of their paperwork offshore, mainly to Puerto Rico, where the cost of clerical data entry is less than in the mainland United States. The rise of the Internet will enable much smaller organizations to exploit similar strategies.

Success in the age of the virtual corporation will hinge on a manager's ability to maintain communications with an increasingly diffuse work force. Building loyalty to a corporation may be an order of magnitude harder in a virtual corporation than in a traditional organization. Maintaining one face to the customer will be a primary challenge in the age of the virtual corporation. The Internet will revolutionize all forms of business communication, including the following:

➤ Internal communications, which include employee-to-employee messages, distribution of organizational news, job postings, and any number of other topics.

➤ Telecommuting, which greatly lessens the need for an employee to be physically present at his or her place of employment; thus offering employees the freedom and flexibility of a variety of nontraditional work alternatives.

➤ Supplier communications, which have traditionally been handled through electronic data interchange (EDI), enabling purchase orders, product information, materials requirements, and the interaction with legal and accounting organizations to be automated.

By examining the way the Internet will change each of these forms of communication, you can see the advantages that a virtual corporation will offer. Given the advantages of a virtual corporation, we feel that it is inevitable that more virtual corporations will dot the landscape.

Internal Communications

Examine your company's internal communications. How much of it really requires face-to-face meetings? How much of it is built on having established relationships? Any type of communications that is already automated internally through e-mail is a primary prospect for being split up into its own unique geographic location as part of a virtual organization. Many times interaction between different departments within a corporation are almost entirely done through electronic means. Although we don't believe that this is necessarily the best way to run a business, it does open up the possibility of splitting these two departments into different geographic locations. If you are in a corporation that has implemented widely varying e-mail technologies, sometimes even within the same building, you will need to standardize your internal communications before being able to disperse these geographically.

Telecommuting

Telecommuting is a precursor to many virtual corporations. *Telecommuting*, allowing employees to work from home rather than driving into the office each morning, offers a variety of advantages to both employees and employers. Telecommuters avoid the hassle of traffic, snow storms, retain the flexibility to deal with personal emergencies, children, and aging relatives. For many employees, their productivity increases dramatically in a telecommuting arrangement.

Although the rise of telecommuting has long been predicted, it only now seems to be becoming a reality. The Internet and Web technology will enable an expansion of this trend. Electronic cash and electronic commerce—by allowing corporations to form contracts and get paid at a distance—will encourage the creation of more virtual corporations. Because more of the necessary work involved in managing a corporation can now be done at a distance, we believe it is inevitable that the market will head in this direction. Telecommuting will certainly not replace the office any time soon. It is more likely that virtual corporations will be groups of geographically dispersed offices for the foreseeable future. The only exception may be the traveling salesman, and since sales is a function done best one on one, it makes sense for a salesman to function independently.

For corporations that are already geographically dispersed, the Internet and other private network companies offer the chance to create a sense of a team that may be missing today. The corporations of the future will exploit the advantages that any particular location offers, placing those parts of the corporation most suitable for that location there. If technical expertise on a product exists in Italy while the marketing expertise exists in Chicago, then that's how a corporation will set itself up.

Supplier Communications

The virtual corporation also implies a closer relationship between a corporation, its suppliers, and its customers. Already suppliers are being given direct access to a company's internal systems, allowing the supplier to manage inventory and/or order taking. Wal-Mart is the prime example of this trend. Wal-Mart has already shifted the responsibility for tracking inventory and restocking its shelves to its suppliers, while at the same time closely tracking the quality and performance of each supplier. Understanding the implications and opportunities offered by the Internet and the Web will be a key competitive determinant in the near future. Companies that invest in learning about the new communications technology will move faster, reach out to more highly skilled employees, and offer and gain competitive advantage. The Internet is a wild and woolly place, and the Web in particular is growing extremely fast. It takes some time to build expertise on navigating and searching the Web, but the pay-off can be quite handsome. Particularly for companies in need of demographic information or competitive analysis, the Web offers the mother lode of information.

The age of the digital storefront, we believe, will lead to more virtual corporations. By providing a consistent face to the customer through a single home page, and managing internal and external communications over the Internet, it is now possible to run a small- to medium-sized business with offices all over the globe. Already many businesses could not survive without the use of networked PCs. In the near future, we predict that companies will look back and wonder how they ever survived without a connection to the Internet. The key to succeeding in the age of the digital storefront will be identifying how your individual organization should best exploit this new technology. Your research should begin by providing Internet access to your employees, enabling them to learn and generate ideas. Setting up a digital storefront is the next step, with the final step being the support of moving into a digital storefront backed by a virtual corporation.

The Future of Internet Culture

The Internet has not been very accepting of advertising and businesses in general. People advertising on the Internet discovered this, to their own dismay. Nearly every book on doing business on the Internet advises merchants to advertise only as an incidental part of their participation in the Internet culture. The Web seems to have a culture completely separate from that of the rest of the Internet. It remains to be seen whether the culture of the Web will spread to the other parts of the Internet, especially the various Usenet groups.

The case of Lawrence Canter and Martha Seagle provide a case in point. They are the husband and wife law firm that sent advertising messages to nearly every Usenet group on the Internet. Armed with an understanding with the way Internet Usenet and mailing lists work and a single IBM PC, they flooded the Internet with their advertising.

What Canter and Seagle did is known as spamming. *Spamming* is a colorful bit of Internet jargon that invokes the dropping of a can of Spam into a fan—filling the surrounding space with meat.

By posting their ad to over 5,000 Usenet groups, Canter and Seagle guaranteed that virtually every person using the Internet would see their advertisement. Many people who participate on the Internet wound up reading the advertisement several times. The response of the Internet community was not surprising. They had their mailbox flooded with junk mail, overflowing the capability of their Internet service provider to handle the volume. In the eyes of Internet regulars, such a move amounts to a declaration of war. A user in Australia retaliated by sending over 1,000 phony requests every day to the couple. After three days, their Internet service provider pulled the plug on their account.

The underlying problem of advertising in Usenet groups is the fear that advertising in commerce could overwhelm the discussion, making it impossible for the people who participate in them to get any meaningful work done. The Internet Usenet groups have a different purpose from the Web. A Usenet group is meant to be a discussion. If there is too much extraneous or irrelevant information, it becomes impossible to hold a discussion. Anyone who has grown up in a large family knows the effect of trying to have a meaningful discussion when there is a half a dozen kids filling the airwaves with distractions. The Web, on the other hand, is meant as a publishing forum. People actively seek out individual Web sites for the information that they may contain. There is no threat that anyone's Web browser will become overwhelmed with advertising since the Web user is in total control of the information that he or she accesses.

We believe that there will be more Canter and Seagles attempting to advertise using Usenets and mailing lists. The fact that they claim to have been successful in reaching many new clients is the key point. If it is successful, more people will do it. This will drive more Usenet groups to declare themselves closed. *Closed Usenets* only allow people who have been invited and cleared to participate.

You can already see the culture of the Internet changing with the recent arrival of the members of America Online, Prodigy, and CompuServe. Most of the people who participate on America Online are relatively new to the online medium. The original culture of the Internet was set by the academic parties who are responsible for its creation. As more of the general population comes to use the Internet, inevitably the sense of community will erode. While it is possible for a small community to be self-policing, large communities need cops. For the Usenet and mailing lists, these cops are moderators. The introduction of moderators, though, means that someone needs to pay for the time that it takes (or you need to find volunteers). Even having a moderator would be a dramatic change for many Internet Usenet groups. We believe that there will be some period of time before the commercial nature of the Web seeps into the other parts of the Internet, particularly the Usenet groups and mailing lists.

To the merchant, the Web represents the first honest way to reach millions of users with overtly commercial information. The Web is the perfect medium for publishing detailed financial information, product literature, or any other information that your company wishes to publish. We foresee a time when companies named in high-profile lawsuits defend themselves partially by publishing research studies and the like over the Internet, particularly the World Wide Web. For now, the culture of the Internet is such that we would recommend confining your overtly commercial operations to the Web. The future may change this recommendation, but we would not expect that to happen during the '90s.

Final Thoughts

The market moves on. Each of us, through our individual actions, helps to shape the technological future. Consumers will pick the winners and losers in the digital marketplace.

The technology is still in its infancy. Changes that seem to be just around the corner may in fact be many years away. We believe that the adoption of the new technology will take considerable time. After all, many corporations are still running their business using twenty year-old technology. Only in the last few years has client-server technology taken off on a broad basis, even though the basic technology has been well-understood for many, many years. Still, once the majority of consumers have made up their minds on digital storefronts, the rest of us will follow along.

Whether you call it evolution or revolution, change is coming. Communications technology will reach into all aspects of our society. The United States is leading the way, but the rest of the world isn't that far behind. The age of the international digital storefront will come. The only question is "When?"

Part V

Appendix

Appendix A

Internet Commerce-Related Organizations

This appendix contains a listing of several of the more common organizations that are associated with Internet commerce today. In addition to the name of the organization, a brief description of each organization's function is included, as well as the Web URL for each.

CommerceNet

http://www.commerce.net.com

Establishing an open Internet-based information infrastructure for electronic commerce by providing the tools that make the Internet secure and easy-to-use, CommerceNet is operated by the CommerceNet Consortium—a non-profit corporation funded by a six-million dollar, three-year cooperative agreement with the United States Government's Technology Reinvestment Project.

Electronic Commerce Association

http://www.globalx.net/eca/

Electronic Commerce Association is a voluntary organization that provides a forum for sharing information, discussing ideas and initiatives, and networking. Some of the technologies addressed by the organization include electronic data exchange (EDI), electronic funds transfer, e-mail, electronic document management, smart cards, and so forth.

Financial Services Technology Consortium (FSTC)

http://www.llnl.gov/fstc/index.html

FSTC is a consortium of financial services providers, national laboratories, universities, and government agencies who sponsor and participate in non-competitive collaborative research and development on interbank technical projects. Their electronic commerce project involves developing a system with a broad architecture to enable all steps in the electronic commerce process over public networks.

Internet Business Center (IBC)

http://www.gnn.com/gnn/wic/bus.23.html

IBC is a resource for conducting business on the Internet. You will find regular updates on business issues, references to the best Internet resources, ways to market on the Internet, new features, and notable examples of business pages through IBC.

Internet Society

http://www.lnisoc.com

Internet Society is a non-governmental international organization for global cooperation and coordination for the Internet and its Internet working technologies and applications.

InterNIC

http://rs.internic.net/index.html

The Internet Network Information Center (InterNIC) lets you know what information sites are available on the system, and what chat components are registered on the system. Contact InterNIC to register your own public domain.

NAFTAnet

http://www.nafta.net

NAFTAnet is an electronic commerce port-of-trade for small business owners and entrepreneurs. This organization implements advanced telecommunications technologies, World Wide Web, and AT&T EasyLink Service to open new communications channels to existing and prospective customers. It also exploits news and information to facilitate and expand the international trade market by reducing trading costs and turnaround time—this is done using electronic commerce and electronic data interchange to target NAFTA trade countries and the Americas.

Premenos

http://www.premenos.com

Premenos, a provider of EDI software, has an extensive list of EDI and EC organizations.

U.S. Department of Commerce

http://www.doc.gov

This Web server is maintained by the Department of Commerce. The site provides entrance to agencies that can affect computing in this country. You can access the National Institute for Standards and Technology (NIST) and the National Telecommunications Information Administration (NTIA) through this resource.

XIWT (Cross-Industry Working Team)

http://www.cnri.reston.va.us:3000/XIWT/membership/agreement.html

XIWT is working to define the architecture and key technical requirements for a national information infrastructure. One of its main areas of focus is electronic commerce.

Index

PLUG YOURSELF INTO...

MACMILLAN INFORMATION SUPERLIBRARY™

que • NRP • SAMS PUBLISHING • alpha books • Hayden Books • Brady • que COLLEGE • ADOBE PRESS

THE MACMILLAN INFORMATION SUPERLIBRARY™

Free information and vast computer resources from the world's leading computer book publisher—online!

FIND THE BOOKS THAT ARE RIGHT FOR YOU!

A complete online catalog, plus sample chapters and tables of contents give you an in-depth look at *all* of our books, including hard-to-find titles. It's the best way to find the books you need!

- STAY INFORMED with the latest computer industry news through our online newsletter, press releases, and customized Information SuperLibrary Reports.

- GET FAST ANSWERS to your questions about MCP books and software.

- VISIT our online bookstore for the latest information and editions!

- COMMUNICATE with our expert authors through e-mail and conferences.

- DOWNLOAD SOFTWARE from the immense MCP library:
    - Source code and files from MCP books
    - The best shareware, freeware, and demos

- DISCOVER HOT SPOTS on other parts of the Internet.

- WIN BOOKS in ongoing contests and giveaways!

TO PLUG INTO MCP: →

GOPHER: gopher.mcp.com
FTP: ftp.mcp.com

WORLD WIDE WEB: **http://www.mcp.com**

Home Page • What's New • Bookstore • Reference Desk • Software Library • Macmillan Overview • Talk to Us

Internet Commerce Home Page

Visit the *Internet Commerce* home page at:

`http://www.mcp.com/newriders.commerce`

Because the software described in this book changes frequently, it is not possible to distribute a CD with the latest versions. Not to worry! You can download the latest software from the *Internet Commerce* home page. In addition, you can also do the following:

➤ Follow hyperlinks to all the sites mentioned in this book (and a few more!)

➤ Get updates on the latest activity in the Internet commerce world

➤ Download instructions for installing and configuring the Netscape Commerce Server for Windows NT

➤ Meet the authors

WANT MORE INFORMATION?

CHECK OUT THESE RELATED TOPICS OR SEE YOUR LOCAL BOOKSTORE

CAD

As the number one CAD publisher in the world, and as a Registered Publisher of Autodesk, New Riders Publishing provides unequaled content on this complex topic under the flagship *Inside AutoCAD*. Other titles include *AutoCAD for Beginners* and *New Riders' Reference Guide to AutoCAD Release 13.*

Networking

As the leading Novell NetWare publisher, New Riders Publishing delivers cutting-edge products for network professionals. We publish books for all levels of users, from those wanting to gain NetWare Certification, to those administering or installing a network. Leading books in this category include *Inside NetWare 3.12, Inside TCP/IP Second Edition, NetWare: The Professional Reference,* and *Managing the NetWare 3.x Server.*

Graphics and 3D Studio

New Riders provides readers with the most comprehensive product tutorials and references available for the graphics market. Best-sellers include *Inside Photoshop 3, 3D Studio IPAS Plug In Reference, KPT's Filters and Effects,* and *Inside 3D Studio.*

Internet and Communications

As one of the fastest growing publishers in the communications market, New Riders provides unparalleled information and detail on this ever-changing topic area. We publish international best-sellers such as *New Riders' Official Internet Yellow Pages, 2nd Edition,* a directory of over 10,000 listings of Internet sites and resources from around the world, as well as *VRML: Browsing and Building Cyberspace, Actually Useful Internet Security Techniques, Internet Firewalls and Network Security,* and *New Riders' Official World Wide Web Yellow Pages.*

Operating Systems

Expanding off our expertise in technical markets, and driven by the needs of the computing and business professional, New Riders offers comprehensive references for experienced and advanced users of today's most popular operating systems, including *Inside Windows 95, Inside Unix, Inside OS/2 Warp Version 3,* and *Building a Unix Internet Server.*

Orders/Customer Service **1-800-653-6156**   Source Code **NRP95**

New Riders Publishing   201 West 103rd Street ◆ Indianapolis, Indiana 46290 USA

REGISTRATION CARD

Internet Commerce

Name _____ Title _____

Company _____ Type of business _____

Address _____

City/State/ZIP _____

Have you used these types of books before? ☐ yes ☐ no

If yes, which ones? _____
_____

How many computer books do you purchase each year? ☐ 1–5 ☐ 6 or more

How did you learn about this book? _____

Where did you purchase this book? _____

Which applications do you currently use? _____
_____

Which computer magazines do you subscribe to? _____
_____

What trade shows do you attend? _____
_____

Comments: _____
_____
_____

Would you like to be placed on our preferred mailing list? ☐ yes ☐ no

☐ **I would like to see my name in print!** You may use my name and quote me in future New Riders products and promotions. My daytime phone number is: _____

New Riders Publishing 201 West 103rd Street ◆ Indianapolis, Indiana 46290 USA

Fax to **317-581-4670** Orders/Customer Service **1-800-653-6156** Source Code **NRP95**

Fold Here

BUSINESS REPLY MAIL
FIRST-CLASS MAIL PERMIT NO. 9918 INDIANAPOLIS IN

POSTAGE WILL BE PAID BY THE ADDRESSEE

NEW RIDERS PUBLISHING
201 W 103RD ST
INDIANAPOLIS IN 46290-9058